THE MANUAL

A Guide to the Ultimate Study Method (USM)

THE MANUAL

A GUIDE TO THE ULTIMATE STUDY METHOD (USM)

•CONCENTRATION •SUPER MEMORY •SPEED READING •NOTE-TAKING •USM •RAPID MENTAL ARITHMETIC

SECOND EDITION

ROD BREMER

FONS SAPIENTIAE

Published in the United Kingdom by Fons Sapientiae Publishing, Cambridge, United Kingdom.

Second Edition

ISBN 978-0-9934964-2-4

Disclaimer

This book is not intended to replace the services of a trained health professional. All matters and circumstances regarding your health require medical supervision and attention. You are responsible for consulting your physician before adopting the procedures and techniques presented in this book. Any applications of the ideas, techniques and procedures set in this book are at the reader's discretion.

The author and publisher of this material are <u>not responsible</u> in any way whatsoever for any liability, loss, injury or risk, personal or otherwise, which may occur, directly or indirectly, due to reading or following the instructions in this book.

To my family

TABLE OF CONTENTS

Introduction 21

A Note Regarding The Writing Convention.....................23

Instructions 24

PART 1   Concentration 27

The Aims of Part 1 28

Why Concentrate? 29

Scientific Evidence..32

Levels of the Mind...34

The Benefits of Meditation...35

Techniques 37

Technique 1: Mantras 39

Variations of the Technique............................. 40

Technique 2: Letters 40

Variations of The Technique 41

Technique 3: Breathing 42

Key points 44

Variations of the Technique.......................... 45

Technique 4: Countdown...46

Variations of the Technique:......................... 47

Technique 5: 3D Objects 48

Variations of the Technique.......................... 49

Technique 6: Smell..51

Technique 7: Touch 52

    Variations of the Technique 54

Technique 8: Relaxing Scene 54

Technique 9: Background Sound 56

    Variations of the Technique 58

Training plan 60

    Training Rules 61

    Training Schedules 63

Summary and Revision Map 65

    Key Points 65

    Revision Map 66

PART 2   **Memory** **67**

The Aims of Part 2 68

The Importance of Memory 69

    Photographic/Eidetic Memory Versus the Memory of a
    Reasoned Understanding 70

    Recorded Feats of Memory 72

Scientific Evidence 73

General Concepts and Basic Tools 78

    Key Principles of Memory 78

        Images 79

        The Link System 79

        Imagination is Infinite 85

        Objects are Best 87

    Rules for Effective Links 87

    The Gluing Toolbox 89

Visualising Words 91

Visualising Numbers and Symbols............................93

   Numbers.. 93

   Symbols.. 102

Adding Dimensions 104

   Adding Three Dimensions 105

The Importance of Revision 110

Being Systematic and Enforcing Order 115

Systems...118

The Link System...119

The Peg System 121

   The Numbers List 124

   The Effigy List.. 126

   The Alphabet List 127

   The Rhyme list.. 129

   The Body list... 129

The Loci System 130

   Houses and Rooms.. 132

   Palaces, Cities and Countries 134

   Imaginary Loci.. 140

The Grid System 145

   The Standard Grid... 146

   The Numerical Grid 150

   The Circular Grid 151

   Empty Spaces and Repeated Data.................. 155

Applications 158

Foreign Vocabulary 159

   Mandarin Chinese 159

   Japanese 161

   French 161

   Arabic.. 162

   Spanish.. 162

   Integration into Daily Life 163

Non-Foreign Vocabulary...164

   Integration into Daily Life 165

Spelling..166

Telephone Numbers...168

Card Memorisation 172

Binary Code 176

Computer Code...178

Mathematical Formulae 182

Chemical Notation..189

Names and Faces 195

   George W. Bush... 197

   Bernard Madoff.. 198

Presidents and Rulers..199

Calendar...203

The Human Organiser 207

   The Lightbulb... 208

   The Trolley... 208

   The Megaphone 209

   The Hammer 209

The Notebook.. 209

Calendar 210

Contacts... 210

Clear the images every day 210

Variations 211

Oenophiles and "Uisgeophiles" 212

Link System Approach 212

Loci System Approach.. 215

Variations 219

Other Considerations 220

Other Applications..221

Chess Openings.. 221

Corporate Hierarchy... 222

Directions 222

Maps.. 223

Morse Code 223

Option Volatility Surface 224

Paintings.. 224

Perfumes 224

Philatelists 225

Poetry 225

Recipes 226

Tube/Train/Underground Map.. 226

Building Your Own System 227

Training plan 229

Weeks 1 to 4: Becoming Familiar with the Systems.........229

Weeks 5 to 8: Introducing the Techniques to Daily Life ..230

Week 8 Onwards 232

Summary and Revision Map 235

Key Points...235

Revision Map...237

PART 3   Speed Reading **239**

The Aims of Part 3 240

Introduction 241

Scientific Evidence...244

The Speed Reading System...................................249

Concentration...252

Regression 253

Skimming..256

Reading: Vertical Line.....................................257

Reading: Text Tracing (optional)........................258

Sub-vocalisation 261

Fixations 264

Skimming..267

Reading: Vertical Line.....................................268

Reading: Text Tracing (optional)........................269

Layered Reading...270

Subconscious Reading (optional) 275

Varying Reading Speeds 279

Training plan 281

Exercise 1: Speed and Comprehension 283

Exercise 2: Speed...284

Exercise 3: Peripheral Vision and Sub-vocalisation..........286

Exercise 4: Comprehension 287

Exercise 5: Fixation Span and Comprehension.................289

Training Schedule...291

Incorporating Speed Reading Into Daily Life (crucial).....293

Summary and Revision Map 295

Key Points...295

Revision Map...297

PART 4   The Ultimate Study Method................................ 299

The Aims of Part 4 300

Introduction 301

Key Concepts 304

Study Materials..306

State of Mind 306

Revision Map...307

Procedure 309

General Considerations 311

Linear Notes 312

Procedure 313

General Considerations 315

Example 317

Unique Identifiers 318

Layered Reading..322

General Considerations 323

Procedure 324

Memorising...326

The Value of Testing 327

Memorising the Revision Map.............................. 330

Memorising the Linear Notes 332

Reinforcing 334

Procedure 334

General Considerations 335

USM 338

The USM Procedure in Full.................................338

Step 1: Study Materials.................................... 338

Step 2: State of Mind 338

Step 3: Layered Reading................................... 338

Step 4: Note-Taking.. 339

Step 5: Memorise 342

Step 6: Reinforce... 345

The USM Procedure (Quick Reference) 346

Summary and Revision Map 348

Key points..348

Revision Map...349

PART 5   Rapid Math.. 351

The Aims of Part 5 352

Introduction 353

World Records...355

Scientific Evidence...356

Techniques 358

Addition..358

Procedure 359

Example 1 360

Example 2 361

Example 3: Nothing to Carry 362

Limits?? 363

Multiplication Tricks 363

Procedure 364

Example 1 366

Example 2 367

Example 3 368

Example 4 368

Example 5: Extending the Technique to Larger Numbers
.... 369

Example 6 370

Example 7: One Below and One Above 100 371

Example 8 372

Example 9: Thousands and Upwards 373

Example 10 373

Contraindications 374

Principal Multiplication Technique 376

Procedure 376

Example 1 380

Example 2 382

Example 3: Numbers of Different Magnitude 384

Example 4: Larger Numbers 385

Squaring 386

Squaring Trick 386

Example 1 387

Example 2 387

Example 3 388

Example 4 389

Example 5 389

Example 6 390

Subtraction...391

Procedure 391

Example 1 392

Example 2 393

Example 3: Solving in Pairs.............................. 394

Example 4: Negative Answers........................... 396

Division 397

Procedure 397

Example 1 400

Example 2 402

Example 3 404

Cube Root..405

Procedure 406

Example 1 408

Example 2 409

Example 3: Approximation............................... 410

Higher Order Roots 411

Procedure 411

Example 1 413

Example 2 414

Example 3: Approximation............................ 414

Square root..415

  Procedure 416

  Example 1 418

  Example 2 419

  Example 3: Approximation............................ 419

Higher Precision 420

  Procedure 421

  Example 422

Decimals 423

Training plan 425

  Training Schedule....................................425

    Level 1: Recommended Starting Point 426

    Level 2 427

    Level 3 427

    Level 4 428

    Level 5 429

  Measure Your Progress 429

  Incorporation into Daily Life............................430

Summary and Revision Map 431

  Key points..431

  Revision Map..432

Afterword 433

Contact Information 435

References and Extra Reading 437

  Concentration..437

Books 437

Scientific Journals 438

Memory 440

Books 440

Scientific Journals 441

Speed Reading 441

Books 441

Scientific Journals 442

USM..444

Books 444

Scientific Journals 444

Rapid Math 445

Books 445

Scientific journals 446

Index..449

INTRODUCTION

There exists a profusion of books written about faster forms of learning and about techniques for greater utilisation of the mind. As with everything in life, some are good, whilst others make grandiose promises that fail to materialise. The aim of this manual, therefore, is to provide the reader with the best techniques: those that achieve the desired goal with the least effort and in the shortest time. The approach taken here is unique. The techniques provided are combined into a precise procedural learning system, whose main goal is the practical implementation of thousands of years of research into the human psyche.

The study system presented herewith is the culmination of the author's 25 years of experimentation. The system builds on the latest research—both scientific and anecdotal—pertaining to the topics of Super Memory, Speed Reading, Concentration, States of Mind, Rapid Math, and Note-Taking. The author has kept the techniques that work; modified the techniques that were not practical, and discarded the techniques that did not provide measurable results. The end outcome is a system that would allow the reader, if he chooses to persevere with the training schedule, to master a powerful tool. This tool will ensure a lifetime of enjoyable learning experiences, as opposed to the drudgery of rote learning and cramming. In addition, the ability to perform monumental feats of mind comes within grasp; for example, memorising a pack of cards in two minutes, or finding the cube root of 912,673 in four seconds. Such feats, once mastered, would make one realise how limited one's intellectual experience of life has been before. More importantly, though, it will highlight how these and other limitations we tend to set ourselves are just an illusion that can easily be dispelled.

The Manual was written in the order in which it should be read. The reader is strongly advised to follow the book's instructions, since earlier techniques are used for subsequent ones. For example, in order to multiply 7,615,234 x 9,854,787, one needs to be able to memorise the result as the computation progresses—which is ultimately a 14 digit number. Without having learnt the memory techniques presented in Part 2 of the book, it would be impossible to perform the calculation—which is later detailed in Part 5.

Contrary to other well-marketed products in this field, the author chooses not to make extravagant claims/promises of abilities such as: to be able to read a book in mere minutes, or to memorise something once and forever retain it. Instead, the exposition in this manual provides the reader with the techniques that work, and the training schedule that needs to be undertaken in order to see measurable progress. We then provide documented and verified feats achieved by other individuals, to allow you to perceive what is possible with perseverance and dedication. The important point here, though, is that your motivation and goals should determine how much time you invest. For example, if you never intend to compete in memory championships, or never intend to play professional poker, then card memorisation should not be high on your training agenda.

The training schedule provided in each part of the book is necessary for mastery of the techniques discussed. The training structure is designed such that a wide variety of tools can be mastered—with the aim of enriching your experience and of demonstrating what is possible with each portion of the system. However, for specific goals, you may wish to tailor the approach by putting a greater emphasis on some exercises compared to others. Nonetheless, it is advisable to do so only after a working knowledge of each technique is attained.

The Manual is self-contained, so extra reading on the topics is not necessary. The References and Extra Reading chapter provides a list of resources that were relied upon for the completion of the work. However, some sections are purely the fruit of the author's work and innovation, and thus have no references elsewhere. The interested reader may wish to explore the references; but, to emphasise the point, for practical use of the techniques, extra reading is not necessary.

A NOTE REGARDING THE WRITING CONVENTION

Firstly, the reader should note that the convention of "he/him" was used rather than alternating between "he/him" and "she/her". This was done in order to avoid confusion when presenting the techniques. The main goal of this manual is to provide a clear set of instructions—avoiding ambiguity is thus paramount. This is the only reason for choosing the "he/him" convention. There is neither a gender requirement nor preference, so the reader can think in whichever term is appropriate to her or him, irrespective of the written word.

Secondly, the writing style chosen by the author mostly follows British English. So, non-British readers who are disturbed by the spellings *memorise* (rather than "memorize"); *learnt* (rather than "learned"); *colour* (rather than "color"); to *practise* (rather than to "practice"); and several others, should keep this point in mind.

Thirdly, the editing style mostly follows *The Chicago Manual of Style*. However, to further eliminate ambiguity and ensure clarity, some modifications were applied.

INSTRUCTIONS

For optimal use of this manual, as well as one's own time, the reader is recommended to follow the instructions below without exception:

1. **Purpose**. Have a purpose in mind: what do you aim to get out of this book, and what do you hope to achieve with the techniques provided?

2. **Read the book in the order in which it was written**. Become well versed in the techniques presented in each part of the book before moving on to the next.

3. **Training schedule**. Ensure that the training schedule of each part of the book is followed exactly as instructed.

4. **Persevere with the training**. This is especially important in the first part of the book, which deals with concentration. There are certain barriers that need to be breached before everything falls into place. The techniques presented work, but practice is necessary for mastery.

5. **Incorporate the techniques into your everyday life**. Just experiment; you do not have to rely on them at first—simply test them out to gain proficiency and confidence.

Much like driving a car, at the beginning it appears to be a smorgasbord of multiple actions, thoughts and techniques put together, which can seem almost insurmountable. But, soon after, with only a little practice, it becomes second nature. The techniques in this book are exactly the same—your aim should be to make them second nature. Just like common drivers in the above analogy, there are mentalists out there who have mastered some of the techniques. If they can do it, so can you. The only components required are a good technique, motivation, and diligent practice.

Character is the ability to follow through on a resolution long after the emotion with which it was made has passed. —
Brian Tracy

Part 1

CONCENTRATION

If you chase two rabbits, both will escape.

—Chinese Proverb

THE AIMS OF PART 1

- To improve concentration by practising attention-focusing techniques and meditation.
- To use meditation to induce deeper states of mind, which facilitate relaxation, learning, reasoning and recall.

WHY CONCENTRATE?

The *Oxford Dictionary*'s definition for *concentration* is as follows:

1. *The action or power of focusing all one's attention.*
2. *Dealing with one particular thing above all others.*

Concentration is the cornerstone of intellectual existence. Without it, no thinking can take place; and, without thinking, there can be no learning.

With the advent of communication devices, as well as entertainment and gaming technologies, modern society appears to be cramming an ever greater amount of tasks into an already multi-tasked reality. As an illustration, picture an executive talking on the phone via Bluetooth whilst reading through his latest e-mails on the BlackBerry. All this performed whilst pedalling on the exercise bike, keeping an eye on the market gyrations displayed on the television above his head. Concurrently, he is also enjoying the background beats of the music played in the aerobics class, which is melodically entwined to the laboured breathing of his fellow gym enthusiasts on their lunch break... This is not an absurd depiction of city life, but rather an almost prototypical example.

Multitasking can be useful when trivial tasks are undertaken. These tasks should be characterised by having little to no need for reasoning (like cleaning the house or washing the dishes). Nonetheless, the habitual use of multitasking as a way of getting more things done, often results in the opposite. Some tasks should not be bundled with others, and the tendency to always attempt to save time by doing more things concurrently, can hinder one's ability to concentrate.

The limits to multitasking are clear when one realises that learning begins by reading from or listening to—both requiring focus—the source of the information. The information then needs to be reasoned, and subsequently it needs to be memorised. The ability to capture the information in the first place is directly proportional to how much attention you provided. Without concentration, the above sequence breaks down. With partial concentration, it takes longer to complete. And because it takes longer, it may cause the student unnecessary frustration, or perhaps even elicit the misguided belief that the material is "too difficult". Such negative cycles can be vicious and self-sustaining; after some time they can affect one's ability to learn, and thus limit potential and performance later in life.

Some mental tasks cannot be completed without absolute attention to the task at hand. For example, a speed-reader boasting a reading speed of, say, 2,000 words per minute, cannot allow his attention to wander. For if it does, every second he lacks in attention to the reading task, he would miss 33 words; for every three seconds, he would miss a key paragraph—and thus a key concept. The overall outcome would be poor comprehension of the material, which will therefore necessitate a repeat of the reading task.

Imagine trying to understand a complex scientific theory while your train of thought keeps getting interrupted by other intruding ideas—generated internally by you or externally by your environment. Every time you sense that you are about to figure out a step in the structure, an interrupting thought enters and makes you lose your focus—instantly derailing your train of thought. The entire portion of that journey thus has to be repeated just to arrive at the same realisation. And it certainly needs to be repeated before you can proceed to the next step in the structure. With constant interruptions, it is simple to see that lack of attention requires the inefficient revisiting of ideas that have already been reasoned. This, in turn, greatly hinders any momentum in the thinking process. Such an approach ends up being costly in terms of time. Nonsensically, it is much like climbing up a treacherous mountain whilst playing *Candy Crush* (or whichever game is addictively popular when you read this) on the phone: this inevitably leads to stumbling or falling down the mountain. And, if luck prevails, it then requires latching on to the nearest rock for safety, before recuperating and heading upwards—needlessly having to cover the same ground all over again.

Concentration is the first part of *The Manual* because everything that follows—individual techniques and the system as a whole—relies on the user's ability to focus his attention on the task at hand. The deeper the ability, the greater the benefit!

It is perhaps the most challenging task to achieve, harder still due to our modern way of life, but it is a challenge that must be undertaken to reap the full benefits from all that follows.

SCIENTIFIC EVIDENCE

As alluded to in the above dictionary quote for *concentration*, it is commonly considered different to, and a refinement/focus of, one's *attention*.

Attention is one of the most heavily researched topics in psychology and cognitive neuroscience. The historical records of the research date back to the 1850s, but, in fact, earlier cultures and religions have experimented with this topic for thousands of years prior to that. They did so through a more spiritual approach to the concept—namely, by meditation. Meditation is one topic that appears to feature equally in most major religions, and proposed paths to spiritual enlightenment are claimed to be paved by the stones of such practice. In this book, we aim to use the techniques of old, which have been experimented with for millennia, whilst relying on the scientific rigor to rationalise our approach.

Meditation refers to the practice of training the mind to induce a deeper state of conscious awareness in order to achieve a goal— be it enlightenment, calm relaxation, deep thinking, or other.

Meditation has been the focus of increased scientific research as early as the 1930s. Since then, a copious amount of publications have suggested links between various meditation methods and changes in: metabolic rates, blood pressure, respiration, brain activation, and attentional allocation. In addition, several studies have suggested that meditation confers improved healing, reduced anxiety, and superior emotional balance. These results have led the scientific community to introduce the use of several meditation techniques in clinical treatments of stress, psychological disorders, and for pain reduction.

Interestingly, some scientific evidence even leads several authors to suggest—albeit with some contention—that the ability to focus our attention today may have been an evolutionary response to the practice of meditation by earlier ancestors. A type of Baldwin effect applied to attention and memory.[1]

Most significantly, at least to the objectives set in this book, recent scientific research also claims that meditation may increase attention spans. It is this evidence, combined with the beneficial side effects listed above, that should motivate us to **use meditation as a method to improve our concentration**—and hence our ability to learn.

When we learn new skills—be it a musical instrument or a sport—even at an advanced age, the brain undergoes physical changes (a process commonly known as neuroplasticity). The same process appears to take place with the regular practice of meditation: a physical transformation and rewiring of circuits results. And the actual changes that take place can vary with the meditation technique being used.

At the time of writing, there are four generally-accepted phases that are considered to take place during a meditation session—each involving a specific brain network. The first phase—that of a distracting thought arising—involves activity in the default-mode network of the brain, an area active in building and updating internal models of the world. The second phase—that of awareness of the distracting thought—occurs in the anterior insula and the anterior cingulate cortex, areas which regulate subjectively perceived feelings. The third phase—that of detaching the awareness from the distracting thought—occurs in the dorsolateral prefrontal cortex and the lateral inferior parietal

---

[1] The Baldwin effect is a theory in evolutionary biology; it posits a selection process in learnt abilities that make them innate for future generations (see "Did Meditating Make Us Human?" by Matt J. Rossano].)

lobe, areas which are involved in executive function and behavioural inhibition. Finally, the fourth phase—that of maintaining attention toward the object of the meditation—continues to take place in the dorsolateral prefrontal cortex.

Each phase in turn improves and rewires the brain areas involved. Furthermore, regular and long-term practice has shown to also alter the volume of grey matter in the areas being activated—in particular, the insula and prefrontal cortices—increasing significantly for veteran meditators with many years of practice.

What is more, it was found that long-term practitioners require less activation in the abovementioned regions of the brain when meditating—suggesting that a more optimal wiring was achieved. This means, at least, for the objectives set in this book, that a much lower effort is required to attain or maintain the same state—in essence, making concentration easier to achieve/maintain and deeper in level.

LEVELS OF THE MIND

The brain is believed to function at different frequencies—each corresponding to a state of mind. Of course, the spectrum is continuous, but there is a generally agreed set of ranges. These frequencies are classified as follows:

1. **Delta**: up to 4Hz, associated with deep sleep.
2. **Theta**: 4-8 Hz, associated with drowsiness.
3. **Alpha**: 8-13 Hz, associated with relaxed awareness.
4. **Beta**: 13-30 Hz, associated with being alert and active.
5. **Gamma**: 30-100+ Hz, associated with cross-modal sensory processing.

Accessing each of the different frequencies above is appropriate and beneficial under different circumstances. It is the alpha frequency that we should aim to attain for the purposes of learning. For the alpha frequency provides a state in which absorption, reasoning, and recall of information are at their optimal rates. It is also a frequency into which the regular practice of entering will lead to the beneficial results highlighted in the previous section. And, pragmatically, the concept of conscious awareness begins to disintegrate at levels deeper than alpha, thus becoming less practical for the objectives of this book.

Mastering the ability to meditate makes the alpha frequency easily accessible to the practitioner. The other frequencies are attained by either *exiting* alpha or by *deepening* the meditation. Exiting is simple: just move around, focus your sight on the objects around you, and let the thoughts take over. Deepening, on the other hand, requires additional techniques depending on the frequencies being targeted, and is beyond the scope and purpose of this book.

THE BENEFITS OF MEDITATION

If the above introduction did not suffice to convince you to continue to the next chapter and introduce a meditation regimen into your life, below is a summary of the scientifically-established benefits that may accompany the improved concentration that is being targeted.

- Lower blood pressure.
- Favourable changes in brain activity.
- Ability to focus more of our attention on a given task. [Our present goal]

- Longer attention spans. [Our present goal]
- Better executive function.
- Joys derived from general relaxation and deep states of awareness.
- Enhanced creativity.
- Enhanced health and well-being.
- Improved healing.
- Reduced activity in inflammation-related genes, and altered functioning of enzymes involved in turning genes on/off—in particular telomerase, which governs the rates of cellular aging.
- Reduced anxiety and improved emotional balance. Reduced risk of relapse for previous cases of depression.
- Enhanced ability to control basic physiological responses (e.g., inflammation and the release of stress hormones) to socially stressful endeavours, such as public speaking.
- Improved sleep patterns.
- An increased volume of the brain's grey matter in favourable areas, and a decreased volume in unfavourable areas (e.g. those for processing fear and anxiety).

The aim of this background information is to highlight the effectiveness and benefits of developing one's concentration through the practice of meditation. It is not meant to cover and evaluate all the scientific information available, but rather to provide a rationale to enhance the reader's motivation to commit to the practice.

TECHNIQUES

This chapter introduces the techniques that will allow the user to improve his concentration and reap the benefits of meditation. The techniques should be practised daily, preferably three times a day—consisting of two short sessions and one long session.

The following instructions should be kept in mind when working on each technique:

1. **Body position**. The techniques should be performed while either sitting on a comfortable chair or lying down. The former is preferred, since the latter can often cause the practitioner to fall asleep (which does not count as a completed training session).
2. **Training time**. Training time should be at least one hour before or at least one hour after a meal (to allow for proper digestion), and at least two hours before going to bed (to avoid a state of high alertness before attempting to sleep).
3. **Meditation is the art of letting go. Thoughts will always arise; meditation is the process, and practice, of letting them go.** [If you take anything away from this book, anything at all, let it be this point! Meditation is not about being in a state of bliss, but rather about the <u>process</u> of letting go of thoughts and feelings. It is this process of letting go that eventually leads to a deeper state of consciousness. In this deep state, thoughts may still arise, but after mastering the ability to let go, they generate neither reaction nor feeling.]
4. **Negative thoughts**. The practitioner should therefore avoid unnecessary anxiety that is commonly caused by thinking: "this is not working"; "my mind is not clear";

"so many thoughts are distracting me," etc. The aim, in fact, is to be in an environment that allows you to notice these interrupting thoughts and having the opportunity to train the ability to let them go. **The more thoughts that arise, the more opportunity you have to master this skill.**

5. **Recurring thoughts**. The thoughts will surely come back—usually within seconds of you letting them go. The practice of meditation is all about letting them go again and again, without reacting to their continuous re-occurrence.

6. **Remember, meditation is essentially time that you set aside for the practice of letting go**. So, do not allow the ego to get in the way by, perhaps, suggesting that you are not deeply relaxed and that hence you are wasting time. Letting go of the thoughts, develops a skill that allows one to easily tune out that which one deems unimportant. This skill can take a while to develop, but the benefits are worth the time spent.

7. **Expectation**. Do not expect anything amazing to happen. Such thoughts will again elicit your ego and desires, and thus hinder your practice. Just follow the technique without thinking too much about it or what it means. Pondering and reflecting can be done before or after the meditation—but never during.

8. **Persevere**. It will be difficult at first, but it will become easier as you progress. And, once the main concept is understood, it will be almost automatic.

TECHNIQUE 1: MANTRAS

Mantra chanting is a very common technique in eastern traditions, which was popularised in the west during the 1960s. The idea is to repeat a phrase, a prayer or a syllable over and over—either vocally or in one's mind. This repetition has a very calming effect on the mind. Moreover, it is a simple tool to use, since sounds are usually easy to repeat either vocally or in the mind (as opposed to the more challenging practice of visualising a scene or recalling a smell in the mind, for example). The procedure is as follows:

1. **Choose a mantra** that you wish to use. Common choices are: Lam, Vam, Ram, Yam, Hum, Sham, and Ohm. (Choose one.)
2. **Alarm.** Set an alarm to ring in 20 minutes.
3. **Position.** Sit comfortably with your feet flat on the floor, your hands resting on your thighs, and your eyes closed.
4. **Breathing.** Take a deep breath, hold it for ten seconds, and then breathe out. Repeat this step three times.
5. **Repeat the mantra.** Now, slowly begin repeating the chosen mantra **in your mind**—do not move your lips nor pronounce it vocally. The pace should be calm and slow. Allow a space of about three seconds between each pronunciation; however, do not count the seconds nor focus on the time—instead, gradually let yourself enter into a natural rhythm. Say, for example, you chose Lam; simply repeat it over and over: "Lam...Lam...Lam...," where the ellipsis represents a pause of approximately three seconds.
6. **The pauses.** The time between each pronunciation will vary with practice. It will vary during the session itself—longer intervals as the session progresses and the state of mind deepens. And it will generally differ across

practitioners. The three seconds indicated above is to provide an initial guide for the beginner.

7. **Let go**. When thoughts intrude (and they will), just let go. When they come back, let go again and again—without reacting, and without analysing the reason behind the thoughts' reoccurrence. Just let go and continue repeating the mantra, all slowly and calmly.

VARIATIONS OF THE TECHNIQUE

1. If the environment permits, you can experiment with a vocal repetition of the mantra. Try to make the pronunciation of each mantra be as long as your exhalation. Then breathe in and repeat the cycle.

2. You can further alter the method by using a word or a prayer instead of a single syllable. The aim should be to stick with what works best for you. The reader should note, however, that in meditation, simplicity is king.

In regard to the selection of a mantra, it is strongly recommended to make a choice and stick to it. Therefore, do not keep changing your mantra: settle on one that is comfortable or meaningful for you, and use it exclusively.

TECHNIQUE 2: LETTERS

Visual techniques are favoured by many, given most people's tendency to rely on this modality (compare how much time you spend in front of the TV, the PC or the tablet, versus the time you spend smelling flowers, for example). However, the technique presented here relies on the ability to picture a letter using the inner eye—an ability that some find difficult at first. Though with regular practice this ability is quickly improved. The procedure is as follows:

1. **Draw**. Take a plain white piece of paper and on it draw, in thick black colour, a letter of your choice. Those with religious beliefs and affiliations may choose a letter from their religion's alphabet (this method was commonly used by Jewish Kabbalists). It is not important (for the purposes set in this book) which letter you choose; the only requirement is that you are familiar with it.
2. **Stare**. Stare at this letter for a minute: just gaze at it intently without any analysis.
3. **Alarm**. After completing Steps 1 and 2, set an alarm to ring in ten minutes.
4. **Position**. Now, sit comfortably with your feet flat on the floor, and your hands resting on your thighs.
5. **Visualise**. Close your eyes and picture the black letter on the white background. **It is not necessary to see it clearly or fully**. It is simply something to focus your attention upon whilst letting everything else go. Do not stress or strain, nor force yourself to see the image. Simply relax and attempt to focus on any glimpse, blur or feeling, which staring at it earlier imprinted in your mind.
6. **Let go**. When thoughts intrude (and they will), just let go. When they come back, let go again and again—without reacting, and without analysing the reason behind the thoughts' reoccurrence. Just let go and continue focusing on the letter.

VARIATIONS OF THE TECHNIQUE

1. When you become more confident in your practice, you can skip the part of drawing the letter (which is only there

to assist your progress in developing inner visualisation skills).

2.   You can change the colour of the letter or the background, but do not change it during the practice itself. For example, if you choose a white letter on a blue background, make this choice before you begin your session, and continue with this combination until the session is complete.

3.   Increase the time gradually to 15 minutes, 20 minutes and, eventually, 30 minutes.

Apart from improving your concentration, this technique trains your ability to visualise images in your mind. Such ability will prove to be very useful when we introduce the memory techniques later in the book—and will increase their effectiveness substantially.

TECHNIQUE 3: BREATHING

Breathing techniques play a key role in the meditative practices of Indian Yoga and Chinese Qigong. There is a great deal of variety in the teaching approaches; so much so, that even within the same branch of each art, there exist radically different schools of thought. The subject is deep, and the subtleties of each technique can take a long time to master. The aim of this manual is to be practical yet effective; hence, the technique introduced below is the one that was found to be the easiest to master whilst still being valuable in terms of the results produced.

The technique is commonly called *Buddhist breathing*, though in the west it can also be found under the name *abdominal breathing* and other variations thereof. The procedure for this technique is as follows:

1. **Alarm**. Set an alarm to ring in ten minutes.
2. **Position**. Sit comfortably with your feet flat on the floor, your hands resting on your thighs, and your eyes closed.
3. **Breathing**. Breathe in through the nose (with your mouth closed, and the tongue touching the top of the palate) whilst allowing your abdominal area to slowly expand outwards. Then breathe out whilst gently pushing your abdominal area inwards.
4. **The breaths should be slow and natural**. You should neither force your stomach in nor force it out: the abdominal movement should be smooth and without any tension.
5. **Minimal sound**. If performed appropriately, the breaths should produce little to no sound (the sound is commonly produced as air passes rapidly through the nose).
6. **Progress slowly and gradually**. Begin the session with five seconds for the in-breath and five seconds for the out-breath. After some practice, if you find that you are able to go further—that is, without tensing your abdominal muscles!—gradually increase the in/out length at the beginning of the session to be ten seconds long. **The key point is not to tense and not to force it to happen.** Tension—mostly due to forced abdominal movements—defeats the purpose and can have undesirable effects. Correct application of the technique requires no external muscular involvement—it is purely diaphragmatic.
7. **There is no need to time or count the seconds of each breath during the practice**. It is to be done for the first few breaths, in order to set the pace for the session; but, thereafter, the pace should be maintained and no counting/timing should take place. You will find that as you enter into a deeper state, as the session progresses,

the pace will also deepen, and each breath will be elongated naturally.

8. **Once settled into the initial breathing pace, with each breath focus your attention on the movement of your abdomen**. Do not vocalise this attention (by, for example, mentally saying "in" or "out"), and do not attempt to visualise the abdominal movement. Only centre your attention on the sensation generated by the movement.

9. **Let go**. When thoughts intrude (and they will), just let go. When they come back, let go again and again—without reacting, and without analysing the reason behind the thoughts' reoccurrence. Just let go and focus on the abdominal area moving in and out with your breathing.

The abdominal movement in this technique is very natural: it is how one breathes from birth until early childhood. And this natural ability can slowly be relearnt and regained with practice.

At the beginning, the physical mechanics of the method need to be learnt (or be accustomed to). With ten minutes every day, a reasonable comfort with the technique can be attained within two to three months. However, each person is different, so time should not be the ultimate gauge: it is whether you feel more relaxed and more focused that should signal whether you are progressing along the correct path.

KEY POINTS

An incorrect application of the technique can cause adverse effects to the practitioner—both mental and physical. For this reason, the key points are reiterated and emphasised below:

1. DO NOT FORCE THE BREATH.

2. DO NOT TENSE: if you feel that you are tensing up, let go (or, if letting go fails, stop the session).
3. DO NOT USE YOUR ABDOMINAL MUSCLES: the breathing should be diaphragmatic.
4. ALLOW THE AIR TO FLOW IN AND OUT NATURALLY: expanding on the in-breath and contracting on the out-breath.

VARIATIONS OF THE TECHNIQUE

1. After practising for six months, and only when you are comfortable with the technique, you can proceed by focusing your attention three inches below your navel (usually measured by horizontally placing three fingers under the navel). According to Traditional Chinese Medicine, positioned there, is a key pressure point (also commonly referred to as a *meridian point*) that is linked to the energy store of the body (the *dantian*). The breathing should continue as before: expanding on the in-breath, contracting on the out-breath, but the attention is now centred on the pressure point.

2. After practising the above navel variation, and if you sense warmth within the **inner** abdominal region when practising this technique, you can proceed to focusing your attention inside your abdominal area (directly behind the pressure point three inches below the navel). This is the location of the *dantian*. As before, simply focus the attention on this point **inside** the body (equidistant from the aforementioned pressure point and the back), and let go whenever distracting thoughts occur. The breathing should continue as before: expanding on the in-breath, contracting on the out-breath.

TECHNIQUE 4: COUNTDOWN

We frequently use numbers in our everyday life, and the notion of counting down tends to solicit an expectation of an event to follow. The following technique makes use of this familiarity and expectation. Owing to the abovementioned properties, the technique is relatively simple to understand and to put into practice. The basis of the method involves dynamic audio and visual processes, which progress or stagnate according to your thought patterns. The procedure is as follows:

1. **Alarm**. Set an alarm to ring in ten minutes.
2. **Position**. Sit comfortably with your feet flat on the floor, your hands resting on your thighs, and your eyes closed.
3. **Count down**. Beginning from 100, slowly count down to 1—waiting approximately three seconds between each number (as a starting pace). Try picturing the number (a black number on a white background is the preferred contrast) as well as saying it in your mind (i.e., not out loud).
4. **The pauses**. Do not count the seconds between each number. Simply get into a comfortable rhythm and count down: "100...99...98...97...," counting in your mind and visualising the number at the same time (where again the ellipsis represents a pause of approximately three seconds).
5. **Adjust the rhythm**. As you get comfortable with the process, you can adjust the rhythm: the slower the rhythm, the better. But, to reiterate, do not count the length of each pause—the attention should be centred on the countdown.
6. **Let go**. When thoughts intrude (and they will), just let go. When they come back, let go again and again—without reacting, and without analysing the reason behind the

thoughts' reoccurrence. Just let go and focus on the countdown.

7. **Restart**. Once you have reached 90, with every thought that distracts you, gently let it go, and then return back to count down from 90. For example:
"...93...92...91...90...89...88...*thought*...90...89...88 ...87...86...*thought*...90...89...."

8. **Avoid analysis**. Do not let the fact that you are going over and over back to 90—because of interrupting thoughts—distract or disturb you. Avoid analysing the frequency of the repetition, and avoid analysing the thoughts themselves—just let go and follow the procedure.

As will become clear when the training schedule is introduced, the added advantage of this technique is that it allow you to measure your progress in improving your concentration. This is achieved by tracking how low you can count down to without any distracting thoughts.

Once you have mastered the technique and can arrive to 1 (starting from 100) easily within the ten minutes session, begin counting down from 200 (or more as you improve) and increase the training session's length accordingly (to 15 minutes, 20 minutes and, eventually, 30 minutes).

VARIATIONS OF THE TECHNIQUE:

1. Among the variations of this technique, there is a popular procedure commonly called *counting the breath*. For each out-breath, you count down (in your mind) one number. For example: *breathe in, breathe out*, "100"; *breathe in, breathe out*, "99"; *breathe in, breathe out*, "98"; etc. Each

time you lose count or allow a thought to emerge, go back to 90. This variation is favoured by some, but it certainly complicates the technique. Hence, it is not recommended to use this variation until mastery of the basic technique is achieved.

2. Other variations include using either only the visual countdown or only the audio countdown—i.e., not together. Again, this should be practised only once the basic technique is mastered.

TECHNIQUE 5: 3D OBJECTS

The following is a visualisation technique that builds on the principles presented heretofore. It does so by introducing the complexity of a 3-dimensional object, as opposed to the 2-dimensional nature of visualising a letter or a number, as was instructed in the previous techniques. Practising visualisation with increased complexity helps the development of the inner eye. Clarity of the inner eye, in turn, is extremely useful for the memory techniques as well as the mental arithmetic system presented later in the book.

The easiest objects to begin working with are items that are viewed on a daily basis. When choosing an object, ensure that there is a lively colour involved and that the dimensions are distinct (e.g., choose a bright yellow box rather than a white piece of paper).

For the instructions below, to better illustrate the principle, an example object (an orange) will be used:

1. **Alarm.** Set an alarm to ring in ten minutes.

2. **Position**. Sit comfortably with your feet flat on the floor, your hands resting on your thighs, and your eyes closed.

3. **Visualise**. Visualise the orange in your mind's eye. Try to make the image as clear as possible, but do not strain or try too hard. Picturing the object against a neutral background tends to help; for example, imagine a white 3-dimensional space with nothing inside it besides a large orange.

4. **It is not necessary to see the object clearly or fully**. It is simply something to focus your attention upon whilst letting everything else go. Do not stress or strain, nor force yourself to see the image. Simply relax and attempt to focus on any glimpse, blur or feeling, which thinking about the object elicits from your mind.

5. **Let go**. When thoughts intrude (and they will), just let go. When they come back, let go again and again—without reacting, and without analysing the reason behind the thoughts' reoccurrence. Just let go and focus on the imaginary orange.

VARIATIONS OF THE TECHNIQUE

1. Experiment with other items that you hold, manipulate, or experience regularly. Common examples are: a lemon, an apple, a strawberry, and geometrical shapes (e.g., a pyramid, a sphere, or a cube). The desired object should have attractive colours (one or two colours, but not more at this stage).

2. Once mastery of the above is achieved, attempt more complex shapes and visualise them with multiple colour combinations. For example, build in your mind, a red and blue *stellated dodecahedron*; then focus your attention on this object and perform the exercise as instructed above.

Though, as with all the techniques presented herewith, it is advisable to slowly and gradually increase the complexity rather than attempt extreme shifts.

3. There are some schools of meditation that attempt to use deep states of consciousness in order visualise higher-dimensional objects (4-dimensional, and higher). Since such a feat is not possible with our conscious perception of reality, this variation of the exercise requires focusing your attention on the "feeling" or "presence" of a 4-dimensional (or higher dimensional) object—pushing away all other thoughts and ideas. Gradually, as the thoughts dissipate and a focus of the "feeling" or "presence" is all that remains, a deeper state of mind is attained. At such deep levels of the mind, one is able to make sense of the concept of higher-dimensional objects and, purportedly, one is able to view a representation that makes one believe a visualisation has been achieved. However, it should be noted that replicating the image is not possible on paper, nor is it possible to replicate mentally at more active states of mind after the session is complete. **This practice is extremely advanced and should not be attempted until the basic technique is mastered.** (Even if mastery of the basic technique is attained, this variation should only be experimented with occasionally: avoiding a large investment of your time unless measurable results occur.)

It is important to note that the item chosen should be easily visualisable—especially at the beginning (referring here, of course, to the basic version of the exercise, not the higher-dimensional variation). If constant thought needs to be invested in trying to rebuild an image of the object in your mind, then the practice is wasted. So, quite naturally, it is advisable to begin with simple objects and then proceed to more complicated ones.

TECHNIQUE 6: SMELL

To the author's knowledge, the following technique has not been covered by previous work on the subject of meditation. It uses an important exteroceptive sense that is often neglected, but whose significance in mental performance is substantial.

The main idea behind the technique is to use the memory of a strong, pleasant smell, and to meditate on its recollection. This method would eventually allow the practitioner to gain the ability to use, in the inner mind, smells and scents as flexibly as sounds or images. It is a truly powerful tool for enforcing some of the memory techniques that will be introduced later in the book.

Olfaction, the sense of smell, is a powerful trigger. Once the technique is mastered, whole scenes (including inputs from the other senses) unfold simply due to the trigger that the smell provided. An example could be a scene of you on holiday, walking on a quiet beach. Trying to recall the precise smell of the ocean often enhances your recollection of the rest of the scene—allowing it to become much more vivid. Mastery of this technique will make the concept of visualisation take a completely different meaning.

The technique is as follows:

1. **Alarm**. Set an alarm to ring in ten minutes.
2. **Position**. Sit comfortably with your feet flat on the floor, your hands resting on your thighs, and your eyes closed.
3. **Choose a pleasant smell** you would like to work with. Make sure that the smell, or scent, is something you can recall easily or have experienced recently. Some examples could be: the smell of wood-fire baked bread, the smell of Grandma's apple pie freshly out of the oven, the smell of cooking pancakes on Sunday morning, the

smell of the recently-cut grass, or the scent of a jasmine flower. Choose one.

4. **Focus your attention exclusively on the smell**. There is no need to visualise or remember the experience or the scene—just the smell.

5. **Let go**. When thoughts intrude (and they will), just let go. When they come back, let go again and again—without reacting, and without analysing the reason behind the thoughts' reoccurrence. Just let go and focus on the smell.

Most beginners find the above technique challenging—mentally evoking the smell on which to meditate seems to be the main hurdle. In order to overcome this, you can begin the session by visualising the scene where the smell was last recorded. Once you lock-in on the smell, let go of the scene and focus on the smell exclusively. This opening introduction to the technique may have to be repeated until proficiency is achieved: when the smell can be retrieved without the scene.

TECHNIQUE 7: TOUCH

Much akin to the smell-based technique above, the following is another technique which, to the best of the author's knowledge, has not been made available in the literature yet. The idea is to train another modality that tends to be ignored in mental activities.

The sense of touch can trigger a very relaxing response. And meditating on a recalled touch-sensation can train the user to solicit such a response without the physical stimulus being present. The procedure for this training is as follows:

1. **Alarm**. Set an alarm to ring in ten minutes.
2. **Position**. Sit comfortably with your feet flat on the floor, your hands resting on your thighs, and your eyes closed.
3. **Attempt to recall a pleasant touch-sensation you might have felt in the past**. Some examples could be:
   a. The sensation generated by the hot sand caressing your feet as you are walking down a deserted beach.
   b. Or the feeling of the ocean's water trickling between your toes as the waves travel to and fro.
   c. Or the feeling engendered by a material, such as silk, that produced a deep sensation of comfort.
4. **Focus**. Once you have chosen **one** sensation that suits you and that you can easily recall, begin focusing your attention exclusively on the sensation.
5. **Ignore the setting**. Do not visualise the setting or the other stimuli that were present—focus only on the touch sensation. In example 3.a. above, it is solely the calming warmth sensation in your feet that should be the focus, nothing else. Your mind knows the origin of the sensation (i.e., that it originates from the sand that is on the beach on which you are walking), so focusing on the other details of the scene is not necessary. Therefore, allow your attention to settle purely on the touch sensation.
6. **Let go**. When thoughts intrude (and they will), just let go. When they come back, let go again and again—without reacting, and without analysing the reason behind the thoughts' reoccurrence. Just let go and focus on the touch sensation.

Similarly to the previous, smell-based technique, initially evoking the touch sensation in the mind may be challenging. Leveraging on visualising the scene where the sensation was last experienced is the interim solution. As before, once you lock-in on the chosen touch sensation, let go of the scene and focus exclusively on the sensation.

VARIATIONS OF THE TECHNIQUE

Variations of the above technique may include whole-body touch sensations; for example:

1. Swimming in tepid water on a hot day.
2. Sunbathing while rocking in a hammock.
3. Being immersed in a mud bath.
4. Being wrapped in a soft fur coat, or lying on a fur carpet.

The concept is simple and can be extended to any touch-sensation you have ever felt—the only requirements are that the sensation was gratifying and memorable.

Other variations of the technique include focusing on more boring or mundane touch sensations, such as:

1. Running your fingers across sandpaper.
2. Feeling the roughness of a tree's trunk.
3. Feeling the coolness of a concrete wall.

Humdrum sensations, such as the three listed directly above, can often offer a reasonable training session. This is frequently the case, for the feelings they invoke are less thrilling—focusing on them, therefore, requires greater effort in concentration.

TECHNIQUE 8: RELAXING SCENE

The following technique builds on all the themes presented thus far. It allows one to experience an entire scene with all the feelings that the senses are able to capture. The procedure is as follows:

1. **Alarm**. Set an alarm to ring in ten minutes.
2. **Position**. Sit comfortably with your feet flat on the floor, your hands resting on your thighs, and your eyes closed.
3. **Try to think of a pleasant, relaxing scene that you would like to experience**. A prototypical example would be: *Lying on a deserted beach by the water, breathing the scented air with relish. Feeling a wave wash over your body and then recede back to the ocean. Savouring the warmth of the sun, gradually enveloping your body, until the next wave washes to the shore with a resonant whooshing sound, repeating the cycle.*
4. **Individual sensations**. You begin the exercise by focusing on each individual sensation (i.e., the smell, the touch sensation, the sound, the visual representation of the scene, and taste, if any is involved) just once and then letting it go. Spend a few seconds on each modality; then, once you have experienced each, go to the next step in the exercise.
5. **Integrate**. Next, feel as though you are inside the scene—this is now your point of focus. Do not try to focus on, nor shift attention from, each individual sensation; instead, focus on being in the scene and experiencing the overall environment. When you are able to feel as though you are truly inside the scene, the individual sensations will slowly return on their own. Until then, all you need to do is maintain the *feeling* of being there as your point of focus.
6. **Let go**. When thoughts intrude (and they will), just let go. When they come back, let go again and again—without reacting, and without analysing the reason behind the

thoughts' reoccurrence. Just let go and focus on the feeling of being there, inside the scene.

The reason for initially cycling through the individual sensations is to create the base feeling onto which you later centre the meditation.

In this technique you are focusing all your attention on a single feeling; it is just that this feeling is, in fact, complex and carries several modalities within it. The different modalities are not apparent at first, but, as the state deepens, they become accentuated.

To reiterate the key point of the technique above: after focusing on each individual sensation very briefly, you let go and focus only on the overall feeling of being there. When a deeper state of consciousness is attained, the individual sensations will permeate back into focus on their own. The main difference, however, is that as they enter back into your conscious awareness, they will be integrated with the entire scene—further deepening the state.

TECHNIQUE 9: BACKGROUND SOUND

The following technique aims to utilise (or, more accurately, to harness) noises that are present in one's environment. And, in turn, it may demonstrate to the practitioner how such sounds, which are commonly a source of frustration, can instead be soothing if a different interpretation takes place in the mind.

Mastery of this technique would provide the practitioner with a substantially improved control over his environment—permitting it to only affect him in exactly the way that he chooses. Thus, it is a valuable tool for competitive performances or for any pressure situations that take place in noisy environments. The procedure is as follows:

1. **Setting**. It is advisable to begin in a relatively quiet setting and progress to noisier surroundings as your skill improves.
2. **Alarm**. Set an alarm to ring in ten minutes.
3. **Position**. Sit comfortably with your feet flat on the floor, your hands resting on your thighs, and your eyes closed.
4. **Listen for any recurring noises in the room or the environment in which you are situated**. It can be the humming of the air-conditioner, the rumbling sound of the trains on faraway tracks, or the fitful noises of cars on a nearby road—essentially any noise that is brought to your attention.
5. **Notice and let go**. Usually, whenever that sound (or sounds, if you are in a noisy environment) appears, you will notice it and begin analysing its meaning. The aim of this exercise, therefore, is to **notice** when you begin thinking about the sound, and then simply to **let go** of these thoughts. So, for example, say the sound of a car driving by is heard, which, in turn, causes your mind to begin to journey on the following type of thought loop:

Why did I choose to live on such a busy road? It's quite noisy, congested and polluted; but, on the other hand, it's good, for it is close to work. Oh, that reminds me, I forgot to file in that report—my boss will be so angry—I better get to work early and do it before he comes in. But, wait, going in early means a long queue for the bus. Oh, and this morning my seat on the bus was wet because it was raining heavily and someone must have had their umbrella placed on it right before I sat down. Ah, yes, I should bring an umbrella tomorrow—the forecast suggests it is going to rain, yet again....

Perhaps not precisely along this anxious line of thought, but the general pattern may seem familiar to the practitioner. The idea, then, is to stop this train of thought before it begins or, at least, before it gathers steam. So the approach should be: whenever you hear the sound, you just let go; i.e., you hear the sound, but you allow nothing else to follow. If thoughts or analyses emerge, just let go; do not analyse and do not search for meanings—simply let go. In the example excerpted above, after the sound of the car is heard, and as you notice you are starting to analyse (i.e., the first line in italics above), simply let go. If the thoughts persist, let go again and again—without reacting, and without analysing the reason behind the thoughts' reoccurrence. The point of the meditation is to spend time **letting go**: hence improving the ability to do so effortlessly.

With practice, external noises will elicit a lesser and shorter thought response, and mastery over your environment would thus become one step closer.

VARIATIONS OF THE TECHNIQUE

As your skill improves, you may choose to increase the challenge by trying noisier environments. However, it is important to ensure you have mastered the simple environment first.

Examples of more challenging environments would be:

- A busy train/bus/underground station.
- The airport.
- A market/bazaar.

(Of course, you must ensure that sitting in such an environment with your eyes closed does not compromise yours or others' security or safety).

The overall approach is exactly the same:

- Do not think of the sounds.
- Do not try and analyse them or figure out where they came from.
- Just allow the sounds to arrive and depart without any effect on your mental process.

Remember: meditation is the art and practice of letting go. So do not expect thoughts not to emerge—you, most crucially, need thoughts to emerge for you to be able to let them go. The key purpose of every meditation session is: to **practise letting go** and to enjoy the relief-sensation that this gradually induces.

TRAINING PLAN

Strategy without tactics is the slowest route to victory.
Tactics without strategy is the noise before defeat.

—Sun Tzu

The previous chapter describes the techniques that would help one improve his ability to concentrate; however, without a training plan, the techniques are worthless. As with most skills, persistent practice is required before mastery is attained. The problem, it seems, is that most of those eager to gain the results tend to stop their practice after a hurdle presents itself. This is perhaps the main reason behind why we are so amazed when we see individuals performing mental feats. We are under the belief that these feats are incredible because few get to achieve them. This is so, indubitably, because few have the character to persist in the face of adversity, not due to the measure of the feat.

It is therefore paramount to have a specific training plan in place, and to set basic rules to enforce compliance with the training. Most importantly, it is necessary to have a tool to measure progress, in order to verify whether the approach taken is effective.

With concentration, measurement of progress is challenging since it is highly dependent on the environment, external factors, general mood of the day, and worries/concerns recently experienced. Moreover, there is a fundamental obstacle: the difficulty in defining the unit of measurement. To circumvent these hurdles and to achieve the task of measurement, we will use the Countdown technique (presented above) to plot how far down the countdown the practitioner was able to descend. Such measurement should not be performed daily, since said period does not allow sufficient time for improvement; doing so fortnightly and plotting the results, may be considered a reasonable frequency.

It should be noted that **initial** results are highly dependent on the personality of the practitioner. Some individuals see quick initial improvement that plateaus rapidly, whereas others may experience no progress until, suddenly, one day all the concepts seem to fall into place and a huge leap in performance is recorded. For this reason, it is advisable to train for at least three months before attaching any significance to the measurements.

In order to maximise the effects of the training plan, the following rules must be adhered to at all times:

TRAINING RULES

1. **Train every day**. The refined skill of concentration is built gradually upon previous days' progress. Missing a day can take you several steps back and cause frustration due to apparent lack of progress. It is therefore paramount that the training be completed every day without fail. If urgent circumstances present themselves, then the training can be reduced to just a single ten minutes session, but avoid at all costs having a day without training.

2. **Do not try to catch up**. Do not try to make up for a missed training day by doing double the amount of training the next day. Such an approach may overload your system and cause frustration, and perhaps even make you feel as though this is a chore. So it is crucial to remember: a chore, it certainly is not! These are

relaxation exercises, and should be viewed with the same relish and zest as one would anticipating a tasty meal, a good movie, or finishing work on a Friday. Regular practice is the key—do not overdo it for the wrong reasons.

3. **Measure your progress every two weeks using the Countdown technique.** As detailed above, progress can be measured using the Countdown technique. This involves recording the lowest number that the practitioner attained during the session, once the full ten minutes have elapsed. The training schedules below only include the Countdown technique from week 5 onwards, as it is advisable to have at least one month of training that does not involve any pressures of achievement. For some, measurement is a crucial component in gaining confidence with the ideas being taught: proof of progress, ergo, proof of understanding.

4. **Follow the training schedules and continue your practice even after mastering the techniques.** Listed below, are simple training schedules that focus the first few months on the core techniques—those that are simplest to perform and that are generally the most effective. Once mastery has been achieved, you can either design your own schedule or continue with the one suggested. The important point here, and crucially so, is that training should not be stopped after the 12th week. To maintain the skill gained would require continued regular practice. And, with concentration, the levels of mastery are not finite: there is always a deeper state and a higher degree of control that one can strive towards.

5. **Do not compare your progress with others'.** Concentration and relaxation are not competitive sports. Once the competitive ego begins to interfere with the training, all efforts would be laid to waste. Competing or

comparing progress is fraught with peril: The person you face may have different views, may not be honest with his experience, may make your progress feel inadequate, or may discourage you altogether by suggesting something else to try. Give yourself a chance by measuring your progress over a three months period. If progress is made, continue with the strategy. If no progress is made, and as long as all the instructions were followed, only then it would be logical to seek further guidance.

TRAINING SCHEDULES

The schedules below require the user to set aside 20 minutes in the morning, 10 minutes at noon, and 10 minutes in the evening. This may not be possible for all readers, but it is certainly encouraged for optimal results. If these three daily sessions cannot be completed on a regular basis, then, at the very least, practise once a day for 20 minutes. Accordingly, it should be noted that practising only once a day would result in a longer period before measurable progress takes place. This is not a bad situation if it is the only available choice. The key, therefore, is to be realistic with what is possible within one's schedule, and to execute regularly on that basis without fail.

For the reader who is blessed with an abundance of free time, the schedules can be amended with longer sessions. The 10 minutes at noon and evening can be amended to 20 minutes, and the 20 minutes in the morning to 40 minutes, for example. It is, of course, advisable to increase the sessions gradually rather than hastily.

Weeks 1 to 4

	Mon	Tue	Wed	Thu	Fri	Sat	Sun
Morning - 20m	Mantra	Mantra	Mantra	Mantra	Mantra	Mantra	Mantra
Noon - 10m	Letter	Letter	Letter	Letter	Letter	Letter	Letter
Evening - 10m	Breathing	Breathing	Breathing	Breathing	Breathing	Breathing	Breathing

Weeks 5 to 8

	Mon	Tue	Wed	Thu	Fri	Sat	Sun
Morning - 20m	Mantra	Mantra	Mantra	Mantra	Mantra	Mantra	Mantra
Noon - 10m	Count-down	Letter	Count-down	Letter	Count-down	3D objects	3D objects
Evening - 10m	Breathing	Breathing	Breathing	Breathing	Breathing	Breathing	Breathing

Weeks 9 to 12

	Mon	Tue	Wed	Thu	Fri	Sat	Sun
Morning - 20m	Mantra	Mantra	Mantra	Mantra	Mantra	Mantra	Mantra
Noon - 10m	Touch	Letter	Count-down	Smell	Relaxing Scene	3D objects	3D objects
Evening - 10m	Breathing	Breathing	Breathing	Breathing	Breathing	Breathing	Breathing

Week 13 onwards

	Mon	Tue	Wed	Thu	Fri	Sat	Sun
Morning - 20m	Mantra	Mantra	Mantra	Mantra	Mantra	Mantra	Mantra
Noon - 10m	Touch	Letter	Count-down	Smell	Relaxing Scene	3D objects	Any preferred technique
Evening - 10m	Breathing	Breathing	Breathing	Breathing	Breathing	Breathing	Breathing

SUMMARY AND REVISION MAP

KEY POINTS

- Concentration is the crux of capturing information.
- Meditation is the approach taken to improve concentration and relaxation.
- Apart from better and faster learning, as well as deeper relaxation, there is also a wide variety of health benefits associated with meditation.
- Common to all approaches to meditation is the art of letting go.
- The techniques should be practised every day, three times each day, according to the schedules provided.
- Persist with the schedules and, after week 4, measure your progress every two weeks, plotting the results.
- Continue the practice after completion of the 12th week. Three times a day is optimal; once a day is the bare minimum.

REVISION MAP

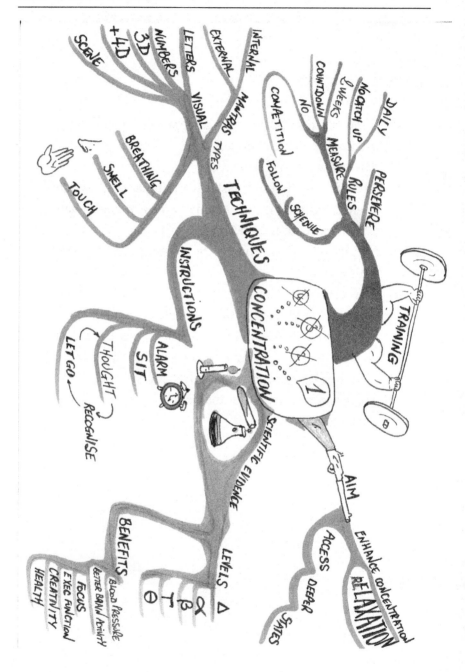

Part 2

MEMORY

Unless we remember we cannot understand.

—Edward M. Forster

THE AIMS OF PART 2

- To be able to immediately commit to memory any type of information.
- To be able to retain the said piece of information for the length of time that is required for its desired use.
- To make the process of memorisation fast yet effective, and, therefore, to avoid the use of rote learning.
- To have incredible amounts of fun whilst memorising—thus making learning a much more enjoyable experience.

THE IMPORTANCE OF MEMORY

There are two advantages of having a bad memory. The first is that traumatic events fade quickly and have a minimal effect over one's future. The second is, as Friedrich Nietzsche put it: "one enjoys several times the same good things for the first time."

Upon further reflection, it is clear that such advantages are also disadvantages when applied to the other extreme phenomena (the first, to major positive events; and, the second, to boring and unpleasant ones).

When considering one's dexterity and intellect, the importance of memory is quite clear: without memory of an event or an experience, no learning can take place. And if no learning takes place, no growth in one's abilities can materialise—one is left in a state of stagnation and inertia. That is indeed a depiction of an extreme scenario, but it is a scenario from which it is easy to deduce that a weak memory will not allow one to reason deeper aspects of a topic—since even the basics remain a mystery. Hence mastery of anything becomes a considerable challenge.

Several of the concentration techniques, introduced in the previous part of the book, will prove quite useful for improving one's memory. For example, the ability to visualise more clearly, or to include smells, sounds and touch-sensations in a visualised scene, are extremely powerful mnemonics. Most importantly though, if the reader has reached this stage—and, by that, has spent at least four weeks following the concentration training schedule—he would be in a better position to focus the mind on (or to pay attention to) the task at hand. And **memory is, in fact, largely driven by attention**.

Essentially, though somewhat loosely described, when we provide our undivided attention to an object or an event, a signal in the brain indicates that an experience of survival importance is being encountered—and thus a record is made for future reference.

The concepts introduced in this part of the book will serve as a complete mechanism for ensuring that the memory of the concept/object/event/experience is retained. It will be achieved by directing one's attention using specific techniques, which are implemented via the syntax of the self-preserving brain.

PHOTOGRAPHIC/EIDETIC MEMORY VERSUS THE MEMORY OF A REASONED UNDERSTANDING

There are some who wish they had a *photographic memory*—the purported ability to simply look at something and be able to recall with clarity the information contained therein (*eidetic memory* carries more than just the photographic/visual information—i.e. it includes sounds, smells, feelings, etc.). Whether such ability exists or not is subject to a great deal of controversy. Some argue that such a recollection can only last seconds, and generally fades shortly after.

Irrespective to its existence, upon further reflection, the benefits of such an ability are questionable when one considers what function our memories serve. The capacity to recall is only one aspect of it; the deeper aspect is actually the imprint a memory makes on our thinking and character. Therefore, it is not sufficient to have a picture of the information in your mind; **it is the imprint of the reasoned understanding of a topic that allows you to then build on its foundation**. Such an imprint is not a picture, but rather a much deeper connection of neurons.

The difference between a photographic memory and the memory of a reasoned understanding is best illustrated by the following analogy: Relying purely on a photographic memory is akin to sitting an examination with a textbook. The person that relies on this approach will have a poorer understanding of the topic. Furthermore, his ability to answer non-fact-based questions would be limited, since the information has not been reasoned and accumulated into the person's conscious awareness.

Consequently, creativity and intuition, which are generally a product of our accumulated understanding, are not likely to result from perfunctory mental scans of text. Hence mastery, further discoveries, and thus deeper knowledge, are likely to be beyond grasp.

Another aspect to consider is that of choice. Those with eidetic or photographic memories usually have limited control over what is captured and retained in their minds. The psychiatric literature is saturated with cases of those tormented by the memories of the mundane and the irrelevant. Having a tool to capture information rapidly and reliably—and solely when one chooses—seems to be a more efficient allocation of finite mental-energy resources, and a psychologically healthier situation.

RECORDED FEATS OF MEMORY

To provide some flavour (and motivation) of what can be
achieved with a trained memory, below is a sample of recently
recorded memory feats.

Category	Result	Record Holder	Year
Reciting pi from memory	83,431 decimal places	Akira Haraguchi	2005
The most binary digits memorised in one minute	240	Itay Avigdor	2006
The most binary digits memorised in 30 minutes	4140	Ben Pridmore	2007
The most cards memorised	59 packs (3068 cards) with only one error	David Farrow	2007
The time taken to memorise a single pack of cards	21.9 seconds	Simon Reinhard	2010
The most numbers memorised in one second	20	Ramón Campayo	2010
The most binary numbers memorised in one second	48	Ramón Campayo	2010

SCIENTIFIC EVIDENCE

There are several competing theories and models for how memory is believed to work. An analysis of the merits of each is beyond the scope, and relevance, of this book. Therefore, this chapter simply provides an overview of the properties of memory that are generally accepted in most models.

First let us detail the stages of memory and the types of memory. There are three general stages to memory:

1. Registering the information.
2. Storing the information.
3. Retrieving the information.

The types of memory are split into three major groups:

1. **Sensory memory**. This type of memory holds sensory information for a very brief period of time. It is generally not under cognitive control, and in most circumstances it is an automatic response. A representative example of this type of memory is glancing at a sheet of data and then glancing away. The first few milliseconds glancing away allows you to still see the data as if it was just in front of you. However, this memory lasts for only a few hundred milliseconds, and, by the time you attempt to recall it, the information is gone.

2. **Short-term memory**. This is a memory that can be recalled between a few seconds to a minute after first being encountered. Some research suggests that the encoding of such information is generally acoustic rather than visual.

3. **Long-term memory**. Through repetition, or the techniques presented in this part of the book, information

can be stored in long-term memory, which refers to periods of years up to a lifetime. Research suggests that long-term memory is primarily encoded semantically.

The scientific views regarding the physiological process for the creation of long-term memory generally agree on the following: the hippocampus is a part of the brain that is believed to be essential in the transferral of memories from short-term storage to long-term storage. And that sleep is considered a crucial component in this process of consolidating information.

Early scientific models for the process of memory postulated that any short-term memory that is kept in short-term storage long enough—through repetition, for example—would automatically get transferred to long-term storage (this is the typical Atkinson-Shiffrin model). However, more recent studies suggest that excitement can enhance memory through the stimulation of hormones that affect the amygdala; whereas excessive stress, which exposes the brain to cortisol, could hurt memory storage. And that inadequate sleep further limits long-term storage and consolidation. It is therefore important to acknowledge the effects that your states of mind and body have on your potential for long-term storage and overall learning performance.

From the basic process described above, it is sensible to realise that lifestyle choices have a strong effect on one's memory capacity (and on cognitive functioning in general). The crucial factors are: an adequate and regular amount of sleep; a balanced diet; frequent physical activity; and, to the extent deemed under one's control, limiting the levels of stress in one's life.

Notwithstanding the above evidence, even when no stress factors are present, forgetting is still a natural process that the brain follows. The main types and subtypes are listed below:

1. **Cue-dependent forgetting**. A failure to remember the information due to the lack of stimuli that was present when the information was first encoded.
2. **Trace Decay**. It is believed that new information causes a set of neurons to create a neurological memory trace in the brain, and it is believed that this trace naturally fades with time. However, with repetition, the synapses experience a structural change, after which the memory moves from being a short-term memory to being a long-term memory. There are several theories for the existence of trace decay:
   a. **Interference theory**. This theory argues for the existence of competition/conflict between old and new information, resulting in the fading of incompatible encoding.
   b. **Decay theory**. This is a broader theory behind the disintegration of the neurochemical trace over time. It is generally believed that this decay occurs in order to ensure that only the most important traces are kept. In essence, it is to ensure that the brain works most efficiently for the processes that are critical for survival (or, in a less evolutionary language, for the processes deemed significant).
   c. **Organic theory**. This theory deals with the decay caused by physiological damage or disease.

Following from the concepts above, *forgetting curve* is the term given to the exponential decay of the memory of newly acquired knowledge. The phenomenon was discovered in 1885 by Hermann Ebbinghaus. The discovery suggested that forgetting has a known, and quite natural, relationship with respect to time. And in order to maintain the information in long-term storage, a rehearsal of the material is necessary before hitting key decay levels on the curve.

The technique of *spaced repetition*, commonly used in language courses (and pioneered for this use by Paul Pimsleur in his eponymous language learning system), revolves around the principles of the forgetting curve. The idea is to make rote learning, or any repetition-based learning, more optimal by reviewing at predetermined periods that are aligned with the forgetting curve. Consequently, less time is spent on repetition overall, yet, to great effect, the method still ensures that the information does not disappear from conscious memory.

The forgetting curve can be described mathematically using the following formula:

$$\text{Memory Retention} = e^{-\frac{t}{S}}$$

Where t represents the amount of time elapsed since learning the material, and S represents the strength of the initial encoding of the information.

Therefore, as time elapses, the retention of the information weakens. However, as the strength of the encoding increases, the retention period lengthens. At the extreme, as S approaches infinity, the retention is unimpeded by time[2]—i.e., there is no apparent decay. A typical example of such a situation occurs in what is commonly termed as *flashbulb memory*. This is a memory encoded under intense emotional stimuli, and where the event or information was materially surprising and with significant consequences for the future—in particular as it applies to the self. Common examples are the assassination of John F. Kennedy and the events of 9/11. Such memories (of

---

[2] Note, however, that even if unimpeded by time, time may have other subtle effects: memories naturally mutate with time to incorporate newly learnt information and to reconcile it with the old.

those who observed the events as they unfolded) persist through time without the need for conscious review.

Upon a short reflection, it becomes evident that one can easily affect one of the variables in this formula and to favourably utilise the other. This is the basis of the techniques introduced in this part of the book.

We increase S by using memory techniques that encode the information as being of high importance and significance—this is done through exaggeration and nonsensical visualisation. We also organically increase S by improving concentration, as was detailed in the first part of the book. The effect of concentration is threefold: the practice of meditation favourably changes the structure and efficiency of the brain; the enhanced attention naturally improves S; and the deeper concentration also improves the application of the memory techniques, which further strengthens S.

It is important to mention that S is also dependent on lifestyle-related factors such as diet, stress and sleep. Improving these is akin to a multiplier effect on the techniques presented herewith.

As for time, we can neither control nor affect t; we can, nonetheless, utilise t by reviewing the information at optimal times. The optimal times being the periods prior to major decay levels. Such reviews further elevate S, hence the rate of decay diminishes with each review.

The optimal review process applied together with the specific techniques to increase S ensures that storage is transferred to long-term memory in an efficient manner. This is the basis of the approach presented in this book.

GENERAL CONCEPTS AND BASIC TOOLS

I mproving one's memory using a specific technique, or a mnemonic, has several key ingredients that appear to be common across the different systems presented in the literature. In this chapter, we introduce these key ingredients and the rules with which they must be applied. It is crucial to point out that these rules were established after decades of research and experimentation. This set of rules and ingredients was shown to be the optimal combination when considering performance in terms of retention as well as speed and efficiency.

The exposition of the material will begin by organising the key principles, tools and ideas, and then proceed to demonstrating their application through detailed examples involving different genres of information.

KEY PRINCIPLES OF MEMORY

In order to remember something, we first need to pay attention to it —hence concentration was covered in the first part of the book. The trouble, however, is that we tend to only pay attention to topics or events that are of interest to us or are of survival significance. The idea behind most memory systems, therefore, is to "trick" the mind into believing that the concept being memorised is out of the ordinary (thus interesting); or that it is so shockingly disturbing that it triggers primal emotions (thus of survival significance).

It is simple to surmise, then, that any memory system would need to take the information and add some spice and emotion to it before it can be reliably committed to memory. We therefore begin by introducing the principles and tools that would allow us to implement such a system:

IMAGES

Images are the crux of the memory techniques presented herein. They are used as an operating language with which we can signal to the memory regions of the brain that certain data is to be retained. The general idea is to use the images of the objects that the words/concepts (which one wishes to memorise) represent; or, if these words/concepts are abstract, to convert the abstract into images. The techniques below are then used to store these mental images into memory. Thereafter, whenever the information is required, the memory can be recalled in a similar way to any other, non-system-based memory.

The reader should duly note that the mental images used for the purposes of memory may have more than just the visual component. Since the construction of such images takes place in the mind, sounds, smells, tastes, feelings and movements can— and should—be incorporated with the visual foundation. For lack of a better term, such synesthetic depictions will be referred to simply as "images" throughout this book.

THE LINK SYSTEM

This is the technique used to input to memory a long sequence of information by connecting two adjacent pieces of information at a time. The system does not rely on previously established knowledge in order to secure new information, but rather anchors information from the sequence to act as pseudo-established knowledge, to which further connections are then made. For example, say you wanted to memorise a list of items; one way to do so would be to *link*, that is, to somehow connect, each item to the next. Take the following list of items:

Shoes, sofa, hose, coffee, iPad, orange, kettle

In essence, we would need to link *shoes* to *sofa*, *sofa* to *hose*, *hose* to *coffee*, *coffee* to *iPad*, *iPad* to *orange*, and *orange* to *kettle*. The idea is to link each item that we do not know to an item that we already know. The result is then a chain whose each element triggers the memory of the elements that precede and succeed it. There are two ways through which we can achieve such a link:

Logical Linking. If a logical connection exists between the items, and if the list does not allow the possibility of confusion, logic can be used to remember it. For example, when all items begin with a certain letter, or all items belong to a certain class, or all items are of a certain shape, etc. Unfortunately, the list above does not have an obvious logical representation; in addition, the list is not particularly short, so a different tool needs to be employed.

Creative Linking (commonly referred to as *linking*). This is the all-purpose tool of memory systems. Using this approach, one can connect any items in any order without the need for a logical relationship between them to exist. The design of this tool is such that the two basic principles responsible for the imprint of any memory are emphatically present. These principles are as follows:

a. **The need to pay attention.** We do so by creating exaggerated mental images that are unusual, that are full of colour, that include nonsensical action, and that are novel and interesting. The key theme is that the images should be absurd—the more so, the better. The act of building such images immediately centres one's attention, and the novelty of such creations further fuels it.

b. **The need to make the memory be of survival significance** (chiefly through emotions). In connection with Clause (a.) above, the images that we create need to evoke emotions; e.g., they could be hilarious, scary, disgusting, confusing, or lustful. If they are boring or mundane, they have no survival significance, they solicit no primal emotions, and they will therefore not be imprinted strongly in the brain.

(Note that attention, subjects of interest, and survival significance are not mutually exclusive concepts.)

Let us use the list of items above to illustrate the practicalities of the Link System. Since logic cannot be utilised to capture these items, we turn to creative linking. We thus begin with the first item, *shoes*. Picture a pair of shoes in your mind; now link them with the next item, *sofa*. To do this, you should create a picture that contains a sofa and a pair of shoes in the most absurd manner you are able to imagine. An example could be: a giant pair of shoes sitting on a sofa with the shoelaces folded behind the back of the top of each shoe— imitating a person with their arms crossed behind their head and their hands providing a resting place for the neck.

The key, when building these images, is to make them vivid, exaggerated, and emotive. So start by visualising in your mind, as clearly as possible, the details and properties of the shoes. That means you should be aware of: their colour; whether they are new; whether they are clean/shiny; whether they are muddy; whether these are sports shoes, etc. And the same applies for the sofa in the image. And, for exaggeration, you should absurdly increase the size of the shoes compared to the sofa, so that it is depiction that is not a reflection of reality. Hence you would picture a hulking pair of shoes resting on a tiny sofa that, helplessly, seems ready to balk under the immense weight that it now bears. Finally, for the emotive factor, feel the sense of dread that the sofa must be experiencing as it realises that its frame is about to collapse.

Note that it is not necessary to go through a checklist of an object's properties or dimensions. The essence of the technique is to naturally make sure that your picture is vivid enough; that is, its key properties are apparent and the exaggeration is blatant.

Let us move to the next item, *hose*. We now need to link *sofa* to *hose*, so picture a hose in the garden that is watering the flowers with sofas flowing out instead of water. Visualise millions of sofas being released from the hose and landing on the flowers, which happily absorb them to help themselves grow. The key here is to imagine lots of sofas (or even better, lots of giant sofas) emerging from the hose. Try to vividly picture the exit point of the hose being stretched every time a bunch of giant sofas emerge from it—sense how painful this experience must be for the hose (notice again how we add emotion to the image).

At this point in the book, if patience prevailed, the reader may question the sanity of the author. However, it is important to realise that this approach to memorising is incredibly efficient and effective—and it is the end goal that matters. It may certainly seem absurd to those who have never encountered it before. But, with practice, this is one of the greatest exercises in imagination one can perform. And it offers the user a pleasurable experience whilst rapidly accumulating the desired information. Readers who have reservations against using this approach due, perhaps, to the ridiculous thoughts it requires, are forgoing an invaluable tool. And if further attestation to the method's efficacy is required, then note here that all mentalists and participants in memory championships use systems that include some form of the abovementioned approach.

Moving on to the next item, *coffee*; imagine a hose on his[3] lunch break sipping a giant Starbucks coffee. Try to smell the aroma that this giant cup is diffusing; try to imagine how pleasurable this hot coffee must feel to the hose.

Proceeding to the next item, *iPad*; imagine yourself having your morning coffee with a stack of enormous iPads on a nearby plate. You then take an iPad, fold it in half with your fingers, dip it in the coffee, and eat it. Try and imagine the flavour it would have. Sense the hard texture and the disgusting taste of metal, hot plastic and toxic chemicals mixed with coffee swirl in your mouth—attempt to feel the disgust this evokes (again, applying emotions).

The next item is *orange*; imagine you receive a present for your birthday, which, once eagerly unwrapped, reveals a massive *iOrange* (an orange that behaves like an iPad). You start tapping along the front of this orange and the internet comes up; you then proceed to surfing the Net whilst playing your favourite songs. Try and attach to this memory how happy you must feel to have received this orange as a present, how cool the touch-screen functionality is, and what an amazing invention it is.

Finally, the last item is *kettle*. Imagine you are walking through an orange grove when, of a sudden, hunger strikes; but, instead of oranges hanging from the trees, you see lots of huge electric kettles. You then climb on a tree, pick lots of kettles, and carry them using a folded portion of the front of your shirt. Imagine how anxious you must feel—again, incorporating emotions into

---

[3] [To personify the inanimate object, we use *his* rather than *its*.]

the memory—while you are hanging onto an orange tree's branch with the front of your shirt loaded full with gargantuan kettles.

Now, a test: what comes after *shoes*?

After following the above instruction, when the word *shoes* is mentioned, you should immediately have the nonsensical image of a giant pair of shoes sitting on a sofa appear in your mind. This image then immediately triggers the next image—that of sofas shooting out of a hose; which issues the next image—that of a hose drinking coffee; which leads to the next image—that of an iPad dipped in coffee; which then elicits the iOrange; and that, in turn, activates the image of you picking kettles from an orange tree.

The system is generally accepted as infallible. Any such image that could not be recollected is usually due to one or a combination of the following factors:

a. **The image was not vivid enough**. Take your time when building the image: visualise it as clearly as possible in your mind's eye. At the beginning this may take a while, but, after some practice, the images will be created as quickly as the information is being processed—almost automatically.

b. **The objects in the image were not exaggerated enough**. Make the image absolutely absurd. The main qualifying criterion is as follows: whatever you are visualising should be something that you would not see in real life or in any of your quotidian experiences.

c. **Your state of mind was not conducive to the formation of a memory**. It is important to be in a relaxed state of mind when learning—hence Part 1 of this book focuses on concentration through meditation. During stressful periods, several combinations of hormones may be released, some of which can affect the chemical activity in the brain, which, in turn, could impede the strength of any connections made at the time.

Continuing with the key principles of memory, it seems natural at this stage to elaborate on the driving force behind creative linking: the imagination.

IMAGINATION IS INFINITE

The most compelling aspect of creative linking is that the possibilities are truly infinite. Any limitations that present themselves are usually due to the degree of freedom at which one allows their imagination to roam. If, at this point, the reader is concerned that the techniques may not be effective on him, for he lacks in imagination—fear not. Imagination is, in actuality, a trait that is available to all. Certain individuals possess personalities that allow them to portray it outwardly more than others; with practice, however, it is a faculty that can be activated and improved in all individuals.

It is important to note that imagination should not be viewed competitively—it is a very personal trait. Creations of your mind should be shared only to the extent you feel comfortable. It is generally preferable to only share innovations in the usage of the imagination. And to do so only with other like-minded individuals, and only for the aim of—through such mutual sharing from everyone in the group—extending the dimensions to which this trait can be expanded in each.

For instance, it may sometimes be beneficial to talk with others regarding the links created for a list of similar items. Such an approach provides one with the opportunity to explore other ideas that could be incorporated into their toolbox. But, to emphasize the point, note that it is not necessary to talk about or share your links, since, with practice, this skill will naturally become freer and will flow to directions you never knew existed (usually via connections with other ideas that are present in your mind at the time).

For those who seek, there are alternative sources for inspiration and for the (re)development of the imagination. For instance, an abundance of absurd ideas and nonsensical action can be found in cartoons; some prototypical examples are:

- *Animaniacs*
- The Ren & Stimpy Show
- Futurama
- Looney Tunes:

  o Bugs Bunny
  o Wile E. Coyote and The Road Runner
  o Sylvester and Tweety Bird
  o Speedy Gonzales
  o Yosemite Sam
  o Daffy Duck

- Family Guy

Cartoons are an excellent resource, so try and spend some time with this form of entertainment on occasion. If you have young children[4], this is an excellent opportunity for bonding whilst at the same time releasing your mind from the imagination limits of adulthood to which it has become accustomed.

---

[4] Children older than two years of age, for TV exposure prior to that age is suggested to have adverse effects on the child's development.

OBJECTS ARE BEST

When converting words/concepts into visual form, it is best to use objects—as these can be visualised quickly and effortlessly (the concentration exercises from Part 1 of the book should serve to make this process even more efficient). However, in some cases the words/concepts will involve abstract ideas rather than a physical object; in such cases, one can apply either one of the following methods, depending on which is more convenient (examples are provided in the Applications chapter):

  a. Convert the word/concept into a similar sounding word that is itself an object.
  b. Convert the word/concept into an object that the word/concept reminds of, or is related to.

The first image that comes to mind is the one to use. For the sake of efficiency, and to avoid wasting time deliberating between trivial choices, it is recommended to pick the first reasonable image that comes to mind, rather than trying to logically reason the ultimate possible permutation.

RULES FOR EFFECTIVE LINKS

The list below provides the key points that should be adhered to when building an image to store information. The rules are there to ensure that the links created are robust, so that they are set to persist in memory. The Applications chapter will illustrate how to apply the rules in practice—using specific examples across a wide variety of topics.

  1. **Exaggerate** your image in:
     a. Proportion,

    b. Size,

    c. Quantity,

    d. The absurdity of the action,

    e. Or all of the above at the same time, if possible.

2. **Colours.** Make the image colourful; avoid the dull, simple black and white.

3. **Make the image shocking and absurd.** The depiction must not be something you would see on any regular day, or in any real-life experience, for that matter. The brain has to believe that this event is something significant that needs to be retained for future reference. By using an absurd and shocking image, you are essentially "tricking" your brain into believing this is indeed the case.

4. **Sounds.** Incorporate sounds with your image in order to reinforce the event or the action taking place.

5. **Smells.** As mentioned in Part 1 of the book, smells are very powerful memory triggers. Therefore, make sure you attach smells to the objects in your image or to the general scenery therein, whenever possible.

6. **Emotions.** Integrate emotions with the image. Obviously, as with the other senses mentioned above, these emotions will have to match the action or scenario taking place. In general, the most effective emotions are fear, lust and mirth (through humour).

7. **See the image vividly!** Do not rush the image-building process; ensure every image is clear and vivid before moving on to the next. At the beginning this may take some time and effort, but, being child's play at its core, it will very quickly become second nature.

8. **Keep it simple.** Do not attempt to coalesce every exaggeration type, every sound, every smell and every emotion into a single image. You only need to get the image to the point where it is convincingly shocking and absurd. Adding details beyond that point is superfluous—

and certainly inefficient in terms of time. Learning to get the balance right will require some practice.

THE GLUING TOOLBOX

A sticking point emerges when considering how to go about linking the separate objects. Closely related to the rules listed above but deserving a separate exposition, the list below covers the various types of "glue" that can be applied in order to link two items together. Different circumstances will require different types of glue—sometimes even multiple glues per link. As with the rules listed above, the practice will become clearer with the examples that follow in the Applications chapter. (For the sake of clarity, *glue* is the term used to describe the method applied in order to effect a link. *Link*, as a noun, is the resulting image; as a verb, it is the act of gluing two items together.)

1. **Substitution**. Replacing one object with another; for instance, we replaced *orange* with *iPad* in the example listed above. We did so by making an orange behave like an iPad—which is an effective glue given the absurdity of such a scenario.

2. **Size exaggeration and the alteration of proportion**. This approach makes one object larger than it really is, especially in comparison to another object in the scene. For example, the shoes in the first image were gigantic in comparison to the sofa on which they were placed. Such a mismatch in proportion is a powerful tool to signal the significance of the image, and thus the need for the brain to retain it.

3. **The law of large numbers**. Involving a large quantity of the relevant object is a potent way to exaggerate an image. In the above example, the sofas that were shooting

out of the hose were in their millions. The reader should here note: thinking "millions" whilst you create your image would make you believe that this is indeed how many there are and would, in turn, immediately register as unusual. There is no need to count or to focus too much on whether it looks enough to be enumerated in the millions. Simply believing that there are millions is sufficient in order to make the brain register this event as important and unusual.

4. **Action**. The action should be exaggerated and nonsensical. It should be an action that would not—or, better still, could not—be performed in real life. It should be something extreme and out of the ordinary. Eating the iPad after dipping it into the coffee is an example from the list presented above.

5. **Emotion.** Involving emotion is an extremely powerful mental adhesive. For example, the fear of falling off the orange tree because you were carrying a shirt full of kettles, as depicted for the list above, was a powerful way to link the two items together.

6. **Involve yourself in the image**. The example above involved you eating iPads dipped in coffee for breakfast. Apart from nonsensical action, this image incorporated emotions (disgust), which already caused it to be more memorable. But, when added to the fact that one tends to better remember events which strongly involve or affect one's self, the combination of the factors—emotion and the self—provides an even better glue. It is your brain after all, and the brain has a selfish survival mechanism: all that affects its existence must be recorded.

VISUALISING WORDS

Words, as opposed to numbers and symbols, are usually easy to visualise since they often provide a concept that is represented by an object or, at least, can be logically associated with an object. And this object can be visualised in their stead. The approach to visualising words is as follows:

1. **If the word directly represents an object**, simply visualise that object. For example, the word *apple* would be visualised exactly as such—i.e., you would visualise an apple.

2. **If the word is not directly represented by an object**—for example, take the word *Friday*—then either <u>one</u> of the following can be applied:

   a. **Convert the word into an object that represents a similarly sounding word or a similarly sounding set of words.** As an example, for the word *Friday* we would use the two words that together sound like "Friday": *fried* and *hay*. This could be visualised as fried hay. Or,

   b. **Convert the word into an object that the word reminds you of.** For example, *Friday* might remind you of the movie *Friday the 13th*, so you may choose to use Jason's mask as your object, or even Jason himself if you can visualise him vividly enough. Or,

   c. **If the word has a personal significance to you which can be immediately associated with an object, you may choose to use that object.** For the *Friday* example: Friday may be the day on which you always go to the cinema. If this is indeed a dominant ritual in your life, you could use *cinema screen* to be the object that represents *Friday*. The key point here is that there are no limits: anything that reminds you of the word—as long as it can be visualised—could be used as the object that represents the word itself.

The larger your vocabulary, therefore, the more choice of objects you have at your disposal, and hence the quicker the image building process can be completed. The reader should note that with the methods presented herein, vocabulary can easily be increased. When one's vocabulary has been expanded using the techniques presented below, one's memory efficacy would immediately improve due to two factors. The first factor is simply the refined ability, which is a consequence of the sheer practice of the method and the training of the imagination that it entails. The second factor is a rather circular mechanism: The accumulation of additional knowledge and vocabulary immediately provides one with more choices when converting words into objects—thus facilitating the build-up of new memories, which then increases the number of choices further, and so on in a virtuous cycle.

A note to multilingual readers: for those conversant with more than one language (even if merely to a basic level), the abovementioned conversion process of words into objects is even quicker. This is the case since the vocabulary that one can utilise for this method need not be restricted to a single language. It can be mixed, so one word can be an object from one language whilst another word is an object from yet another language. Mixing vocabularies does not hinder the method! The reason for that is as follows: the act of attention through exaggeration embeds—subconsciously deep within the memory—the relevant information necessary to interpret the picture in the way that was intended.

VISUALISING NUMBERS AND SYMBOLS

NUMBERS

Words, as detailed in the previous section, are simple to visualise since they already represent a concept, which, in turn, is either associated with an object or could easily be converted into an object. Numbers and symbols, on the other hand, require a different approach. This is where the memory system comes into play. The key word is *system*: one needs to systematise the information into bits that can be used with the tools presented thus far. What follows, therefore, is the conversion process for numbers and symbols into bits of information to which the memory tools can be applied.

Let us first begin with the key themes:

1. **For each number and symbol, create a unique identifier** that can be easily visualised (again, preferably an object). The term *unique identifier* is used here, and in the rest of the book, in a very specific manner. When recalling a piece of information by summoning a previously created image, it is paramount that the image can be decoded to mean exactly what was intended when it was created. For that to be the case, there can be no ambiguity: each component in the image must uniquely translate into a piece of information.

2. **Keep this unique identifier consistent:** once it is created, do not change it or replace it—it will forever represent that number or symbol. It thus becomes a consistent unique identifier.

3. **Avoid using similar identifiers** that are related in concept. For example, a *cup* and a *mug* are quite similar

when visualised as objects. It would be preferable to only use one of these as an identifier, in order to avoid confusion when interpreting (i.e. recalling) images.

A word representing an object has a natural unique identifier: the object itself. The preceding section detailed how to convert abstract words into their unique identifiers. For numbers, the way to create a unique identifier is to convert the number into a word that represents an object. This object, from that point forward, will be used in constructed images to represent the number. However, in order to convert the number into a word in the first place, we must begin the exposition by introducing the phonetic alphabet:

№	Phonetic Sound	№	Phonetic Sound
1	T,D	6	SH, CH, J
2	N	7	K,G
3	M	8	F,V
4	R	9	P,B
5	L	0	S,Z

Note from the table above that each phonetic sound can represent only a single number—i.e., the number is uniquely identified through the sound. Therefore, if a series of phonetic sounds is stored in a memory, it can only be decoded into one unique number.

The idea behind this approach is to associate with each number from zero to nine a consonant sound that exists in spoken language. One can then look at a sequence of numbers and immediately be able to convert it into words, which, as previously demonstrated, can be readily visualised. For example, say we are presented with the number 131485. Using the phonetic alphabet presented above, this number can be converted into a simple sequence of letters. The resulting sequence of letters could be one of the following permutations: *TMTRFL, TMTRVL, DMDRFL, DMDRVL, TMDRFL, TMDRVL, DMTRFL,* and *DMTRVL*. The chosen permutation can then be transformed into words by adding vowels. For example, *TMTRVL* and *DMTRFL* can be transformed using vowels to become *TiMe TRaVeL* and *DoMe TRuFFLe*, respectively. The former can be visualised as a time machine (e.g., think of the flying DeLorean from the *Back to the future* trilogy); the latter, as the London Millennium Dome constructed out of truffles.

It is simple to notice that, using this technique, any number can be converted into a set of letters, and these into a set of words, which, subsequently, can be transformed into an image. The image, when recalled, can then only be decoded to mean one number—thus the number is uniquely identified.

The reader may note that the above approach is based on creating manageable building blocks (the letters representing the numbers zero to nine) from which the unique identifiers of larger numbers can be derived. We could have simply set about providing each number with a unique identifier by some other process—say, by the shape of the number, or the sound it resembles. However, having basic building blocks means that any possible number sequence—irrespective of its length—can be uniquely defined without additional preparatory work at the crucial time when memorisation is taking place. This is a general theme in the memory system of this book: **design an optimal set of uniquely-identified building blocks with which all other data can be uniquely identified.**

Given the new terms introduced thus far, for the sake of clarity, let us affirm the parlance. The term *unique identifier* is used to describe an object that can be interpreted as only a single piece of information (be it a word, a number, a symbol or other). The term *building blocks* is used to describe the most basic components from which the abovementioned unique identifiers are constructed. For words this is the syllable sounds or the word itself; for numbers it is the phonetic alphabet. Building blocks should themselves be uniquely identified; and, vice versa, unique identifiers larger than the basic building blocks can, as progress is made in a given topic, act as building blocks themselves. (The latter statement will become clearer as we discuss applications.) Lastly, the term *consistent unique identifier* is used to indicate that the unique identifier is applied consistently—that is, whenever a certain piece of information is encountered, the same object is used to represent it. For unique identifiers to become building blocks, they must be applied consistently.

A system then consists of a set of building blocks and a set of rules with which they are to be applied so that each piece of information is uniquely identified—and consistently so.

Continuing with the exposition for numbers, the key rules for the process are as follows:

1. **Memorise the table above and do not change it**. Building blocks must remain consistent for the system to work. An easy way to memorise this table is by applying some logical linking and some creative linking:

   1- *One* represents sounds that are due to letters which consist of <u>one</u> vertical stroke (*T* and *D*).
   2- For *two* we use a letter that consists of <u>two</u> vertical strokes: *n*.
   3- For *three* we utilise a letter that consists of <u>three</u> vertical strokes: *m*.
   4- *Fou<u>r</u>* is represented by *R* since its last letter is *R*.
   5- *Five* offers no logical connection, so link *L* (e.g., *L* sounds a little like "hell", so use *hell* as the object in

the link) with *5* (e.g., there are five fingers on the hand, so use *hand* as the object).

6- Pronouncing *six* with a full mouth can sound like "shix" or "chix" or "jix", thus reminding you that *six* is represented by either *SH* or *CH* or *J*.

7- *Seven* offers no logical connection, so link *K* and *G* (e.g., *K+G* sounds like "keg") with *7* (e.g., seven rhymes with "heaven").

8- Again, no logical connection, so link *F* and *V* (e.g., *F+V* sounds like "thief") with *8* (e.g., eight sounds like "hate").

9- *Nine* can be rotated into a *b* and reflected into a *p*.

0- *Zero* sounds like "z-ro" or "see-ro", which reminds one of *Z* and *S*.

Review the table several times and test yourself to ensure complete familiarity with the material. Do not proceed further until the phonetic alphabet is committed to memory.

2. **Vowels and silent letters are ignored**. So, for example, *14* could be converted into *TyRe* or *ToweR* or *TeaR*, etc.—and it would make no difference which. For when an image needs to be converted back into numbers, the list of words that make the image can only be interpreted in one unique way once the vowels are ignored. Therefore, had we linked *tyre* or *tower* or *tear* with some other piece of information, it would always mean *14* and no other number—thus there is no ambiguity.

3. **It is the consonant <u>sound</u> that matters, not the letter itself**. For example, the *c* in *lace* would represent zero since it sounds like "leis"; whereas the *c* in *cat* would represent seven since it sounds like "kat".

4. Then choose either one of the following approaches:

a. **Convert the desired number into its component phonetic sounds,** and then find words containing these sounds in order to construct an image (as was shown for 131485 above). **Or, and preferably so,**

b. **Create a list of numbers and appoint an object—a unique identifier—to each number.** Then split the number to be memorised into its constituent numbers, and use the newly created unique identifiers list to memorise it. It is advisable to follow this approach, so that, after the list is set, the practitioner would never again need to break down numbers into letters and then search for words that fit those letters. The aim here is to increase the size of the building blocks. If the practitioner has a list of objects for all the numbers up to 100, then any two digits in a sequence can quickly be converted into a word—thus a step of thinking/searching is eliminated, and, ergo, general memorisation speed is improved.

In the system developed here, following Clause (4.a.) above is only intended for the purpose of initially setting the unique identifiers for the numbers 0 to 100, or to extend the list from 101 onwards. Attempting to find an appropriate object to fit a sequence of letters is not recommended while actual memorisation is taking place. It is only in the preparatory phase—that is, in preparing the memory toolkit—that this approach is used. During the learning phase—that is, of actually learning desired pieces of information—it is approach 4.b. that should be used. It is materially faster, and, more importantly, it sets the unique identifiers in advance, whereas 4.a. requires coming up with new identifiers on the fly. The likelihood of confusing, or being inconsistent with, an identifier created on the fly is significantly higher. In which case it fails to be a consistent unique identifier, and thus a key principle that governs efficiency is violated.

Provided below, therefore, is an extended list up to 100, with a suggested object to represent each number. Let us name it the Numbers List. It was derived using the phonetic alphabet combined with the rules presented above. The list should be memorised in the same manner as the previous table was: with logic, creative linking or rote. In most cases very little effort is required, as the phonetic alphabet already determines the consonant sounds that make up each word. Note also that this is the only time we would excuse using rote learning. The excuse stems from the fact that, at this stage, we are in the process of building a system that would eliminate any further use of this less efficient approach (rote) to memory.

A reasonable manner by which to proceed would be to break the list into ten groups of ten numbers—memorising ten numbers each day. While doing so, it is important to every day test the ability to recall what was learnt during the previous days. Perfect recall of all 100 words makes everything else that follows below much more efficient, and it is highly recommended for the reader to do so.

The reader can use the list below as given, or he can use the list for inspiration—through which he ultimately implements unique identifiers that better suit him. The list includes popularly selected objects, but it is always better to make this more personal; so alterations, subject to the general rules highlighted above, are highly recommended.

№	Object	№	Object	№	Object
0	Saw	34	Mare	68	Chef
1	Tie	35	Mule	69	Shop
2	Knee	36	Match	70	Case
3	Moe (from Simpsons)	37	Mac	71	Cat
4	Row (Rowing oar)	38	Movie	72	Coin
5	Lee (think Bruce Lee)	39	Mob	73	Gum
6	Shoe	40	Rice	74	Car
7	Key	41	Rot	75	Coal
8	Foe	42	Rain	76	Gauge
9	Paw	43	Rum	77	Coco
10	Taz (Tasmanian Devil)	44	Roar (think lion)	78	Cave
11	Toad	45	Rail	79	Cape
12	Tin	46	Ridge	80	Vase
13	Dummy	47	Rock	81	Fat
14	Tower	48	Reef	82	Fan
15	Till	49	Rib	83	Foam
16	Dish	50	Lace	84	Fur
17	Duck	51	Latte	85	Fly
18	Dove	52	Looney (think cartoon)	86	Fish
19	TP (Toilet Paper)	53	Lamb	87	Fog
20	Nose	54	Lorry	88	Fava bean
21	Net	55	Lily	89	Fob
22	Nun	56	Leech	90	Bus
23	Gnome	57	Log	91	Boat
24	Honour (think Godfather)	58	Leaf	92	Bone
25	Nail	59	Lab	93	Palm (L is silent)
26	Hinge	60	Cheese	94	Bear
27	Nike	61	Sh*t (vulgar but effective)	95	Bull
28	Knife	62	Chain	96	Beach
29	Knob	63	Jam	97	Pig
30	Maze	64	Shower	98	Bath
31	Mad	65	Jelly	99	Pipe
32	Moon	66	Shisha	100	Thesis
33	A Mummy	67	Jockey	101	...etc.

Note that memory championship competitors tend to extend their lists further into the thousands, in order to have a ready-made representation of larger chunks of numbers. Such approach speeds up the process of converting numbers into images, and, as an added benefit, also requires fewer images to memorise a given number. It is the difference between memorising 314159 as:

Mo, Tie, Row, Tie, Lee and *Paw*—as single digits,

Versus

Mad, Rot and *Lab*—using the 100 objects listed above,

Versus

Meteor and *Tulip*—using a list extended to 1000 objects.

This, clearly, is an important feature for competitive mentalists. The ability to cut the total number of images by half—or, better still, by two-thirds—greatly improves speed, frees up space for storage (c.f. the Loci System section below), reduces the likelihood of error when recalling, and, ultimately, requires less effort.

It is important to clarify here that extending the list to 1000 is not a necessary part of the system, but rather a method of applying it more competitively. For most purposes (except for memory competitions), 100 is an optimal list size to work with. It is considered optimal since it can be learnt relatively quickly, so as not to be too onerous a step in the learning of the system. Yet, at the same time, it still fulfils the purpose of encoding numerical data into images far faster than the untrained memory.

A final point to mention here is that the list—be it up to 100 or up to 1000—can be expanded less laboriously by simply adding dimensions such as colour, location, smell and sound. This approach effectively increases the list tenfold with each single increase in dimension. We expand on this method later in this chapter.

SYMBOLS

As with words and numbers, symbols can be converted into images as per the following rules:

1. **If the symbol is a representation of an object, then visualise that object.**
2. Otherwise, convert the symbol into an object by attempting to associate it with:
    a. **The concept that the symbol represents.** For instance, the dollar sign, *$*, can be associated with *wealth*—which can be represented by *sacks full of money*, for example.
    b. **An object to which the symbol resembles.** For example, the asterisk sign, *, looks like a snowflake—so *snowflake* can be used to visualise the symbol. (For those familiar with the French comic book series *Asterix*, the eponymous hero can be used instead of *snowflake*.)
    c. **An object that the <u>name</u> for the symbol sounds like.** For example, the plus sign, +, sounds a little like "pus", which can easily be visualised. As an added benefit, it is a rather unpleasant item to visualise, since it evokes feelings of disgust—thus an excellent memory trigger.
3. **The image chosen for each symbol needs to be unique and consistent (i.e., a consistent unique identifier).** Once all the symbols that need to be learnt for a particular topic are gathered, the reader is advised to draw a table listing the object which will represent each symbol. It is

important to avoid duplication and to remain consistent. Each object can only represent one symbol, and will, going forward, always represent just that symbol. And, vice versa, the symbol will always be represented by the aforementioned object and none other. Doing so will save time and reduce the likelihood of errors. To give an example of such a table, in the Mathematical Formulae section we will use the following:

Symbol	Object	Why
+	Pus	*Plus* sounds like "pus".
-	Dennis the Menace	*Minus* sounds like "menace".
=	Eagle	*Equal* sounds like "eagle".
Division (÷)	Machete	Division can be associated with cutting, which, in turn, can be represented by a machete.
Power (^ or x^y)	Bodybuilder	Power can be associated with muscles.
Integration ($\int$)	Interrogation light	*Integration* sounds like "interrogation".
Differentiation (∂)	Sock	One needs to differentiate between pairs of socks when sorting the laundry. This trifling association can then be used to determine that differentiation is represented by a sock.

The key is to fix a single object to represent each symbol, to then write it down—so that a source of reference is readily available. And then to consistently apply it without improvising or altering that which had been fixed. In Part 4 of the book, which introduces the Ultimate Study Method, we provide more details on how to systematise this process.

ADDING DIMENSIONS

Let us assume that a practitioner has mastered the list of objects that represent the numbers 0 to 100. It is then possible to multiply the entire list by a factor of ten—thus yielding a list for 0 to 1,000— without having to fix and memorise an additional list of objects that correspond to the numbers between 101 and 1,000. And this can be extended further by a factor of ten with each application of the method.

The approach simply takes the current object that the number (any number from 0 to 100) represents and adds the following dimensions:

1. Location
2. Colour
3. Action
4. Sound
5. Smell
6. Texture
7. Emotion
8. Shape

The concept of dimensions is best illustrated through examples. Below is a demonstration of how to apply the first three dimensions listed above in order to expand a thousandfold the 0-to-100 list. Broadening further to the other dimensions is then straightforward, but it is excluded from the examples for the following reasons:

a. Extending the list by adding dimensions makes the image much more complex, and thus more difficult to memorise. So there is a trade-off to be optimised.
b. The more dimensions present, the more time it takes to build each image.
c. Going past the first three dimensions requires accessing modalities that are not pictorial. These are, generally, more difficult to keep fixed in the mind for the purpose of memorising using systems. It is certainly possible to apply all eight dimensions effectively, but it requires persistent training in combination with the concentration exercises— introduced in Part 1 of the book—that train these non-pictorial modalities.
d. In sum, the added effort, difficulty and time required can hinder the overall performance.

ADDING THREE DIMENSIONS

For a five-digit number, the first three dimensions will be added using the following formula (where each letter represents a digit):

VWXYZ

1. **VW** represents the numbers we already know from 00 to 99.
   a. The practitioner can use the object for *0* to be the identifier for *00*, the object for *1* to be the identifier for *01*, and so on all the way to *09*, This is fine as long as, from this point forward, *0* is always viewed as *00*, *1* is always viewed as *01*, and likewise up to *09* whenever these figures are encountered.

b. Alternatively, a more versatile approach is to extend the Numbers List to include unique identifiers for the numbers 00 to 09 (using logic for *00* and the phonetic alphabet for the numbers 01 to 09).

№	Object
00	Toilet
01	Suit
02	Sun
03	Zim (think *shipping container*)
04	Syria
05	Silo
06	Sage
07	Sick
08	Safe
09	Soup

2. **X** is the *location* dimension. It will determine where the image shall be taking place.
3. **Y** is the *colour* dimension. It will represent the colour of the objects, the colour of the location, or the colour of the entire image.
4. **Z** is the *action* dimension. It will represent the action taking place within the image.

For each dimension, each digit from zero to nine is depicted by a predetermined representation which belongs to that dimension. The list below provides examples for the first three dimensions.

№	X	Y	Z
0	Jungle	Grey	Parachuting
1	Desert	Red	Showering
2	Lake	Black	Freezing
3	Field	White	Burning
4	Pigsty	Blue	Vomiting
5	Outer Space	Orange	Bleeding
6	Ocean	Green	Sweating
7	Mountain	Pink	Frying
8	Cloud	Brown	Sneezing
9	Football pitch	Yellow	Exploding

As with the preceding lists, the one above needs to be memorised if the practitioner wishes to apply the higher-dimensional technique. It should be noted that memorising this list of 30 items allows one to increase their original list of objects from being 100-long to being 100,000-long. A more than fair return on investment.

EXAMPLES

To best demonstrate the concept of dimensions, let us focus on some examples. Say we wanted to memorise the number 33980. One way to do so would be to split the number into three parts: *3, 39* and *80*, and then to memorise these by linking them together, as we already know the objects representing 0 to 100. The technique presented above, however, allows us to capture this five-digit number with just a single depiction, instead of three. It is equivalent (in result, but not in effort) to having a fixed list for all numbers from 0 to 99,999. The procedure for building such an image is as follows:

1. Begin with *33*, which is **VW** in the formula above. The object which represents this number is that of *a mummy*.

2. The next number is *9*, which is **X** in the formula above. The dimension corresponds to a location, so this *9* determines that the image takes place on a *football pitch*.
3. The next number is *8*, which is **Y** in the formula above. The dimension corresponds to colour, which is *brown* for number *8*. So the mummy's colour is brown, and the image takes place on a football pitch.
4. The last number is *0*, which is **Z** in the formula above. The dimension corresponds to action, which in the case of *0* is *parachuting*. So the brown mummy is parachuting onto a football pitch.

To complete the example, assume that this number represents an internal telephone extension number at one's office. This fact could easily be memorised by linking the number to the person to whom it belongs. For example, say the person's surname was Jones; then all that is required is to link *Jones* to the image we created for the number. An example link could be to think of a football pitch that is covered with lots of Indiana Joneses (instead of the usual football pitch's green grass). And these Joneses are all screaming out of fear and pain as a gigantic brown mummy is parachuting atop of them, crushing them mercilessly.

Try the following number: 28762. What image would this number generate? [Pause to try and then read on.]

A *green knife freezing* its blade off—i.e., shaking uncontrollably due to the freezing cold—at the top of a *mountain*. Say, for example, it was your boss's extension. To memorise this fact, you may wish to picture your boss climbing a mountain, and, just as he arrives to its summit, he locks eyes with a menacing gigantic green knife that is shaking the frost off its blade. You then hear a loud shriek of utter dread emanating from deep within your boss's lungs.

Please note that the example above is neither meant to be cruel nor to encourage rebellious feelings towards authority. It is simply there to demonstrate that in the realm of imagination, the possibilities are infinite, and that there **you should not be bound by the same rules that govern your everyday (real-life) behaviour.** Wherefore, set your imagination free and let fantasy take over. The more extreme the image is, the better the link—hence the stronger the engraving of the memory becomes.

OTHER APPROACHES

Instead of three dimensions, one can extend by less dimensions or more dimensions, depending on the user's preference and the comfort with higher-dimensional visualisation. Below are two such examples to demonstrate the flexibility.

Extending by only two dimensions. The formula here is **VWYZ**: **VW** is as before, **Y** represents *colour*, **Z** represents *action*, and **X** was removed.

Extending by four dimensions. The formula here is **VWXYZA**: **VWXYZ** is as before, and **A** represents *sound*.

There exists a large number of possible permutations of the eight dimensions listed above. The permutation one chooses ultimately depends on which modalities provide the best results—a property that tends to differ across individuals and, for that reason, it remains a personal choice. The key is to settle on a single permutation that works well, say **VWYZ**, for example, and to apply it consistently thereafter. If one keeps changing the permutation used, confusion will quickly set in and spoil the efforts made. (This is again the concept of consistent unique identification.)

Needless to mention that, in order to apply this method for a given permutation, the table listing the relevant property that each number represents for each dimension needs to be memorised.

Using this approach can take a while to master, but it is extremely useful to do so, as will later be demonstrated with specific applications.

The reader may by now have deduced that for a practitioner who has memorised objects for all the numbers between 0 and 9,999, this method allows the possibility of stretching a single image to contain a number that is seven digits long (if extending by three dimensions). In some countries, this would correspond to a telephone number. It is extremely impressive to be able convert a large chunk of numerical data (such as a telephone number) into a single image. If the practitioner wanted to beat the current world record for memorising pi, he would only have to create 11,919 images, whereas, without the extra three dimensions, he would need 20,858 images. Furthermore, extending the same list by eight dimensions would mean only 6,953 images are required for the same feat.

THE IMPORTANCE OF REVISION

The topic of Revision[5] is frequently overlooked in the presentation of novel memory systems. It is true that with memory systems, by creating powerful mnemonic links, a strong bond is created between bits of information. The likelihood, then, of forgetting them is substantially reduced, even after a long period of time has elapsed. While writing this, the author recalls the first time he applied a memory system to remember a face, a

---

[5] *Revision* is used here in the educational sense of the word; that is, "The process of rereading a subject or notes on it, esp. in preparation for an examination" (source: *Collins English Dictionary*).

portrait that was in a memory book. The name and the face of the one who bears it are still clear in his mind even though he only looked at the picture once—that is, in addition to the fact that more than 20 years have elapsed. The reason for this eventuality is likely due to the image created being ludicrous, combined with the great deal of attention that was dedicated given the novelty of the exercise. However, this is an exception rather than the norm. The process by which common memories are stored usually results in the elimination—at least from conscious awareness— of anything that is not of extremely high significance to the individual.

By repeating an action or revisiting a topic, the memory can become entrenched in long-term storage. The act of repetition invokes chemical and structural changes in the brain, making the connections between neurons more efficient—thus requiring less energy to be used when recalling the information at future points in time. It also has the effect of signalling the importance of a factor/task/fact that has become, given its repetition, significant in a person's life. The brain responds to such signals by transferring the memory into long-term storage.

Most images constructed using creative linking, as presented above, begin to fade after 24 to 48 hours. Although this property ranges across individuals, the aforementioned period appears to be the common eventuality. Therefore, in order to reliably incorporate data into long-term memory storage, a revision will have to take place before the abovementioned window closes. The goal is to perform the least amount of revision (for the sake of optimal use of time) while still achieving the task of long-term storage. This is accomplished by ensuring that each round of revision is scheduled just prior to the memory fading away.

Research on this topic, as highlighted earlier in this part of the book, indicates that memory decay appears to follow a defined set of windows; by knowledge of these, one is able to optimally time the revision periods. For the long-term storage of memories, it is therefore recommended to follow the procedure below:

1. Memorise the data with the techniques discussed above. The point in time at which this is performed is defined as T_0.
2. Repeat the scene or image in your mind immediately afterwards, to ensure the data has been absorbed.
3. An hour later, that is, $T_0 + 1$ hour, attempt to recall the data and review the scene/image.
4. Ideally, a couple of hours before going to bed, that is, $T_0 + 12$ hours (assuming that the data was learnt in the morning; otherwise, simply perform 12 hours after T_0), review again.
5. Review again the next day, i.e., $T_0 + 24$ hours.
6. Review once more a week later, i.e., $T_0 + 1$ week.
7. Review once more two weeks later, i.e., $T_0 + 2$ weeks.
8. Review once more a month later, i.e., $T_0 + 1$ month.
9. Review once more three months later, i.e., $T_0 + 3$ months.
10. Review once more six months later, i.e., $T_0 + 6$ months.
11. Review once more twelve months later, i.e., $T_0 + 12$ months.

The reader may look at the monolithic list above and feel disheartened or overwhelmed. At this point, to make such feelings worse, it is crucial to re-iterate that: for long term storage, extra stimulation is absolutely necessary. However, the task is much simpler than it appears in the list above. All that is really required is a brief glimpse at an image that is funny, absurd, enjoyable, fantastical and, most satisfyingly, of your own creation. It takes mere seconds, and it should be seen as entertainment rather than revision.

The list above is designed to ensure long-term storage—that is, it is a sufficient condition—though in most circumstances, and largely depending on the strength of the links created, what is necessary may be much shorter. Nonetheless, without knowledge of the individual's forgetting curve and thus the precise measurement of each link's strength, we must be pragmatic and rely on the sufficient condition provided by the list above. But we do so by adjusting the depth of each revision based on the level of retention: speeding through where the practitioner feels the material was fully absorbed, and focusing more on information whose retention feels weaker.

According to the author's experience, memory systems that promise long-term memory results without the review of the image/scene are simply not realistic. Such an omission is certainly helpful for marketing purposes: it is much less impressive to place on the cover of a self-improvement book that several repetitions would be required for long-term memory storage. An omission without sinister intentions, perhaps, but the effects are detrimental nonetheless.

The difference between the repetition proposed above and the repetition which is used in rote[6] learning, is that the repetition in the latter must be performed just to be able to absorb the information in the first place. Whereas in the system presented above, the information is absorbed effortlessly on the first read-through.

Furthermore, for long-term storage, information learnt using rote learning would still require repetition as per the list presented above. It is a consequence of the fact that even information learnt by a large number of repetitions on day one, notwithstanding the

---

[6] Rote learning, as referred to here, pertains to the standard approach of rereading or repeatedly covering the information until it is committed to memory.

effort involved, is susceptible to elimination from longer-term storage if it is not deemed sufficiently important. It is therefore clear that the system provided herewith is far superior (to rote learning) for absorbing information. In this system, repetition is only required for very long-term storage. It is not, however, required for acquiring the information in the first place.

The reader is strongly recommended to evaluate the importance of the information being studied before dismissing the revision stage. It would be lamentable to initially spend time and effort studying and memorising, only to find that after a few months the memories had dissipated, and that only a mild trace of "knowing that you once knew" has remained. A small effort invested in revision would allow you to maintain the memories for a very long time. And this, in turn, would increase the general knowledge available for you to leverage on when learning new topics, when making decisions, when planning, when thinking, as well as when generating new ideas or solutions to problems.

Ultimately, it is one's intention that should determine the length of time during which a memory is to be retained. If the purpose of the memorisation is short-term, for example, when performing mental arithmetic (as illustrated in Part 5 of the book), revision is not necessary. For studying, research or general knowledge accumulation, revision is essential.

Given this section's focus on long-term memory, it is perhaps fitting to briefly mention the topic of sleep and its contribution to the process. Sleep is an important, if not absolutely vital, component in long-term memory storage. It is recommended to regularly obtain at least eight hours of uninterrupted sleep per day—preferably going to sleep at the same time every night, and doing so before[7] 11 p.m. It is believed that memory consolidation occurs mainly during sleep, and that interrupted, irregular, or inadequately short sleep can cause memories not to be transferred to long-term storage.

BEING SYSTEMATIC AND ENFORCING ORDER

For the techniques to function optimally, order and clarity must be established. The goal is to maximise efficiency and to ensure that there are no ambiguities between the components of the system. As an example touched upon earlier, assume that the number 37 was converted into *mug* and the number 79 was converted into *cup*. Clearly, these choices present an ambiguity: whenever the practitioner recalls an image that involves any form of drinkware, the possibility of misinterpreting the image increases ("Was the pink tiger drinking from a cup, or was it from a mug?").

It may not be feasible to completely remove all ambiguities, especially when several data types are being studied across numerous topics. Nevertheless, the aim should be to systematically design the memorisation approach to minimise the possibilities of ambiguity and to impose order for maximal efficiency. This will be clearly demonstrated when the applications of the system are discussed in detail below. For now, the reader is advised to ensure the following requirements are fulfilled:

---

[7] To better understand the importance of both the start time and the length of one's sleep, the interested reader may wish to peruse the topic of *circadian rhythms*.

1. **Building blocks**. Before memorising a major topic, break down the information into building blocks that can be uniquely identified by easy-to-visualise objects. For example, each letter, symbol, number, syllable, sound, smell, radical, etc., should have a unique identifier.
2. **Unique identifiers**. The building blocks can then be used to construct unique identifiers for the pieces of information contained in the topic.
3. **Consistency**. The unique identifiers should thereafter be applied consistently.
4. **No conflict**. Any building block or unique identifier should neither conflict nor present an ambiguity across topics. To that end, it is advisable to use a notebook to write down the list of building blocks, and, where feasible, the list of key unique identifiers. The phonetic alphabet presented earlier in this part of the book is an archetypical example for a list of building blocks. The table listing unique identifiers for the numbers 0 to 100 is a quintessential example for a list of key unique identifiers.

The crux is to break down the topic into its most basic building blocks. For each such building block, a unique identifier should be assigned. Through this approach, any complex piece of information that is a combination of these building blocks can easily be visualised and thus memorised. Thereafter, the unique identifier for the complex piece of information can be used as a building block for pieces of information that are more complex still (and so forth).

To eliminate any confusion around the principle presented here, note that it is absolutely not necessary to tabulate each item being memorised and the unique identifier to represent it. The idea is to generate a set of building blocks of which there are far less than data in the entire topic. This far smaller set of elements is then tabulated and used to organise the entire topic and to systematically derive other unique identifiers. For example, the phonetic alphabet was the set of building blocks for any topic involving numbers. It is finite in size and easy to tabulate, yet it is able to transform any number into a unique identifier.

Then, once progress is made in a topic, to further improve speed and efficiency, larger building blocks become desirable. In the case of topics involving numbers, tabulating the unique identifiers for 0 to 100 achieves such a task.

In this approach, the assignment of objects to represent information follows a methodical and efficient allocation. This minimizes the overall efforts required to memorise a topic, eliminates the possibility of confusion, and allows usability across similar or related topics.

The Applications chapter will provide clear examples of this instruction and will clarify, through practical observation, precisely what is required.

SYSTEMS

Having covered the general concepts of memory in the previous chapter, the reader should by now be familiar with how to convert pieces of information into visualisable objects, should be cognisant with what to do with those objects, and should be comfortable with the key ingredients required to make the memory persist.

This chapter focuses on the major systems that facilitate the fast and effective filing of information. The author introduces the different possible filing approaches, where each tends to serve a different purpose and is optimal under different circumstances. The circumstances and their matching systems are then detailed in the Applications chapter.

Except for the Link System, all other systems involve filing the data away by linking a new piece of information to something that is already known. This is commonly termed *pegging*, and the item that is already known is aptly named the *peg*.

The gluing toolbox and the rules discussed thus far remain the same. The only difference is in the method with which the images are filed in the brain.

In general, there are two possible approaches to filing:

1. **Link System (new to new).** Link the first piece of new information to the topic's name. Subsequently, connect all other pieces of new information together by linking each piece to its neighbour.

2. **Peg, Loci and Grid systems (new to old).** Link each piece of new information to something that is already known—this can be one of the following:

a. **An ordered list of items.** A list that is already present in conscious memory; for example, the list of objects for the numbers from 0 to 100 (presented earlier in this part of the book).

b. **A room.** The room's contents as well as their position within the room need to already be available to conscious memory. Any room in your home could serve this purpose.

c. **A palace, a city or an entire country.** The monuments or key attractions, and their order of appearance, must already be available to conscious memory. Some examples could be: a museum you frequently visit, a favoured public park, a main road traversing the city in which you reside, or key monuments in a country you have recently visited.

d. **An imaginary room, palace, city or country.** The figmental contents, monuments, or key attractions, and their order of appearance, must already be available to conscious memory. This is similar to items 2.b. and 2.c. above; however, there is one fundamental difference: it is purely imaginary. More details on how to design such locations are presented later in this chapter.

e. **A grid of items.** The items' location within the grid must already be available to conscious memory. More details on how to design such a grid are presented later in this chapter.

THE LINK SYSTEM

The Link System, which was utilised to introduce the basic principles of memory techniques (and *linking* in particular), is a very free approach that is not limited by the size of the lists/places you have available to you. Size limit is generally a constraint in other filing systems.

The approach allows connecting, at least theoretically, an infinite list of items in a desired order. The system also allows one to recall the data either backwards or forwards. But, unfortunately, it does not allow numerical positions to be specified or recalled easily. So, for example, one could memorise a list of 1,000 items and know that *fridge* comes after *TV*, but one would not be able to recall that *fridge* is the 923rd item and that *TV* is the 922nd. Consequently, the application of this system is only appropriate when recollection of the precise numerical position is not required.

An illustration of this system was already covered in the Key Principles of Memory section, but, for completeness, a detailed explanation of the steps involved is included below:

1. **What does the information to be memorised signify?** As an example, it could be a simple shopping list. Knowing this detail is crucial for correct filing and retrieval; without it, the reminder of what is the first item on this list would be lost, and hence the entire recollection could be jeopardised.

2. **Link the first piece of information to the representation of what the information signifies (from Step 1 above).** For example, if shoes were the first item on a shopping list, one would need to link *shoes* to *shopping list.*

3. **Continue linking each item to the next until you reach the last item on the list.** This should be performed in the same manner as the linking illustrated in the Key Principles of Memory section.

4. **Repeat the list in your mind to ensure that the links are strong,** and, if necessary, fortify the links that are deemed weak. This is essentially the first step of the revision process, as was detailed in The Importance of Revision section.

Step 1 of the above procedure is absolutely crucial. And, in being so instrumental, it also points out the disadvantage of the system: if a single item is forgotten, the rest of the list could be lost. Generally, such an extreme scenario does not transpire, since knowing any other item on the list would trigger the memories of its neighbours on either side, and these, in turn, to their neighbours, and so on. For example, in a list of 1,000 items, if one had forgotten the first item but remembered that one of the items was *fridge*, the links to the next and previous items (i.e., those on either side of *fridge*) immediately come to mind. Thenceforth, one can work forwards and backwards from *fridge* to retrieve the rest of the list.

Perhaps a demonstration would better elucidate this point: if you hear "iPad", what are the two images that immediately come to mind?

[Assuming that the reader followed the visualisations detailed by the example in the Key Principles of Memory section, images involving *orange* (to the right of *iPad*) and *coffee* (to the left of *iPad*) should spontaneously appear.]

THE PEG SYSTEM

The Peg System differs to the Link System in two ways. The first is that the Peg System specifically defines the numerical position of a piece of information. The second is that the Peg System requires the pegs, i.e., the items in one's already-known list, to have been previously determined and fixed in one's mind. Consequently, the Peg System is limited by the length of each list, as well as by the number of such lists one has available.

Creating a list of objects whose order (both relative to each other as well as in numerical terms) you are familiar with, allows you to thereafter peg—that is, to file into previously-established compartments—information in a way that would allow you to retrieve the fact, the order and the precise numerical position with which it was meant to be memorised. It is appropriately named the Peg System: we are essentially pegging a previously unknown item onto another item that is fixed and known. The clear advantages of this approach over the Link System are:

a. Both the order of the items as well as their exact numerical positions can be recalled.
b. Forgetting one item does not jeopardise the entire list.

The mechanism involved here is fundamentally the same across all the memory systems: **the act of linking something new to something that is already known**. In the Link System, known items are created on the fly: once an item is linked to the item that precedes it, it becomes known, and thus a following item can be linked to it—and so forth. For the Peg System, new items must be established prior to applying the system. This means one needs to create in advance plenty of lists with items that can be easily visualised, while ensuring their numerical order of appearance is also captured. The rules for the creation of such lists are as follows:

1. **Easy to visualise**. Each item on the list must be easy to visualise—preferably a common object.
2. **Numerical position**. The numerical position of the object within the list must be known.

3. **No conflict**. There must be no conflict with other lists previously established that are still in current use; i.e., the same object should not appear on more than one list.
4. **Logical connection**. There should be a logical connection between the items on the list. That is, they should all belong to some group, or type, or they should all be derived using a certain technique—e.g., the objects representing the numbers 0 to 100 were derived using the phonetic alphabet.

In terms of actually attaching the new information to the list of pegs: **The act of pegging involves the very same glue that is used for linking**. The procedure is exactly identical: make images that are wild, absurd, exaggerated, emotional, colourful, etc. Again, to emphasise, the only differences between using the Peg System and using the Link System are that the peg list is known in advance, whereas the link list is new; and that the former has established numerical values for each item, whilst the latter does not.

Detailed below are examples of lists that can be easily constructed for the application of the Peg System. The reason for establishing more than one list should be evident. It is to ensure a more efficient filing of the information by avoiding the use of the same list for remembering everything. Perhaps the apt analogy of utilising a small clotheshorse to hang and dry all the clothes in one's household could better illustrate this point. It is glaringly obvious that having several such frames will make the task of drying faster and more efficient. In the same way, pegging many new sets of items onto one list, all at the same time, might cause confusion about which items belong to which set. This, in turn, would require more time to be spent strengthening the images.

For example, say one wanted to memorise the shopping list, the day's schedule, the list of presidents and some recent cricket scores using just a single peg list. It is inevitable that some of the images would blur, since each object on the peg list has four separate items pegged to it. The images would then need to be repeated and strengthened—which would be an inefficient use of one's time. Far better would be to have several prepared peg lists, which could then be used more effectively for the same task.

The examples below should provide some inspiration on how to approach the creation of a new peg list. However, for most day-to-day uses, the below-discussed lists more than suffice in capturing and filing information without conflict. The creation of additional lists may therefore not be necessary—it is ultimately dependent upon the individual's needs.

As with other portions of the memory system, consistency contributes to efficiency. For example, it could be decided that the Numbers List (see below) should always be used for the shopping list, and that the Effigy List (also detailed below) should always be used for the day's schedule. Once the decision on which list should be used for which purpose has been made, it should be applied henceforth without further changes.

THE NUMBERS LIST

The list of numbers from 0 to 100 with their corresponding objects derived using the phonetic alphabet has already been presented. For peg-related applications and to avoid confusion while instructing, let us name it the Numbers List. It can be utilised to remember any other list (consisting of less than 101 items) by pegging each item in the new list to an existing object in the Numbers List. For example, say you have the following shopping list:

1. Eggs
2. Beans
3. Minced Beef
4. Milk
5. Soap
6. Lettuce

As demonstrated in earlier sections, with the Link System this list can be memorised by linking each item to the next. With the Peg System, however, the process involves pegging each item in the shopping list to its corresponding item on the Numbers List.

Let us begin with the first item on the shopping list: *eggs*. The corresponding item on the Numbers List is *tie*, so peg *eggs* to *tie*. Perhaps try to imagine cracking a tie on the frying pan's rim, when, all of a sudden, a smaller tie falls out and starts to sizzle in the hot oil (make sure that the tie which you crack is enormous and disproportionate to the setting in which it is imagined).

Moving on to the second item on the list: *beans*. The corresponding item on the Numbers List is *knee*, so peg *beans* to *knee*. You could try to visualise—and feel—how it would be like to walk around with a knee that is made out of a bean. Imagine the bean as large yet soft while still connecting the thigh to the shin; exaggerate the image and feel the discomfort that such a scenario would bring.

Proceeding with the rest of the items on the list:

Minced beef should be pegged to *Moe*; *milk* should be pegged to *row*; *soap* to *Lee*; and *lettuce* to *shoe*.

Once the above images have been created and, say, the number two is called out, it should immediately summon the image of a knee, which, in turn, should trigger the nonsensical image of a person that has a massive overgrown bean where a knee would normally be. And, by that, immediately indicating that the second item on the shopping list is *beans*.

It is clear, therefore, that the user can either recall the items in their intended order—i.e. by going through the objects of the Numbers List seriatim—or by looking up an object in a particular numerical position that is of interest.

THE EFFIGY LIST

The Effigy List below, as the name might suggest, was created by trying to find the object that most resembles the shape of each number in the list. Upon further inspection, the reader may decide on better choices of objects for some of the numbers—this is fine as long as it is applied consistently going forward.

№	Peg
0	Smoke ring
1	Tree
2	Swan
3	Ant
4	Sail
5	Hook
6	Elephant Trunk
7	Boomerang
8	Grand Prix/Racing Track
9	Seahorse
10	Basketball net

As applicable to all peg lists, the list above can be extended to the length desired by the practitioner.

Even for the short list provided above, it is still possible to find a useful application—the day's calendar, for example, where each number can represent an hour's session of a working day. This example, therefore, should highlight that having a few short lists which are there just to serve a specific purpose, is quite a reasonable approach. By that token, extending all lists to a high number, say 100, is not necessary. Some should be short and some should long, in order to correspond to the different types of data one may wish to memorise.

THE ALPHABET LIST

Much as the Numbers List serves both as a list of unique identifiers for the numbers from 0 to 100 as well as a peg list, the Alphabet List serves a dual purpose too. These are listed as follows:

1. It provides a unique identifier to each letter. This is useful when memorising abstract ideas that involve letters positioned in an illogical manner (from a language's perspective). A typical example would be mathematical formulae, which will be addressed in the Applications chapter.
2. The list, given that the letters have a natural numerical order, can also serve as a peg list.

It is simple to remember the Alphabet List—as should be the case with all peg lists—since the underlying elements that form the list have a logical aspect or rule which connects them. In the case of the Numbers List, it was the use of the phonetic alphabet; in the case of the Effigy List, it was the shape of the number; and here, for the Alphabet List, it is the most distinctive object that sounds similar to the way in which the letter is pronounced.

Letter	Peg
A	Ape
B	Bee
C	Sea
D	Dill
E	Eel
F	Elf
G	Gin
H	Hedge
I	Eye
J	Jail
K	Cane
L	Hell
M	Ham
N	Hen
O	Ho, ho, ho! (think *Santa*)
P	Pea
Q	Cue
R	Arrr! (think *pirate*)
S	Ace
T	Tea
U	Hugh (think *Hugh Grant*)
V	Veal
W	"Dubya" (think *George W. Bush*)
X	Eggs
Y	Wine
Z	Zit

THE RHYME LIST

Similar to the previous lists, the following list was derived by finding an object that rhymes, or nearly rhymes, with the number. Employing perfect rhymes is not necessary; being close in sound is sufficient. Having a single logical element that unites all the objects in the list is the key point. Applying such an element loosely is therefore permitted.

№	Peg
0	Zorro
1	Gun
2	Zoo
3	Tree
4	Door
5	Hive
6	Vicks
7	Heaven
8	Slate
9	Mine
10	Zen (think *meditating monk*)

THE BODY LIST

The Body List is ordered according to each body part's location from the head downwards. This list does not immediately provide a numerical reference for each peg, but such a reference can be added by remembering which are the 5th, the 10th and the 15th pegs on the list. These are called *markers*.

For example, in the list below, *tongue* is the 5th body part, *stomach* is the 10th , and *toenails* is the 15th—this is straightforward to remember, as each belongs to a different section of the body (the tongue belonging to the upper third;

stomach to the middle third; and toenails to the lower third). The three pegs then become markers for the numerical order of the list.

After new information has been pegged onto the list, if a numerical position needs to be recalled, it is simple to work it out from the nearest marker to each peg. For example, say that the item pegged to *mouth* was *mosquito*. It would be simple to work out that *mosquito* is the fourth item in the list, since the nearest marker, *tongue*, is the fifth peg and is immediately successive to *mouth*.

Body Part
Forehead
Eyebrows
Nostrils
Mouth
Tongue
Neck
Chest
Arms
Fingers
Stomach
Groin
Thighs
Calves
Foot
Toenails

THE LOCI SYSTEM

The Loci System is treated separately even though loci are, in principle, peg lists, since loci incorporate a spatial dimension that distinguishes them from abstract peg lists.

Upon further reflection, a more nuanced difference emerges from the Loci System's reliance on a memory of a place (locus), be it a city, a road, a house or a room. The location does not have to be created artificially using a unifying rule or theme, as was the case for the peg lists presented above. Instead, the location should be somewhere extremely familiar to you, and it should contain plenty of visually distinct objects or monuments that can be used to deposit information—i.e., to be used as pegs. And it is this familiarity with the location that ennobles the Loci System: the spatial dimension focuses the mind on a specific place (and activates the brain regions responsible for spatial awareness) rather than an abstract ethereal location where other links or pegs are imagined. The act of focusing the mind using a specific location and the consequent activation of additional (sensory-integrating) regions of the brain, together result in stronger memories. Deploying loci thus gives rise to sinewy pegs.

The Loci System permits the storage of an incredibly large amount of data, which, in practice, is only limited by the size of the location chosen. The information can be stored and recalled almost as fast as one takes to mentally travel around the said location. And, as an additional benefit, the topic being memorised can be self-contained within the location chosen. This means that revision of a topic can be performed without any notes for guidance, since all such a revision would entail is to walk through the aforementioned location (that is, walk through mentally) and review the items pegged along the way.

The order of the information can be recalled as easily as the journey itself, as long as the rules below are adhered to. However, if the intention is to use this method while still being able to recall the numerical position of each item, then markers, as introduced for the Body List, will have to be placed at fixed increments along the way.

There are several common choices of loci; these are described in the subsections below.

HOUSES AND ROOMS

A classic example for a locus would be a room in your house. To prepare the locus, simply choose a room and travel through it (mentally) clockwise while recording all the significant objects to which information may be attached.

Being systematic is important for accurate recollection of the order of the information being memorised. When using your house as a locus, the requirements to achieve this are as follows:

1. **Clockwise through the house.** Starting the journey from the front door, navigate clockwise through the house—travelling from the lowest floor to the highest floor (completing a clockwise circuit of each floor before proceeding to the next).
2. **Clockwise through each room.** At every room along the way, navigate clockwise starting from the room's entrance.
3. **Set the pegs.** Perform the journey (mentally) a few times before using the locus for the first time to store information. During these practice journeys, record in your mind the items you will be using as pegs according to the following criteria:
   a. Each item should be fixed to a position in the room (e.g., a cupboard, a fridge or an oven); or, at least, the place where it is deposited is always the same (e.g. a coat on a coatrack or a book on a bookshelf).
   b. Each item needs to be distinct and easy to visualise.

c. Avoid using the same type of item multiple times in each room. For example, using several individual books—each as a peg—would not be effective and may cause confusion; using the entire bookcase would be far better.

4. **Place markers**. If numerical order is desired, place a marker at every fifth peg. For the marker, you will need to use an object that represents the number which the marker aims to signal. For example, linking, in a very absurd manner, a *rail* next to the 45th peg in the chosen location, would be a good marker. The reader should note that doing so is not necessary if numerical order is not important for the memory task, or if a marker every five pegs is too granular. You may choose to instead place a marker every ten pegs or place no marker at all—it all depends on the intended use of the locus. A common choice is to have some loci with markers and some loci without markers. The former can then be applied to memory tasks that require numerical positioning, whereas the latter can be used for everything else.

5. **Review**. Once established, review the journey through the locus—and any markers along the way—in your mind a few times to ensure it is firmly fixed.

You can always extend a locus, but **do not alter the portion of the locus that has already been established** (even if the actual physical location—for example, a room in your house—changes with time).

To better illustrate the implementation of a room as a locus, let us outline an example. Take a room in a house—say, the kitchen; navigating clockwise you notice the following items:

A *fridge,* a *microwave,* a *toaster,* a *sink,* an *oven,* a *cupboard,* a *bin* and a *blender.*

You now have a locus to which new information can be attached. As an example, you may decide that you wish to use your house, going clockwise through each room, clockwise through the house, and travelling from the lowest floor upwards, in order to memorise the list of presidents of the United States. Using the example room above (and assuming, somewhat implausibly but without loss of generality, that it is the first room in the house), you would then peg George Washington to the *fridge*, John Adams to the *microwave*, Thomas Jefferson to the *toaster*, and so on. The challenge of converting the president's name into an object that can be visualised will be clarified in the Applications chapter. The only concept that the reader should understand at this point in the book is: all you are doing here is using a location—which is known and firmly fixed in your mind—in order to store new information.

Note that, as with all memory techniques, the glue for connecting the unknown item (i.e., the new piece of information) to the known item on the locus is the same: use absurd imagery and ludicrous action as detailed in the previous sections.

PALACES, CITIES AND COUNTRIES

To remember long lists of items or comprehensive topics of study, one would require larger loci than mere houses and rooms. The principle, however, remains the same. All that is needed is to have locations that are already known and clear in one's mind, and then to apply the same technique as for the rooms of the house.

The core requirement is to be systematic: the journey through the locus must always be the same. So, for example, say one would like to use the journey to work as a locus. The most important point is to always follow the monuments along the journey in the same manner and not to change the order as and when one feels the wish to do so. If the order is changed, the method will still work, but the ability to recall sequences will be diminished. As a consequence, it will no longer be possible to summon the concepts of the topic in the order with which they were memorised, and, furthermore, the revision process will become more laborious. This is of greater concern when the practitioner uses a city as the locus (rather than a room, where the number of paths is strictly limited). Where one is able to travel the city via different routes and side streets, if no systematic procedure is imposed, the aforementioned effects will be severe.

The practitioner is therefore recommended to follow one route that systematically passes through all the main roads, streets, and alleys. One approach could be as follows:

1. **If the city has a ring road**, start the journey by travelling the entire ring road clockwise from the south-easternmost point.
2. **If the city does not have a ring road**, or after completing the journey along the ring road, start at the south-easternmost position and travel towards the north in a systematic east to west (followed by west to east) sweep. Viewed from above, it would appear as a snake crawling northward.
3. **Travel through each main road once**, taking the monuments on both sides as pegs.
4. **Travel through streets and alleys clockwise**: covering one side and its monuments on the way in, and then the other side and its monuments on the way back to the main road.
5. **If at its end a main road does not connect to another main road**, the last street connecting to the next main

road is used. However, it is not travelled clockwise, but rather traversed directly to arrive at the next main road.

Note that the entire procedure above can be applied to smaller units of a city—for example, a city divided into quadrants or neighbourhoods. These smaller units can then be connected by the rule of travelling from east to west (followed by west to east for the next row up), starting from the south-easternmost point and heading north.

The crux, as for simpler loci, is to impose general rules that guarantee order in the loci.

The above procedure should provide a template for any type of reasonably flat locus, be it a round structure or a grid. Another approach, which can be useful for round loci, is to travel in circles either from the inside outwards or the outside inwards.

Note that the procedure above is merely an outline, it is not meant to be fully exhaustive—its purpose is to illustrate how appropriately designed rules can impose order in the locus. Modifications can be made to the above general procedure to account for topographical subtleties and other road types. The preferred method remains to be the choice of the practitioner. Irrespective of the choice made, however, the following rules must be adhered to:

1. **Same route**. Always travel along the locus via the same route; do not change or improvise along the way.
2. **Efficient route**. Cover the territory by following an efficient travel route that captures the entire locus. In doing so, you will be using up most of what the locus has to offer. Note that when rules are imposed, some portions of a locus may need to be ignored. This is the cost of imposing order; though in most cases it will be minimal. (E.g., if the rule is to follow the last street leading to the

next main road [say, main road B], then the main road currently being travelled [call it main road A] will not be completed to its end point, as the street connecting A to B may be placed prior to that end point. The untraveled portion of main road A, however, is likely to be small in comparison to its entirety.)

3. **Set the pegs**. Decide which of the monuments along the way you will be using. Once decided, do not make changes or alterations.
4. **Peg information**. Peg the new information being studied to the monuments chosen for the locus—using absurd images and nonsensical action, as before.
5. **Review**. Review the new information memorised by mentally travelling along the established journey across your locus.

Below is a list of some more capacious ("more" is in comparison to a room or a house) common loci. The journey through enclosed loci should be bound by the same rules applied to the locus of a house. Outdoor loci should be subject to the same rules applied to the locus of a city.

1. **The journey to work**.
2. **The journey to a friend**.
3. **An art gallery**.
4. **A neighbourhood**. The area you grew up in or the one in which you currently reside.
5. **A palace**. If you have had the pleasure of roaming through a palace, or have seen a documentary of such a journey, this would make a good locus.
6. **A museum**. With all the exhibits, artefacts and statues contained within, a museum represents an excellent choice of locus.
7. **A village**.

8. **A town or city**.
9. **A country**.

The list above is ordered by a progressive level of difficulty. It is relatively simple to walk through a palace or a museum, become familiar with the items along the way, and then use these with the system explained above. Whereas, when one considers whole cities and countries, the task becomes much more exacting.

For most purposes, the need to have a whole town as one's locus is superfluous—this is usually reserved for the memorisation of very large chunks of information in competitive situations. For example, memorising as many decks of cards as possible within a given time frame is one of the challenges in the World Memory Championships; using a town locus would be ideal for such a task.

The level of difficulty notwithstanding, the task of mapping out in one's mind an entire town is not impossible, and doing so can, in fact, be a rather pleasurable undertaking. All that is needed is the desire to go for a walk (or a bicycle ride) and systematically cover the desired location, enjoying the scenery whilst noting any monuments that can become useful pegs.

So building a locus is essentially sightseeing—an activity most of the population performs for leisure. Enjoying more of this fun activity would provide more storage space for other bits of data. The procedure utilised could be a variation of the following:

1. Go sightseeing (museums, towns, cities, etc., as detailed above) and note the monuments that are of interest to you. Be systematic in the way with which you cover the territory. Taking brief physical notes of the monuments along the way—like writing them down, taking a photo, or filming a video—can be useful when first establishing the locus as well as for future reference.

2. Or, choose a topic that you wish to memorise and take your notes of the topic along with you on a sightseeing journey. At each monument you encounter, attempt to memorise a new piece of information from your topic by pegging it to the monument you see in front of you. Again, proceed systematically through the territory to ensure an orderly coverage. This approach allows one to create a new locus at the same time as memorising a new topic.

3. After you complete either one of the two approaches above, mentally review your journey a few times, observing the monuments along the way (and the pegged information, if the second approach was followed). Once you are comfortable with the journey and the monuments along it, do not change or alter them. The journey can then be used to memorise temporary information, or it can be used to contain the entirety of a specific topic.

To better illustrate the principles involved, let us use an example journey—the route taken to go to work. In the journey's note-form description below, the words in italics are the monuments of the locus, to which new information can be pegged.

1. Exiting the *building* in which the practitioner resides.
2. Traversing the road at the *zebra crossing.*
3. Walking past an *old pub* with a blue wooden sign (names of monuments are not necessary—it is the visual representation that matters).
4. Crossing the *bridge* to enter the wharf.
5. Passing by the *ferry station.*
6. Saying good morning to the waiter at the *Chinese restaurant* that is next to the *long flight of stairs.*
7. To the left stands the *Four Seasons hotel.*
8. Continuing straight, entering *a circular garden.*

9. Past the garden and onto the *main road.*
10. Crossing the road, arriving in front of *high rise building* made of steel and glass.

The above description is meant to illustrate all that is required, in terms of detail and order, of a typical locus. The key, again, is to utilise your own journey—one you have personally experienced and can recall well.

Once you have gained some practice with this method, you would come to appreciate its power. The enjoyable feeling generated by mentally touring through pleasant sceneries, outpouring while revising a topic, is priceless, and it makes studying that much more enjoyable. And, as an added benefit, the emotions already present in the journey, as well as the concreteness of the spatial dimension, causes any pegged information to be deeply implanted.

IMAGINARY LOCI

The Imaginary Loci technique is an extension of the Loci System that uses one's creative powers to build loci mentally. The idea is to simply relax and mentally construct a house, a palace, a town, a city, a country, or even an entire world. It is much like the *SimCity* game; the difference, however, is that you are not limited by the variations that a computer allows—you are only limited by your imagination, which, for all intents and purposes, is infinite.

This method is more difficult to apply since one must become familiar with the newly imagined place before it can be used as a locus. And it is crucial that the locus be as vivid and clear as any real physical location that is stored in one's memory. When one physically visits a location, the memory of the scenery is automatically captured. But, when one creates in the mind a location that does not exist, the memory requires more effort to become established. Nonetheless, with practice this process, too, can become automatic.

An example application of an imagined locus could be to create a neighbourhood—create mentally, that is—for the purpose of grouping together and memorising all books of a certain genre. More specifically, say you wanted to memorise a group of ten leadership books you have recently read; the procedure would be as follows:

1. **In your mind, create a small neighbourhood.** Whichever type of neighbourhood you wish to build is fine (urban, suburban, historic, gated, rural, etc.)—there are no limitations, but mixing the different types across loci is a good idea.

2. **Build a road traversing the neighbourhood.** Visualise clearly the colour of the road, the width of the pavement, the trees along the way, etc.

3. **Visualise a "leading" book**—for this is the genre of the books you will be depositing here—dressed in military uniform and carrying a sword. Imagine how he is leading the army of books that is marching behind him: vividly picture the billions of books marching to this leader's commands on the new road you have just created.

4. **Now build a house at the entrance to the neighbourhood.** Whichever type of house you wish to build is fine—let your imagination flow and create whatever you feel fits well in the location.

5. **Give this house a mailbox, and peg the name of the book being memorised to the mailbox.** The book could be, for example, Sun Tzu's *The Art of War*. As a peg, you may then decide to picture a *mailbox* that is at *war* with a

canvas (*canvas* is to remind you of Art, and *war* is for War). Picture, in front of the house, the mailbox and the canvas warring each other using machine guns, tanks, fighter jets, atomic bombs, etc.—i.e., make ludicrous vivid images in order to link the items together.

6. **Next, walk on the footpath leading towards the house and begin to vividly picture its architecture and properties.** At this stage you can further refine the house in any way you wish: making it modern, western, eastern, new, old, large, small, colourful, plain, etc. Once completed, you should, at the very least, be able to answer the following questions: What colour is the main door? What colour is the house painted in? How many floors does it have?

7. **Then proceed with creating the interior.** As you enter the house, what is the first room you walk into? Is it the living room? What objects are inside this room? What colour are the walls?

8. **Once the first room has been created, work your way clockwise through the items inside it, making sure each item's position is vivid and clear.** After establishing the room's contents, to each item in the room peg one key piece of information from the first chapter of the book (*The Art of War*, to continue with the previous example). Always travel clockwise through the room to maintain a clear order, and remember to use exaggerated and ludicrous imagery when pegging.

9. **Proceed by applying the same approach to the other rooms of the house:** each room corresponds to a chapter, and each item in the room captures—via pegging—one piece of information from the chapter. (Travelling through the house is performed in the same order as for non-imaginary house-type loci.)

10. **After depositing all the information contained in the first book, exit the house and walk to the next house on the road**. It could be on the opposite side of the road or it could be that the houses are all placed on one side of the road, with, perhaps, a view towards the sea on the other—the choice is yours, design the locus as you please.

11. **Give this house a different mailbox or no mailbox at all**. You can create a variation here, where you peg the name of the book to the footpath leading to the house instead of using the mailbox. Again, it is up to you; the possibilities are infinite. You can even design the front of the house to be painted in the same pattern and colour as the front cover of the book. The main point is to peg the name of the book to any item outside of the house so that you are clear on what information is contained inside the house. It is analogous to the naming of folders prior to filing information within them.

12. **Enter the second house and allocate each room to represent a chapter**, memorising the key points of the chapter by pegging each bit of information being memorised to an item inside the room.

In the example above, the new information was being memorised at the same time as the imaginary locus was being created. This is one approach to using an imaginary locus. The other approach is to establish the imaginary locus two days prior to deployment, reviewing it a few times a day (two to three times would suffice) for these two days.

The first approach is generally more convenient, as the locus grows just enough to accommodate the new information (i.e., a house is added with each new book; the number of rooms in each house directly corresponds to the number of chapters; and the number of items in each room is sufficient to memorise the key points in the room's matching chapter). On the other hand, the second approach results in stronger pegs, as the locus is firmly established before information is deposited. Also, in terms of speed, the second approach is superior, for having the locus prepared in advance is obviously crucial for timed memory tasks (e.g., for memory competitions).

After constructing a basic imaginary locus (as in the example above), there are several avenues through which you can further extend it. Here are some ideas:

a. Once you have created a road, you can connect it to the next road, which may, for instance, store books you have read about history, where each house corresponds to a different era being memorised.

b. Once your first neighbourhood is established, you can place a major road connecting it to the next neighbourhood, where, perhaps, each road corresponds to a general topic of study. For example, one road may be dedicated to computer languages, with each house storing the syntax and rules of one language. Or, alternatively, for larger topics and areas of speciality, each neighbourhood could correspond to a field of study (e.g. mathematics), with each road representing a different branch of the field and each house representing a sub-branch.

c. You can proceed in this manner until a city is established.

d. Then, proceed further by creating more cities, then countries, then worlds, and so on.

The reader is advised to regularly visit these locations and to walk through them (mentally, of course), so that the pegs are reviewed and eventually stored in long-term memory. The reader should refer to the earlier section about The Importance of

Revision in order to apply the optimal times at which such a review should be performed. If a locus already contains the contents of a topic, the review of the pegs belonging to the locus is performed automatically during the revision of the said topic.

Once the loci are filled with the desired information, in order to revise a topic, all that is required is to lie down in your bed, or, even better, in a hammock between two palm trees, and mentally walk through the imaginary universes you have created. Using imaginary loci for studying offers a very gratifying experience; it enhances creativity, it improves spatial awareness, and, above all, it facilitates storage of vast amounts of information. Compare that to rote learning, and the beauty of mnemonic systems quickly becomes apparent.

THE GRID SYSTEM

The Grid System is primarily used to memorise visual data in the shape and order with which the data is presented. It can also be used as a standard peg list, but, since simpler peg lists are generally easy to derive, the Grid System is most often used for its visual data applications.

Some typical examples would be to memorise: a map, the particular placement of a deck of cards, a graph or the periodic table. A modification of the Grid System into a circular representation permits applications for rotund depictions of information—the world map (being elliptic) or a maze, as examples.

The approach taken to memorise information using the Grid System is exactly the same as the method utilised for the Peg and Loci Systems. It requires one to simply peg the new piece of information to the known item that represents its position on the grid (the examples below will further clarify the procedure involved).

THE STANDARD GRID

The Standard Grid is the main operating tool of the Grid System: it can be used to capture any two-dimensional visual data. The procedure for the creation of the Standard Grid is as follows:

1. **Draw.** Draw a grid with the desired dimensions.
2. **Label.** Label the first row with letters and the first column with numbers.
3. **Name.** Each cell is then named using the **letter first followed by the number**. For instance, starting from the top-left corner, A1 would be the first cell.
4. **Set the unique identifiers**. The unique identifier to each cell is then created by finding a word that begins with the cell's letter followed by the phonetic sound of the cell's number. (See the phonetic alphabet in the Numbers subsection for details; remember, in the phonetic alphabet, it is the sound that matters, not the letter.)
5. **Be consistent**. Ensure that each object chosen to represent a cell cannot be confused with any of the other unique identifiers you have (e.g. in other peg lists), and do not change it once it is established.
6. **Extensions.** Thereafter, you can increase the grid size, if required, by adding rows and columns. But, again, do not alter that which has already been established (i.e., the objects representing already-existing cells).

To better illustrate the procedure, provided below is a five-by-five version of the Standard Grid, which was created according to the steps above:

	A	B	C	D	E
1	Ad (e.g., think of a funny TV commercial you know)	Bat	Cod	Dodo	Eddie (Frasier's dog)
2	Annoy (e.g., visualise someone banging a spoon on a pot)	Bono (the U2 singer)	Can	Dean	Eon (e.g., visualise a sandglass)
3	Ammo	Beam	Comb	Dam	Emmy (e.g., picture the Emmy Award statuette)
4	Air	Bar	Crow	Dry (e.g., think of a hair dryer)	Ear
5	Ali (e.g., visualise Muhammad Ali)	Ball	Clay	Doll	El (e.g., think of El Niño)

This grid can be further extended across columns or rows or both. The key requirement is to have a unique identifier for each cell in the grid.

A classic example demonstrating an application of this system is to memorise the elements in the periodic table as well as its structure. In the illustration below, in order to apply the example five-by-five grid created above, we will only include the first 25 elements. Extending the approach to cover the entire periodic table can be performed by simply using a larger grid.

	A	B	C	D	E
1	Hydrogen				
2	Lithium	Beryllium			
3	Sodium	Magnesium			
4	Potassium	Calcium	Scandium	Titanium	Vanadium
5	Rubidium	Strontium	Yttrium	Zirconium	Niobium

In order to memorise the portion of the periodic table presented above, all that is necessary is to peg each element in the periodic table to the corresponding object that represents its position in the Standard Grid. For example, lithium is in cell A2, which is represented by *annoy*. And so to remember lithium's position in the table, simply peg *lithium* to *annoy*. You could visualise an annoying lithium battery banging on a pot, annoying all those around it (hear the noise and feel the discontent present in the scene).

Another example could be vanadium, placed in cell E4, which is represented by *ear*. To capture this piece of information, peg *vanadium* to *ear*. Perhaps do so by visualising Jean-Claude Van

Damme[8] in a street fight, trying to high-kick a gigantic muscular ear.

Proceed in a similar manner with the rest of the table: at each cell peg the element being memorised to the object that represents the cell.

If there is interest or need to then further memorise the atomic number of each element in the table, either one of the options below can be applied to achieve this goal:

1. After pegging the element to its position in the table, link the element to the atomic number. In the example for vanadium, you would link *Van Damme* to *gnome*, since the atomic number of vanadium is 23, and the number 23 is represented by *gnome* (as detailed in the Visualising Numbers and Symbols section).

2. Or, if the entire periodic table has been memorised, the atomic number can be worked out by finding the element's position in the table relative to another's. That is, by counting the number of steps—travelling horizontally left to right from top to bottom—from a known element, which essentially acts as a marker. For example, if you know that calcium has an atomic number of 20, it is simple to work out that titanium would have an atomic number of 22, as it is two cells away to the right.

Clearly, for the second method to work, markers should be placed at regular intervals—say, every five elements. This means that only a fifth of the atomic numbers would need to be memorised, with the rest inferred from the markers.

---

[8] *Van Damme* is used to represent *vanadium*, for the former sounds similar to the latter, yet is easier to visualise. (See the earlier section titled Visualising Words.)

In general, the first approach is preferable, as it allows for quicker recall of the necessary information.

THE NUMERICAL GRID

In a similar manner to the Standard Grid's derivation, the Numerical Grid can be created using the following procedure:

1. **Draw**. Draw a grid with the desired dimensions.
2. **Label**. Label both the first row and the first column with numbers.
3. **Name**. Each cell is named using the number of the column followed by the number of the row. For instance, 3_1 would represent the cell in the top-right corner of the table below.
4. **Set the unique identifiers**. Use the phonetic alphabet to convert the label into a word that can be easily visualised. To do so, the phonetic sound of the column number forms the first part of the word, and the phonetic sound of the row number forms the second.
5. **Be consistent**. Ensure that each object chosen to represent a cell cannot be confused with any of the other unique identifiers you have (e.g. in other peg lists), and do not change it once it is established.
6. **Extensions**. Increase the grid size, if required, by adding rows and columns. But, again, do not alter that which has already been established (i.e., the objects representing already-existing cells).

	1	2	3
1	Tot	Knot	Mat
2	Ton	Neon	Man
3	Dame	Anime	Mime

The application approach is then precisely the same as for the Standard Grid.

The reason behind having more than one grid of the same form—taking the Standard Grid and the Numerical Grid as an example—is to ensure that a single grid is not used for too many memory tasks all at the same time. Using the same peg list, the same locus or the same grid for a large number of memory tasks can result in slower execution, confusion, and hindered recall. Therefore, having a large number of peg lists, plenty of loci, and several grids improves performance.

THE CIRCULAR GRID

The derivation of the Circular Grid is similar to that of the rectangular sort, which was demonstrated above for the Standard Grid and the Numerical Grid. The underlying principle is to cut the shape into specific sectors, and then represent each sector uniquely using an object.

For the Circular Grid, each sector is represented by a letter first, followed by a number. The direction for the labelling of the circles is from the middle outwards, so A is the innermost circle; B is the next, and it encompasses A; and so on for C, D, E, etc.

The numbers are then allocated clockwise from the 12 o'clock mark, starting with the number one and dividing the shape into as many sectors as desired.

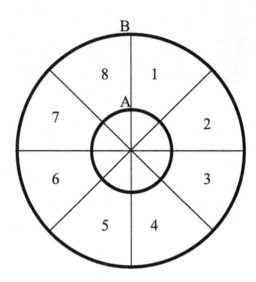

Since the Circular Grid would be used for a different format of data than the Standard Grid (circular, as opposed to rectangular), it is acceptable to utilise the same naming convention. For the practitioner is unlikely to be confused about the general shape of the data being recalled. From this viewpoint, the Circular Grid can be seen as an application of the Standard Grid for circular pieces of data. To further emphasise this point, let us look at two examples: the first sector in the A-circle is A1, which would be represented by *ad*. The final sector in the B-circle is B8, which would be represented by *beef*. Both are objects used to represent the same-named cells of the Standard Grid.

It is possible to name the sectors in the Circular Grid differently to the cells in the Standard Grid, quite simply, by employing separate objects for each. For instance, A1 could be *ad* for the Standard Grid, but would then have to be either one of the following for the Circular Grid: *AUD* (Australian Dollar), *Audi* (the car brand), or *Auto* (which can be visualised either as a car [*auto*mobile] or as a robot [*auto*maton]). However, for large grid sizes, it can be rather challenging to find two words that can be easily visualised and that are in accordance with the naming rules detailed above. The process of building several such grids can therefore be time consuming. And the possibility of confusing objects between two grids that are using the same naming rules is not insignificant.

Another approach would be to use the Standard Grid naming convention for rectangular data, and the Numerical Grid naming convention—applied to the Circular Grid—for circular data.

In most cases, grids are used for fewer applications than standard peg lists. Accordingly, having a single naming template that can be applied to two different shapes seems to be an optimal solution. Nonetheless, as with all the techniques in this book, it is for the reader to decide what is most appropriate for his specific needs and intentions.

An example application of the Circular Grid could be to memorise the map of London's inner boroughs. Superimposing this map onto the Circular Grid would look like the following figure:

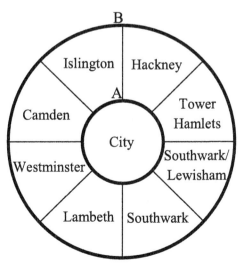

To memorise the map, simply peg each borough's name to the object representing the sector it is in. For example, Hackney is in B1, so peg *hacked knee* (to represent Hackney, for they sound alike and the latter is easier to visualise) to *bat*. Visualise a bat with a knee that was hacked at savagely; vividly picture this poor bat painfully limping on its gigantic knee, which appears to be partially hacked off. This image may be absurd, cruel and disturbing, yet it is precisely these ingredients that make it memorable.

Another example could be sector B8, which is represented by *beef*; the corresponding borough is Islington. Hence, picture a juicy beef steak walking through Grizzly Town (*Grizzly Town* to represent Islington: picture a town populated by hungry grizzly bears). Feel the fear this steak must be experiencing as it begins to accept its inevitable fate.

Note that the inner circle, that is, circle A, was not broken down into sectors, since the entire circle represents City borough. To remember this fact, simply peg the object representing this letter, *Ape* (see the Alphabet List subsection), to the borough's name, *City*. Perhaps visualise a city of apes instead of people: imagine boarding the Underground at Leicester Square only to realise it is filled with apes on their journey to work, busy reading their morning papers. [No offense intended towards the city's dwellers.]

Once the above two-level Circular Grid is established, it is straightforward to then extend it by adding more circles. Simply add another circle to the outside of the last circle drawn, and then extend the diameter lines further outwards to cover the new area.

The Circular Grid can be used to memorise circular cities, circular maps, mazes, pie charts, planet orbits, etc. The procedure to do so is exactly the same as for the rectangular grids:

1. Superimpose the grid onto the information that needs to be memorised.
2. Figure out what piece of information resides in each sector of the grid.
3. Peg the information in each sector to the object that represents the sector.

A common modification of the above Circular Grid is to use more sectors so that the shape is divided into 12 pieces, which corresponds to a clock-type decomposition of the circle. The user is free to experiment or design the grid with whatever granularity he deems appropriate for his goals.

Another modification of the Circular Grid is to use a numerical labelling approach. So instead of each circle being represented by a letter, it is represented by a number. This is analogous to the Numerical Grid's derivation, only here it is applied to circles rather than rectangles.

EMPTY SPACES AND REPEATED DATA

At this stage, a note regarding empty spaces and repeated data is in order. For example, in the periodic table above, cells B1 to E1 were empty (in the sense that no information was contained within them). In most cases, familiarity with the topic would allow the practitioner to just ignore such areas when recalling. For someone familiar with the basic properties and shape of the periodic table, memorising the empty areas is not necessary, as it can be discerned from previously established knowledge.

Nonetheless, for unfamiliar topics or to gain confidence over the material being studied, it is always possible to memorise the grid points that are empty. To do so, simply peg the empty areas to a *baseball players' bench* (commonly located in the area known as the *dugout)*. This object was chosen since the individuals sitting on such a bench are not participating in the game, in much the same way as the empty spaces are not participating in the memorisation of the topic.

To illustrate the approach, let us again look at the periodic table example above. In order to memorise the empty spaces therein, we would start by pegging the image for B1, *bat*, to *bench*. Visualise lots of baseball-playing bats—wearing their team's uniform—sitting on the bench, looking onto the field, eagerly awaiting their turn to play. Then continue by linking B1 to C1, C1 to D1, and so on for the rest of the empty cells.

Alternatively, if every cell is empty between B1 and E1, instead of linking together each individual cell that is empty, one can simply bundle the start and end cells into a single image that acts as a reminder that the whole section is empty. In this case, that is for B1 to E1, we need to peg *bat* and *Eddie* to *bench*. The image could be lots of bat-shaped creatures with gigantic heads that resemble Eddie's (a dog-bat hybrid), all sitting on the bench, eagerly awaiting the chance to go onto the field.

The overall procedure is as follows:

1. Visualise the bench.
2. Peg the first empty cell's representative object to *bench*.
3. Link the next empty cell's representative object to the previous empty cell's representative object.
4. Or, if a whole section is empty, create a single image by bundling the start- and end-cell's objects into one, and link it to *bench*. Then proceed by linking the next empty section's image to the previous empty section's image, and so on.

For a grid point (cell or sector) that contains data which is also present in another grid point, as in the London map example, where B3 and B4 both contain Southwark, simply peg the data (e.g., Southwark) to each grid point's object independently—as you would any other grid point. However, if a large section contains the same piece of information (for instance, the oceans on the world's map would take up large sections of the grid), simply bundle the start and end grid points of the overlapping data, and peg the object representing the overlapping data (e.g., the oceans) to this bundle.

Note that, when bundling, it is not necessary to stick to rows only or columns only—using rectangles or other shapes is perfectly reasonable. The choice should largely depend on which shape captures the intended area with the least amount of images. For instance, in the periodic table, cells C1 to E3 are empty; this rectangular section covers most of the empty points, and should therefore be bundled to create the image that would be pegged to *bench*.

APPLICATIONS

The best way to complete the exposition of a topic is by providing examples. Given the self-improvement nature of the topics in this book, a further focus should also be given to how the examples can be practically incorporated into daily life.

The examples that were provided thus far for each system should have served the purpose of explaining the general approach and principles. The sections below are intended to reinforce the key concepts, to focus on and explain specific memory tasks, and to elucidate the rules behind the memorisation of different types of data.

The examples below will illustrate how different techniques should be used under different circumstances, and will detail which technique is optimal for each type of information. The reader should note that the choices assigned here are based on the author's experience. These choices have been made based on performance, which was measured in terms of speed of memorisation, speed of recall, as well as the accuracy achieved. After mastery of the techniques, the practitioner may choose a different matching approach between each task and technique than the one presented below. It is advisable to verify whether any improvement is achieved by doing so, especially before applying the modifications in this manner permanently. To emphasise the point: especially for a beginner, it is advisable to adhere to the methodology discussed below—alterations should only be applied once experience is gained (and only after careful assessment of their performance).

FOREIGN VOCABULARY

With the application of the Link System, learning foreign vocabulary is simple, fun and effortless. The procedure is as follows:

1. **Convert the foreign word** into a similarly-sounding native word that represents an object which can be easily visualised.
2. **Convert the translation** of the foreign word into an object that can be visualised.
3. **Link the two** objects together by using a ludicrous image containing absurd depictions and nonsensical actions.
4. **To optimally achieve long-term storage, review the link** from Clause (3.) above by testing yourself immediately after creating it. Thereafter, test yourself subsequent to the following intervals elapsing from the time of the initial memorisation: 1 hour, 12 hours, 24 hours, 1 week, 2 weeks, 1 month, 3 months, 6 months, and 12 months.

To illustrate the first three steps of the procedure, let us look at some specific examples from different languages.

MANDARIN CHINESE

Ying hung—[a] bank

Ying hung sounds similar to "ink hung", which can be visualised as an *ink*well (the vessel used to store a fountain pen's ink) being hung. All that remains, therefore, is to link *inkwell*-being-*hung* to *bank*, the translation. Picture an inkwell being hung in the middle of the bank by a very violent and menacing bank clerk—perhaps because the inkwell has taken an unauthorised overdraft (using such nonsensical background reasoning improves the link). Picture the scene vividly, with the noose being tightened around the inkwell and the fear in its eyes. Visualise the scene taking place in your bank, or your idea of what a typical bank looks like on the inside. It could be in a vault full of gold, for example, with the inkwell trying to place its foot on one of the stacks of gold in order to avoid being strangled by the rope.

Fung chien—[a] room

The first part of the word, *fung*, sounds similar to the beginning of "fungus"; *chien* sounds similar to "chain". Therefore, to memorise this foreign word, simply link *fungus* and *chain* to *room*. For instance, picture a hotel room that is being occupied by a chain that is made out of fungus links instead of metal links. Visualise this fungus-chain jumping out of the room's double bed and stepping into the complimentary hotel slippers, then making its way towards the en-suite bathroom to wash its face. As always, exaggerate the image: visualise the fungus-chain as enormous, so much so, that when it is lying in bed, its lower links extend over the edge of the bed. And when it jumps out of bed, the whole room shakes, and the neighbouring hotel guests respond by shouting for it to quiet down.

A crucial principle needs to be articulated at this point. An optimal application of the technique above would be to use the same objects for identical sounds encountered in other foreign words. For example, in Chinese, a relatively small number of key syllables can be ordered into various permutations to generate different words—with each permutation carrying a distinct meaning altogether. To memorise these, it would be optimal to proceed by consistently representing each key syllable using the same object.

The general approach is as follows:

1. If the entire foreign word sounds similar to an easy-to-visualise object, then use this object to represent the word.
2. Otherwise, break the foreign word down into its component sounds and convert these into similarly-sounding objects.
3. Thereafter, when new words are encountered, convert the sounds into objects in a consistent manner. So, from the example above, whenever the sound "ying" is encountered in any new Chinese word (or a word in any other foreign language, for that matter) that you learn, make sure to use *inkwell*, as was derived above. It is strongly advisable to maintain a notebook to ensure that key sounds are defined and applied consistently (i.e., create and maintain a list of unique identifiers).

JAPANESE

Chumon—to order

Chu sounds similar to "chew"; *mon* sounds similar to "moon". Therefore, to remember the translation above, link *chew* and *moon* with *to order*. Picture a patron in a restaurant chewing on a moon while raising his hand to order more food. Visualise the gigantic moon in this human's mouth and his poor attempts at chewing it down into ingestible pieces. Yet he is so hungry, or just gluttonous, that he tries to order more such moons.

FRENCH

Colère—anger

The word *colère* sounds similar to "collar". Hence, to remember the translation above, link *collar* to *anger*. Picture a dog's collar getting angry at the owner for tugging on him the whole day. Visualise the large and scary collar turning red with anger, with steam emanating from the metal studs along its periphery. Clearly visualise the owner cowering in fear from the gigantic monster he has now unleashed.

ARABIC

Tabeeb—a doctor

The word *tabeeb* can be broken down into the similarly sounding "tab" and "hip". Thus the translation above can be memorised by linking *tab* and *hip* to *doctor*. Picture the hip of a tab (using the *restaurant bill* definition of the word) as damaged, and visualise the tab limping slowly towards the doctor's clinic. There the doctor inspects the hip and writes the tab a prescription for the pain. Visualise the absurdity of a tab having a hip, and clearly imagine how the doctor is examining the hip with care, as much as he would for any human. Exaggerate the sizes and proportions, and feel the pain the tab must be experiencing.

SPANISH

Sellos (pronounced as "seyos")—stamps

The foreign word *sellos* sounds similar to "cellulose". (The reader should note here, if it was not already deduced from the examples presented thus far, that finding a native word that sounds precisely the same as the foreign word, is not necessary. As long as the native word chosen is capable of reminding you of the foreign word, the choice is appropriate.) To remember the translation of the Spanish word above, simply link *cellulose* to *stamps*. Picture a plant writing a letter; then, suddenly realising he has no stamps at home, he begins to violently scratch at his cells' walls until a stamp finally peels off. He then proceeds to affix this bloodied stamp onto the letter's rightmost corner.

INTEGRATION INTO DAILY LIFE

If you are in the process of learning a new language, or always wanted to do so, choose a popular study course and work through the lessons described therein. Then, when new words are encountered, use the system above to memorise them.

It is advisable to write down the new words in a notebook and to record the images chosen—for future reference, if required. This notebook can then be utilised for the revision of the material at the optimal times suggested earlier in this part of the book. The notebook can also be used to keep track of key syllables/sounds, so that their unique identifiers are clearly defined and consistently applied. Each entry in the notebook should carry the following information:

1. The foreign word followed by an em dash.
2. After the em dash, write down the translation.
3. Next to the translation, enter square brackets in which you note the image for the foreign word. (You are to enter a brief description of the image, not a drawing of it.)
4. Next to the description of the image for the foreign word, enter an em dash followed by the image for the translation. After that, close the brackets.

5. It is preferable to use black ink for the foreign word; blue ink for the translation; and green ink for the description of the images.

To better illustrate the format, let us use examples. The two Chinese words detailed above should be portrayed in your notebook as follows:

Ying hung—a bank [an inkwell being hung—inside a bank]

Fung chien—a room [a fungus-chain—inside a hotel room]

NON-FOREIGN VOCABULARY

The techniques used for foreign vocabulary can equally be applied to native words. The procedure is identical, as the examples below will illustrate:

Pejorative—A word expressing contempt or disapproval.

The word *pejorative* sounds similar to "Peugeot-rat-Eve". To memorise the definition of the word, link *Peugeot, rat* and *Eve* to *contempt*. Picture a rat driving a Peugeot: as he stops next to the Garden of Eden, he rolls down the window and begins to express his contempt for Eve's behaviour with Adam. Vividly see the large rat in the Peugeot shaking its head in disapproval whilst Eve's head is bowed in shame. Exaggerate the image, and sense the feelings being expressed in the scene.

Hegemony—Leadership or dominance, esp. by one state or social group over others.

The word *hegemony* sounds similar to "hedge-money". To memorise the definition, simply link *hedge* and *money* to *leadership*. Picture a hedge of shrubs made out of money (instead of leaves) leading an army of smaller hedges to war. Vividly capture the huge banknotes that grow on the branches of the leading hedge, and sense the tense, unsettled atmosphere, as the leader is gathering his hedge-troops for war.

INTEGRATION INTO DAILY LIFE

To profitably integrate the above procedure into your daily life, a simple approach could be to record in a notebook any word that you come across whose meaning you do not know. This could be a word heard on the radio, spoken on TV, read in a newspaper, a book or a magazine, or used in conversation. Gather all such words into a notebook in the format described below. As you add each word, memorise it using the technique presented above. And, for long-term retention, ensure you review all the words in the notebook using the optimal revision schedule, as was instructed for foreign vocabulary.

The suggested format for the vocabulary notebook is as follows:

a. Write the new (previously unknown, or whose definition is unknown) word followed by an em dash.
b. After the em dash, write down the definition of the word.
c. Next to the definition, enter square brackets into which you insert the image that represents the new word. Again, as for the foreign vocabulary notebook, you are to enter a brief description of the image, not a drawing of it.
d. Next to the image that represents the new word, enter an em dash followed by the image that represents the definition of the new word. Finally, close the brackets.
e. It is preferable to use black ink for the new word; blue ink for the definition; and green ink for the descriptions of the images.

To better illustrate the format, let us use examples:

> Pejorative—a word expressing contempt or disapproval [Peugeot, rat and Eve—"dissing" and shaking his head in disapproval]
>
> Hegemony—leadership or dominance, esp. by one state or social group over others [hedge-money—leading an army to war]

SPELLING

This section deals with the spelling of words that have a challenging and confusing combination of letters. Such combinations, oftentimes, appear to follow fuzzy logic when compared to the pronunciation of similarly-sounding tones.

These spellings can be remembered by applying the Alphabet List, which was presented earlier in this part of the book. This list allows you to convert each problematic letter into a unique object. The objects, in turn, can be used to remind you which letters feature in the spelling of the word, and thus remove the confusion from the spelling. The procedure is as follows:

1. **Unique identifier for the word**. Find an object to represent the word whose spelling is being considered.
2. **Unique identifier/s for the letter/s**. Find an object/s to represent the problematic combination of letters. This can be retrieved from the Alphabet List.
3. **Link**. Link the objects from (1) and (2) in an absurd manner.

For combinations involving repeated letters (which are indeed quite common), it is advisable to create unique identifiers for the common pairs in the language being studied and utilise these instead. It is more effective than memorising the same object twice. The list below provides some typical examples of such pairs:

Letter combination	Unique identifier	Reason/logic behind the choice
cc	Syringe	*cc* being the unit of measurement on a syringe.
ss	Nazi	*ss* is the common name for the Schutzstaffel, which was a paramilitary organisation under the Nazi party.
ll	LL Cool J	The beginning portion of the famous rapper's name.
mm	Road Runner	The cartoon character that calmly articulates his signature "**meep-meep**" sound before speeding away from Wile E. Coyote.

Let us take an example:

N-e-c-e-s-s-a-r-y—the spelling of this word is often confused with n-e-c-c-e-s-a-r-y, n-e-c-e-s-a-r-y or n-e-c-c-e-s-s-a-r-y. To remember that there are two *s*'s and only one *c*, we follow the procedure detailed above.

First we need to find an object to represent *necessary*. The word sounds similar to "NASA-sari", so we can think of a sari made of a NASA design, and carrying its logo. Next we need to find objects to represent the problematic combination of letters. Using the Alphabet List we find that *c* is represented by *sea,* and, from the table above, we find that *ss* is represented by *Nazi*. We therefore visualise a sea of Nazis to represent the problematic combination of letters.

Finally, to put it all together, we need to link *NASA-sari* with *Sea-Nazi*. Perhaps visualise a NASA astronaut wearing a sari—instead of a space suit—whilst walking on the moon. He then jumps into a sea of Nazis and tries to swim to the shore. But, alas, these violent Nazis are not letting him pass; they insist he be punished for wearing such a ridiculous sari. And, as should be becoming habit by now, incorporate emotions into the scene. Feel the <u>fear</u> that the astronaut must be experiencing and the <u>hate</u> displayed towards him. Exaggerate everything: imagine the sea as a collection of billions, or even trillions, of Nazi soldiers, and clearly visualise the resulting Nazi-splash as the astronaut jumps in.

It is now easy to recall that the word *necessary* is spelled with one *c* and two *s*'s.

To some readers *necessary* may have been an apt example, whilst, to others, it may have appeared as a trivial one. The key here is not the example but the technique: it can be applied to any word and any spelling.

TELEPHONE NUMBERS

To memorise telephone numbers, we employ a technique that uses the Numbers List, which was introduced earlier in this part of the book. The aim is to convert something abstract, such as numbers, into objects that are easy to visualise—and that are therefore easy to link together. The Numbers List acts as our vehicle of conversion. It avoids the need for creating new objects to represent the telephone number (via the phonetic alphabet), which would generally take longer to do. The Numbers List essentially becomes the set of building blocks with which longer numbers can be uniquely identified (much as the phonetic alphabet was the set of building blocks from which the unique identifiers of the Numbers List were derived).

The procedure is as follows:

1. **Unique identifier for the contact**. Find an object to represent the person (or company) to whom the number belongs.
2. **Unique identifier/s for the number**. Find an object, or a series of objects, to represent the telephone number (use the Numbers List).
3. **Link the contact to the number's first object**. Link the object representing the person (or company) to the first object representing the telephone number.
4. **Continue linking the number's objects**. Proceed by linking the first object representing the telephone number to the rest, until all the objects that together represent the number have been linked.

Let us look at some examples (note that the telephone numbers below are fictional—for obvious reasons):

555-3495—Flower Shop

Flower Shop requires little effort in conversion, as it is already an easy-to-visualise object. Next, let us proceed by breaking down the number into the objects that will thenceforth represent it: *lily, lamb, rib* and *Lee*. These were derived by looking for the object in the Numbers List that corresponds to each pair of digits from the telephone number above. If, by now, you have committed the Numbers List to memory—as is highly recommended!—the process of conversion should be very swift.

Lastly, to complete the process, proceed to linking *flower shop* to *lily, lamb, rib* and *Lee*. Begin by picturing a flower shop where the shop assistant is a gigantic lily. Next, visualise a lamb whose wool is made out of lilies. Then picture a lamb sitting at a table and eating human ribs. Finally, visualise a rib practising the *nunchaku* (Bruce Lee's weapon of choice, with which he is commonly depicted) whilst yelling menacing warrior cries.

Henceforth, to recall the telephone number, all that you need to do is think *flower shop*, and the rest of the images will be triggered to flow through your mind to remind you of the number. Since each image will contain an object that can only represent a specific number, the recall should be faultless. For example, after thinking *flower shop*, you should suddenly see the pleasant, gigantic *lily* that is working as a shop assistant. *Lily*, using the phonetic alphabet or the Numbers List, can represent only one number: 55. The same applies for the rest of the images.

(As before, for long term storage, a revision will have to take place according to the optimal revision schedule.)

+44-666-6219—Nigel

Another example: Say you would like to memorise the telephone number that belongs to a friend who lives in the UK. If you already know that the UK's country code is 44, then there is no need to include this piece of information when linking the objects together— simply skip it and proceed with the rest of the digits. **The aim should always be to only memorise that which is unknown.**

Therefore, in this example, you can begin by memorising from *666* onwards. Here, however, instead of using the Numbers List, you can opt to utilise a simple association that uniquely identifies the number 666—namely that of the Devil. It is generally advisable to use such opportunistic simplifications whenever you spot them. Doing so amounts to packing more information per image: in the above example, three digits are used instead of two.

The person's name, Nigel, sounds similar to "Nike-gel". We must therefore link *Nike-gel* to *Devil, chain* and *TP*. Start by picturing the Devil smearing a protective layer of Nike gel (perhaps a gel-like substance made by pestling Nike shoes in a mortar) over himself before entering the hot climes of hell. Then picture the Devil appearing on the shoulder of a chain, and, standing there, surreptitiously whispering in its ear, advising the chain to commit an evil deed. Continue by picturing a toilet-paper roll that is made out of thick metal chains rather than paper (ensure you incorporate the feeling of discomfort that will be experienced by the hapless end-user).

Note that, instead of the above approach, the practitioner can choose to use the higher-dimensional methodology (for example, by adding two dimensions). In this case, the images would be as follows: *Nike-gel* linked to *Devil,* and *Devil* linked to *a red chain that is exploding* (using the **VWYZ** convention). We already covered the first link (*Nike-gel* to *Devil*). For the second link, one could picture a red chain that is made out of Devils (instead of metal links). The chain, under the intense pressure and heat conditions of hell, seems to be rapidly increasing in size until it suddenly explodes.

Whatever approach is ultimately taken, the key is to be consistent. For instance, if the higher-dimensional method is utilised, it is important to decide which dimensional convention is being used for which portion of the number, and to continue to use this convention without exceptions or changes. Say, for instance, we have several seven-digit telephone numbers. One must not use **VWYZ** for the first four digits of one telephone number and then use it for the last four digits of another telephone number. Doing so would introduce confusion during recall. By contrast, if the convention is applied consistently, say, by assigning **VWYZ** to only the first four digits, there can be no confusion.

To instil consistency, a simple generic rule would be to apply **VWYZ** to every four digits until it is no longer possible, at which point the Numbers List takes effect. So, for a nine-digit number, **VWYZ** would be applied to the first eight digits, while, for the ninth digit, the Numbers List would be called upon to retrieve the object. Using such a generic rule avoids the need for prior knowledge of the length of the number to be memorised.

To solidify the understanding of the technique, the reader is advised to practise with phone numbers that are encountered during the day. Practise by attempting to recall phone numbers mentally before accessing them from a cellular device, smart phone, tablet, or rolodex. With practice, you will gain confidence and mastery.

CARD MEMORISATION

To memorise cards, we require a systematic conversion of each element in a pack of cards into an easy-to-visualise object. The simplest approach is to use the Numbers List along with the following rules [The reader may have noted the pattern by now: the Numbers List is an invaluable workhorse in the memory toolkit.]:

Suit	Suit's Range
Spades	1 to 13
Hearts	21 to 33
Clubs	41 to 53
Diamonds	61 to 73

Using the Numbers List, the method presented here assigns a unique object to each card in the deck. The convention applied is as follows:

- The first number of a suit's range is equal to its Ace (i.e., the numbers 1, 21, 41 and 61, are equal to the Aces of Spades, Hearts, Clubs and Diamonds, respectively).
- The second to tenth numbers of a suit's range represent the numbers two to ten of that suit.
- The 11th number of a suit's range represents its Jack.
- The 12th number of a suit's range represents its Queen.
- And the 13th number of a suit's range represents its King.

With the rules above we essentially assign a number to each card, and, using the Numbers List, we retrieve an object to uniquely represent that card going forward.

For example, the Jack of Clubs would be number 51, since the suit's range is 41 to 53, and the 11th number in that range is 51. And, after consulting the Numbers List, it can be concluded that this card is represented by *latte*. Similarly, the Five of Diamonds would be number 65, which is represented by *jelly*.

Memorising a deck of cards is now a trivial task. We can apply the Loci System to capture the sequence of cards with the order in which it was memorised. To better illustrate this application of the Loci System, let us use an example journey (across a locus) that has, in order of appearance, the following monuments along the way (this is just to illustrate the card memorisation technique; you are, as mentioned previously, advised to use your own loci):

A *bar,* a *church,* a *gym,* a *bridge,* and a *shoe shop.*

And say the sequence in the pack of cards begins as follows:

Ten of Diamonds, Jack of Clubs, Queen of Diamonds, King of Clubs, and *Ace of Spades.*

This sequence of cards is represented by the numbers 70, 51, 72, 53 and 1, respectively, and the corresponding objects are *case, latte, coin, lamb* and *tie.*

Now, to memorise the sequence of cards, begin by pegging the first card to the first object in the locus: i.e., peg *case* to *bar*. For instance, picture a gigantic briefcase walking through the swinging doors of the bar. And, as if by cue, everyone in the bar stops what they are doing, the music pauses, and all eyes are fixed on the strange briefcase slowly making its way towards the bar.

Next, peg *latte* to *church*. Visualise a hot latte dressed in preacher's clothes standing in the entrance to the church, vociferously urging you to come in and repent your sins.

Continue by pegging *coin* to *gym, lamb* to *bridge* and *tie* to *shoe-shop*. Walk (in your mind's eye) the journey a few times, vividly seeing the pegs you have just created along the way. Thereafter, in order to recall the sequence, all that is required is to mentally walk through the journey, at which point the pegs will jump out and provide the details of the card sequence that was memorised.

In order to memorise a longer sequence of cards (hundreds or thousands of cards, say), the practitioner would need a locus that contains as many items. Though it may seem arduous, it is actually quite simple to create such loci (as detailed earlier, in the Loci System section). And it is useful to always have at least two loci with at least 100 items in each. Note, however, that for memory championships, 100-item loci are not, in general, sufficient. One would require journeys through large portions of towns or cities, to allow for the pegging of the thousands of images that would be created along the course of the competition.

To reduce the need for larger loci, it is always possible to use the higher-dimensional technique—capturing the information of two or more cards at a time. For example, we could use the **VWYZ** convention to capture two cards in each image, by converting two cards into a single number[9]. From the example above, this would mean combining the Ten of Diamonds and the Jack of Clubs together to become 7051. And the image to represent this number would be an *orange briefcase that is having a shower*. We would then peg this image to *bar*, which is the starting point of the journey. Visualise, perhaps, that you walk into a bar and see that there is a humongous orange briefcase that is having a shower in the middle of the room.

Using higher dimensions reduces the required length of the journey, since more information is being attached to each object of the locus. This is very powerful, and, with practice, it can give the practitioner a serious edge over other competitors.

An obvious extension of this idea would be to expand the Numbers List from 0-100 to 0-9,999 and then to add four dimensions. This would allow the practitioner to peg four cards to each object along the journey. With memory systems, as with Abraham Lincoln's famous quote[10], the more you prepare and refine your toolkit, the more effective and rapid the actual memorisation process becomes.

---

[9] **VW** to represent the object from the Numbers List; **Y** to represent the *colour* dimension; and **Z** to represent the *action* dimension.

[10] *Give me six hours to chop down a tree and I will spend the first four sharpening the axe.* —Abraham Lincoln

[Note that there exists some uncertainty around whether this quote is correctly attributed to Lincoln.]

Translating the cards into numbers, the numbers into images, and then quickly pegging these images to the items along the journey, requires some getting used to. The process needs to be internalised; it needs to become automatic. This will require practice.

When adding dimensions, it is usually the step of translating into numbers that tends to hinder speed. When working with one card at a time, after having used the technique for a while, the object that represents the card emerges as soon as the card is revealed—without the interim step of converting the card into a number. When working with two or more cards at a time, the step of converting the cards into a number begins to emerge again—hindering the overall speed. Nonetheless, with diligent practice, this too can be made automatic.

BINARY CODE

Sequences of binary digits can be easily memorised using the Loci System. Again, the crucial first step is to allocate a unique identifier to each combination of digits. These representations can then be pegged along the journey through the locus in an absurd manner. The unique identifiers for binary digits—up to second order—are presented below (these were derived using logic for *00* and using the phonetic alphabet for the rest):

Binary Digit Combination	Unique Identifier
00	Toilet
11	Date (the fruit)
01	Suit
10	Toes

Let us take an example. Using the same journey as in the Card Memorisation section (a *bar,* a *church,* a *gym,* a *bridge,* and a *shoe shop*), memorise the following binary sequence: 0111010100.

Utilising the list of unique identifiers in the table above, the binary number in the example can be converted into: *suit, date, suit, suit* and *toilet.* All that remains is to peg these along the journey through the locus. That is, peg *suit* to *bar,* *date* to *church,* *suit* to *gym,* *suit* to *bridge,* and *toilet* to *shoe shop.*

Similarly to the approach detailed in the Card Memorisation section, extending to higher dimensions would reduce the number of images required.

Another approach with which the technique can be improved is by creating a higher-order list of unique identifiers. The table above is only of second order. Expanding to the fourth order, for instance, would mean creating a list of all the binary permutations that can be contained in a four digit sequence (e.g., 0000, 0101, 0111, 1000, etc.) and assigning a unique identifier to each. Using a fourth-order list would mean that the sequence is being memorised in chunks of four digits at a time. Furthermore, it is then also possible to add dimensions to make the chunks bigger still—for example, by adding a colour dimension and an action dimension. Each image would then represent six digits.

Better still, we could create dimensions that are specific to binary digits. For example, we could allocate the **VW** in **VWXY** to be represented by the unique identifier from the list above. And we could allocate **XY** to be represented by a colour that is preassigned (again, to ensure unique identification) to each of the four possible combinations of two binary digits (e.g., 00=white; 01=green; etc.). In this setting, the binary sequence 0001, as an example, would be represented by a *green toilet.*

Finally, it is simple to notice why the Loci System was chosen for the task of memorising binary numbers. Say, for instance, one tried to use the Link System instead. For a long sequence, this would likely result in errors and confusion, as the same images will be repeated and linked many times over along the chain. In a journey through a locus, however, repetitions are irrelevant. Even if the same binary digit combination appears very frequently, it is pegged to distinct items along a journey—hence, each image is unique, and confusion dare not encroach.

COMPUTER CODE

In order to memorise computer code, we need to decompose the subject into its constituent key components. And to each such component we need to allocate a unique identifier, which will represent it—when building nonsensical images—going forward.

Once the unique identifiers are established, the general procedure is as follows:

1. **For a language used infrequently**:
   a. Utilise the Link System to memorise each element of the code.
   b. Review.
2. **For a language used frequently**:
   a. Memorise the syntax rules using the Link System.
   b. Memorise only the key steps and the functions being called in the code, skipping punctuation and other components that can be discerned through knowledge of the syntax.
   c. Review.

Since each computer language uses a different syntax, provided below is a prototypical example based on C++ code, from which the reader can easily adapt the ideas to other computer languages.

As always, let us begin by assigning unique identifiers:

Component	Unique Identifier
int	An Inn
main	A Menu
()	The Twin Towers
{	A Spider
}	A Spider
cout	An Axe (as *cout* sounds a little like "cut")
<<	*Pac-Man* (the popular arcade game from the 1980s)
\	A Slide
"	A Snake (as it resembles a snakebite)
return	An Urn full of Rats
;	A Winking/Twitching Eye

With the above identifiers, we can memorise the following code using the Link System:

```
int main()

{

    cout << "Hello World\n";

    return 0;

}
```

We begin by linking the name of the program, *Hello World*, with the code. *Hello World* can be visualised as a *world waving hello*.

And the code starts with **int**, which, from the identifiers detailed above, is represented by *inn*. So we need to link *world waving hello* to *inn*. Perhaps visualise a small inn gladly welcoming a new guest: stepping into the inn's tiny reception area is a gigantic world waving hello.

We then proceed to linking the rest of the code by order of appearance. The next part of the code is **main**, so we need to link *inn* to *menu*. Perhaps visualise a large restaurant menu and his[11] girlfriend checking into an inn.

The next part of the code is **()**, so we need to link *menu* to *twin towers*. Maybe picture two gigantic menus towering over New York.

Next we have **{**. We thus need to link *twin towers* to *spider*. Consider using the image of a large spider that has twin towers for legs.

The next portion of the code is **cout**. We therefore need to link *spider* to *axe*. Think of a logger-spider that is cutting trees in the forest with an enormous gossamer axe.

Next we have **<<**. So we link *axe* to *Pac-Man*. Visualise a forest full of Pac-Mans being felled with an axe.

Next we have **"**. We must then link *Pac-Man* to *snake*: Picture Pac-Man viciously biting a snake.

Proceed by creating images for the rest of the code: link *snake* to *world waving hello*; *world waving hello* to *slide*; *slide* to *hen* (using the Alphabet List); *hen* to *snake*; *snake* to *winking eye*;

---

[11] [To personify the inanimate object, we use *his* rather than *its*.]

winking eye to *urn full of rats; urn full of rats* to *saw* (using the Numbers List); *saw* to *winking eye*; and *winking eye* to *spider*.

If the reader was patient enough to follow the example above to its conclusion, then a critical concept may have been noted. The C++ example focused on breaking down the code into its most basic components, which meant that a large number of individual images was required. **Such should be the approach only when there is absolutely no familiarity with the topic.**

Fortunately, knowing the basic syntax rules of the language substantially reduces the amount of information that needs to be memorised. Using the above example of C++: knowing that each beginning { should end with a corresponding }; that every statement inside the subroutine's/function's brackets should end with a semicolon; that each " should be terminated with a corresponding ", and that a text string is inserted between these quotation marks, would together substantially reduce the amount of data that needs to be memorised in any code encountered.

Knowing the key rules of a language means that all that needs to be memorised are the main features of the code, rather than the precise script and punctuation. **The optimal strategy, therefore, is to first learn and memorise the rules of the language, and thereafter only memorise the key commands/steps of any particular code.**

For C++, you could, for example, link *winking eye* to *statement*. This link captures the rule that each statement should end with a semicolon. Thenceforth, the semicolons (*winking eye*[s]) no longer need to be considered when memorising C++ code.

Another, somewhat unpleasant, example: visualise a vicious axe striking Pac-Man, with yellow blood gushing out, spraying a computer screen—forming blood-dripping words. This link captures the purpose of the function `cout` `<<`, namely that of outputting a data stream to the console. Henceforth, just memorising the data to be outputted is sufficient, since you already know what function to call to effect this.

Experienced programmers will not, in general, need to memorise the precise script of the code, since most of the script can be inferred from accumulated knowledge of the logic required to achieve the intended goal. Instead, experienced programmers may use the technique to:

1. Memorise the syntax rules of a new language.
2. Memorise the key steps of a complex program—in particular the key function calls. As above, this is performed using the Link System.
3. Memorise the name of a function, the inputs it requires, and what the function performs (again, using the Link System). Advanced forms of coding generally focus on calling other functions throughout the code—having a vast mental database of functions thus speeds up code-writing considerably.

MATHEMATICAL FORMULAE

The Link System is commonly used in order to memorise mathematical formulae. The procedure, as always, starts by deriving a unique representation of each element. For the example detailed below, we will use the following table of unique identifiers:

Symbol	Unique Identifier	Reason/Logic Behind the Choice
+	Pus	*Plus* sounds similar to "pus"
-	Dennis the Menace	*Minus* sounds similar to "menace"
=	Eagle	*Equal* sounds similar to "eagle"
2π	Two pies	It is the Greek letter pi, and there are two
μ	Cow	The letter is pronounced "mu"
√	Root	It is the square root symbol
( )	Twin Towers	Visually it looks like two leaning towers
σ	Sigmund Freud (visualise a white beard)	The letter is pronounced "sigma", which sounds similar to "Sigmund"
Division (÷)	Machete	Division is associated with cutting
Power (^ or x^y)	Bodybuilder	Physical power is associated with muscles and size
Integration (∫)	Interrogation light	*Integration* sounds like "interrogation"
Differentiation (∂)	Sock	Differentiating between the pairs of socks when the clean laundry returns.

Note that some of the unique identifiers were chosen through a whimsical, silly thought process. There should be no shame in that. The only criterion is whether the chosen unique identifier effectively reminds you of the data it is supposed to represent.

The reader may be daunted by the size of the table required just to memorise a shorter-looking formula. However, it should be noted that the table was designed in order to form a unique and consistent structure that can be applied to all basic formulae. It is a one-time investment that is applicable to all similar problems thereafter. (Note that for more complex formulae, the table will need to be extended. The reader can do so by following the principles detailed in this book.)

Without using a table, certain duplications or inconsistent representations may inadvertently be utilised at some point during the study, which could lead to confusion and inaccurate recall.

Only a small effort is required in maintaining a table of unique identifiers. The reward is a more systematic approach—which means rapid encoding, with faster and better recall.

As always, the best instruction is through examples. To demonstrate the application to mathematical formulae, let us memorise the equation for the *normal distribution density function*. The procedure is as follows:

1. **Unique identifiers**. Create a unique identifier for each element.
2. **Link the name**. Link the name of the formula to the first element in the equation.
3. **Link the elements**. Proceed by connecting the rest of the elements using the Link System.
   a. Travel from left to right,
   b. From the top downwards.
4. **Review**.

Taking the formula for the normal distribution density function as the example:

$$f(x) = \frac{1}{\sigma\sqrt{2\pi}} e^{-\frac{(\mu-x)^2}{2\sigma^2}}$$

We have already created a set of unique identifiers for the symbols in this equation. The letters in the equation will be represented by the objects from the Alphabet List.

We proceed by converting the name of the equation into an image. For *normal distribution*, perhaps think of a wide bell (since the distribution resembles a bell; in fact, it is informally called the "bell curve").

Now link *wide bell* to the first element of the equation, *f*, which is represented by *elf* (using the Alphabet List). Imagine a little elf tolling a gigantic, wide bell to alert everyone that dinner is ready.

The next element in the equation is $\boxed{(x)}$. Therefore, proceed by linking *elf* to *an egg that is being crushed between two towers*. Perhaps, with the severe pressure being applied by the two towers, the gigantic egg finally breaks, and out comes an elf.

Next in the equation we have $\boxed{=}$. So link *an egg that is being crushed between two towers* to *eagle*. Consider visualising the violent scene of an egg being crushed between two towers taking place in an eagle's nest; and the eagle, pacifist that he is, is pleading for the towers to stop.

The next element in the equation is $\boxed{1/\sigma}$. We therefore need to link *eagle* to *a white beard that is cutting a tie using a machete*. The *tie* represents *1*; the *white beard* represents σ, being an easy-to-visualise object to remind us of Sigmund Freud; and the *machete* represents the division that is taking place. Imagine an eagle trying to pull at the tie it is wearing in order to save its own life, as the vicious white beard is cutting away at the tie using a machete.

Next is $\sqrt{2\pi}$. We need to link *white beard* to *two pies that are made out of roots*. Perhaps the beard is sampling the two pies and is disgusted by their "rooty" taste.

Next is e. Thus link *two pies that are made out of roots* to *eel*. Consider visualising the two pies being electrocuted by the eel, causing their "rooty" innards to set on fire.

Proceed to the next element, $-$. We need to link *eel* to *a bodybuilding Dennis the Menace* (bodybuilding, since the minus and what follow in the equation are applied to the power). Visualise a massive bodybuilder version of Dennis the Menace that has gigantic eels instead of biceps.

Next we have $(\mu$. We thus link *a bodybuilding Dennis the Menace* to *a tower that is made out of cow's skin*. Visualise Dennis riding, rodeo style, a tower that is made entirely out of cow's skin.

Proceed to the next element, $-x$. So we need to link *a tower that is made out of cow's skin* to *a Dennis that has a gigantic egg-shaped head*. To that end, picture a Dennis that has a gigantic egg-shaped head trying to eat a tower that is made out of cow's skin.

The next element is $)^2$. We thus link *a Dennis that has a gigantic egg-shaped head* to *a tower with extremely muscular knees*. Try visualising a tower with extremely muscular knees bouncing the egg-headed Dennis upon them.

Penultimately, we have $/2\sigma$. We therefore need to link *a tower with extremely muscular knees* to *two white beards cutting with a machete.* So visualise two white beards nefariously cutting the tower's muscular knees with a machete.

Lastly, we have the $\boxed{2}$, i.e., the power of two. We need to link *two white beards cutting with a machete* to *a giant muscular knee.* So visualise a giant muscular knee lying on a psychiatrist's couch (a location which further reinforces the fact that the beards represent Sigmund Freud, which represents σ) as two white beards try cutting away at it with a machete.

The reader may have noticed that, rather than working with one parameter at a time, some of the parameters in the equation were combined to form a more complex image. This process is called *bundling.* It is similar, in principle, to adding higher dimensions to the Numbers List, and amounts to reducing the overall number of images necessary. This advantage, however, comes with the cost of added complexity.

For example, the element $\boxed{)^2}$ was visualised as *a tower with extremely muscular knees.* It was created by combining the leftmost symbol (the RHS parenthesis), which is represented by *tower*, with the rightmost symbol (the power of two), which is represented by a *bodybuilding knee* (the *bodybuilding* portion is due to the number two being set to the power). Performing such bundling avoided the need to create two separate links (linking *tower* to *bodybuilding knee*, and then *bodybuilding knee* to the next element).

It is recommended to bundle items in order to reduce the number of images required, but not to the point of having such complex images that recall is hindered. With practice, the balance between complexity and ease of recall becomes clear.

When a topic (say mathematics, to follow from the abovementioned example) becomes familiar, a portion of the information (e.g., some of the parameters in the equation) can be omitted, since prior knowledge of the subject provides you the information needed to complete the picture. (This point was already alluded to in the Computer Code memorisation section.) Viewed in this way, *linking* simply serves as a tool to **capture the data with which one is not familiar**, while prior subject knowledge serves as the structure onto which this data is assembled.

For example, in the equation above it would not have been necessary to memorise (x), had prior knowledge of the topic made it obvious that the formula is a function of x (as mu and sigma are the mean and variance respectively, and the only other variable on the right-hand side is x). Such shortcuts should always be used; only that which is unknown should be memorised.

Another important point to note is that once information is learnt, it should be utilised as a shortcut to memorising larger pieces of information in which it appears. For the example topic of mathematics, it means that once basic components (e.g. functions) have been memorised, committing to memory equations that contain them in expanded form becomes very easy, since images of the components already exist. For instance, say we wanted to memorise the *normal cumulative distribution function*:

$$\Phi(x) = \frac{1}{\sigma\sqrt{2\pi}} \int\limits_{-\infty}^{x} e^{-\frac{(\mu-t)^2}{2\sigma^2}} \, dt$$

Relying on basic knowledge of the subject, all that is required to memorise the *normal cumulative distribution function* is to notice that it is simply the integral of the *normal distribution density function*. Thus, all we need to do is link *camel* (as it sounds similar to the beginning portion of *cumulative*) to *interrogation light* (which represents the integral, using the unique identifiers in the list above), and then *interrogation light* to *wide bell* (which represents the normal density).

From the above exposition (and obvious logical deduction), it is clear that a subject should be learnt from its basic principles up towards its complex theories. This way, basic data learnt early on can be used to more easily memorise the more complex ideas. And, in addition, having better structural knowledge reduces the amount that needs to be memorised in the first place, as observance of the basic rules of the topic makes certain pieces of information immediately obvious.

CHEMICAL NOTATION

The main approach used for chemical notation employs the Link System. However, in some cases either bundling or using the Loci System becomes necessary, as will be demonstrated below.

As usual, the motivation should be to break down the compound to be learnt into subcomponents whose images are established and can therefore be easily linked. The procedure is as follows:

1. **Unique identifiers**. Ensure that each symbol in the compound is represented by a unique identifier. (Write it down in a list to avoid inconsistencies.)
2. **Convert the name of the compound** to be memorised into an image.
3. **Convert each component of the compound** into an image, utilising the names of sub-compounds if you are familiar with them (in the example below, we do so for amine).

4. **If using the Link System**:
   a. Link the image for the compound to the image of its first constituent component.
   b. Then link each subsequent component to the one that precedes it.
5. **Or, if using the Loci System**:
   a. Peg the image for the compound to the entrance of the locus (be it the door to a room, the main entrance to a house, the beginning of a road, etc.).
   b. Peg the images of the constituent components of the compound to the rest of the items in the locus.
6. **Memorise the compound**:
   a. From left to right.
   b. From the top downwards.
   c. For circular portions to be memorised, work clockwise.
7. **Review**.

The table below lists the unique identifiers we will be using for the example.

Symbol	Unique Identifier	Reason/Logic Behind the Choice
Double bond	James Bond with two heads.	Representing a chemical bond, of which there are two.
Single bond	N/A	Assume it is a single bond unless otherwise specified.
Letters	The corresponding object from the Alphabet List.	N/A
NH₂	Preacher	*Amine* sounds like "amen".

The reader should note that we have used the name of NH_2 to represent it where it appears in the compound below, rather than memorise each of its constituent elements separately. This principle was already alluded to in the Mathematical Formulae section and is again—for its importance—reiterated here:

1. **Previous knowledge of the topic should be used to make the conversion of data into images simpler**. For example, any collection of items that are already known by name as a group, should be memorised as a group rather than the individual components. (E.g., NH_2 is memorised as amine, rather than the individual chemical elements. And in the Mathematical Formulae section's example, it was the *normal density function* that was utilised when memorising the *cumulative distribution function*, rather than the individual parameters within the integral.).

2. **Structural knowledge of the topic should be used to avoid memorising data that can be reasoned**. In the chemical example below, we do not memorise single bonds. Thus, unless an image of a double bond appears, we should assume a single bond is present. Further such reductions in data actually memorised are possible the more the practitioner is familiar with the general rules of the topic. As was the case with a computer language's syntax, learning the rules first reduces the data that needs to be memorised.

We proceed with the example of melamine:

Melamine sounds a bit like "melon-mean"—which can be visualised as *a mean-looking melon*. Begin, then, by linking *a mean-looking melon* to *preacher*. Perhaps this mean looking melon is preaching in front of a congregation of terrified melons.

Proceed by linking *preacher* to a *two-headed James Bond*. Perhaps a gigantic two-headed James Bond is sitting with the congregation, nodding his heads along to the preacher's sermon.

Continue by linking *two-headed James Bond* to *hen*. Maybe the hen is the archvillain, Bond's nemesis, standing over the two-headed James Bond, boasting about the success of its evil scheme.

Next, link *hen* to *preacher*. You could visualise a hen preaching to the other hens in the henhouse about the nearby crafty fox.

Then, link *preacher* to *two-headed James Bond*. Perhaps this time the congregation consists of billions of such two-headed James Bonds.

Proceed by linking *two-headed James Bond* to *hen*. Think of a two-headed hen schmoozing at an exclusive dinner party, wearing an elegant tuxedo and drinking a vodka martini.

Next, link *hen* to *preacher*. Visualise a preacher on a farm picking grains by pecking his nose at the ground.

Continue by linking *preacher* to *two-headed James Bond*. Perhaps the two-headed James Bond is walking around a dinner party dressed in preacher's robes.

Finally, link *two-headed James Bond* to *hen*. Visualise the two-headed James Bond picking grains by pecking his two noses at the ground.

Tired and confused yet? The example above was deliberately utilised to illustrate a subtle point: the Link System approach works, but there are plenty of repeated links. These repetitions test the limits of the Link System. The Link System works well when there are few pieces of information that repeatedly appear adjacently. Where such repetitions are abundant (as they certainly are in organic chemistry), there are two possible alternatives:

1. **Use the Loci System instead.** Repetitions in this system cannot be confused.
2. **Use bundling (with the Link System),** as was illustrated in the Mathematical Formulae section. The aim is to bundle items in such a way as to ensure that there are few repeated links.

In most cases, and if wisely applied, bundling is the optimal approach. Nonetheless, some structures (which result in repeated bundles) make it rather challenging to deploy—in which case the Loci System should be used.

With bundling, the above example is transformed into:

Link *mean-looking melon* to *two-headed preacher; two-headed preacher* to *hen preacher*; then link *hen preacher* to *two-headed hen*; and, lastly, link *two-headed hen* to *two-headed hen preacher*.

An alternative—and superior—bundling approach would be to bundle the circular portion into a single image. For example, we could think of a *hen ball*: a hen being used as a football (a soccer ball). If this approach is taken, any future circular structures should be treated in a similar manner—that is, using a uniquely-identifiable convention. The example above used the letter on the circumference (*N* in the case of melamine) to determine the type of ball it was. A ball with *C*'s on its circumference would be a *sea ball*, for example. (Note that implementing this approach requires some basic knowledge of the topic, so as to be able to infer the types of bonds in the ball.)

This approach leads to a single image that captures the entire structure: picture three preachers standing in a triangle formation, kicking a gigantic hen ball around in an extremely vicious manner— punishing it for its sins. Visualise billions of feathers flying about, and sense the visceral pain felt by the hen following every kick.

For users who prefer to use the Loci System, it is advisable to be organised and, thus, assign a set portion of your loci to be dedicated to the subject. For example, in order to memorise chemical compounds, the practitioner may choose to use a palace that he had once visited. Each room in the palace would then correspond to a single compound. However, it quickly becomes apparent that, for a serious study of the subject, one would require a very large palace—with lots of rooms. Imaginary palaces or towns may work well here, but, as discussed in the Loci System section, these first require construction and familiarisation before they can be used effectively.

NAMES AND FACES

It appears to be simple to remember a face, but the corresponding name tends to come less naturally. The former is likely due to the survival necessity of being able to identify friend from foe; the latter is likely due to the insignificance of abstract representations to one's survival. The brain is optimised for survival: energy and resources are prioritised to tasks necessary for survival.

Ironically, for economic survival—which is the relevant sort in our portion of the Anthropocene—remembering a name has become just as important as remembering a face. Our genes, however, have yet to naturally select that trait. And, perhaps, our ability to find ways/tools to overcome our natural endowments circumvents the need for such selection.

Evolutionary speculation aside, and whatever the cause may be, in comparison to the other senses, our brains have substantially more resources devoted to processing visual stimuli. So the vocal cadences of a name are already less memorable than the visage of the one who bears it. Furthermore, when meeting someone, the face features throughout the encounter, whereas the name makes an appearance at the start and, possibly, at the end. So the period of exposure to the name is substantially shorter than the exposure to the face.

Lastly, the region of the brain that processes visual stimuli differs to the region that stores the name (which is generally the region devoted to words). So weak connections between the pieces of information are a further impediment to recall.

The method to remember names exploits the reliability of facial recall in order to be able to capture the name at the same time. The procedure to remember names is therefore as follows:

1. **Look for a distinctive, unusual or funny feature of the face**. Try to avoid focusing on jewellery or glasses, as it is better if the feature is a permanent fixture on the person's face or head. For example, look out for:
   a. Big ears. Pointy ears.
   b. A wrinkly forehead.
   c. A thick or connected set of eyebrows.
   d. A long nose. A crooked nose.
   e. Very thin or very fat lips.
   f. A crooked chin.
   g. Any visible scars, birthmarks, or moles.

   (Key principle: Think like a caricaturist.)

2. **Choosing the distinctive facial feature of the person is analogous to deciding on a key monument within a locus.** The facial feature and the monument are both items stored in memory onto which further information—which is yet to be committed to memory—can be pegged. For this reason, the facial feature is also commonly known as "see-peg".

3. **Listen attentively to the name.** As indicated earlier in this part of the book, attention is principal in the formation of any memory.

4. **Convert the name into images**. As always, maintain consistency by defining unique identifiers. For example, if the first Donald you meet is represented by Donald Duck, ensure that all future encounters with persons named Donald receive the same treatment.

5. **Peg** the image that represents the forename to the distinctive facial feature.

6. **Then link** the image that represents the surname to the image that represents the forename.

7. **Review**.

The procedure utilises the Peg System combined with the Link System: we peg the forename to the distinctive facial feature, and then we link the forename to the surname. As always, it is important to be consistent with the breakdown of the constituent components. In this case, it is the names that should always be converted consistently into the same images. This, by now, should feel logical and congruent, given the exposition of the topics presented thus far.

It should be noted that finding a distinctive feature is neither meant to degrade nor perceive a fault with the person whose name you wish to remember. It is merely a deliberate act to solicit attention to something you wish to memorise.

Detailed below are some examples to illustrate the procedure. To ensure that the reader is familiar with the facial features, let us focus on famous figures.

GEORGE W. BUSH

The 43rd President of the United States.

Distinctive features: the side-swept grey hair, the small light blue eyes, and the thin-lipped horizontal smile. [Choose one.]

The forename, George, can be converted into the similarly-sounding *gorge*.

The surname, Bush, can be converted into *bush* (as in shrub).

Proceed, therefore, by pegging *gorge* to *side-swept grey hair*. Perhaps you are walking near a gorge that is filled with gigantic side-swept grey hairpieces instead of water. Then continue by linking *gorge* and *bush*. Visualise that you are walking near a row of bushes that have gorges on their stems instead of leaves.

It is important to utilise in your image the precise "see-peg", as you would when using the Loci System. So, in the example above, the gigantic side-swept grey hairpieces filling the gorge must be precisely the same as the hair on George W. Bush's head. Using a generic *side-swept grey hair* would yield a weak peg; using the precise form of the hair you noticed in an image, in a video, or in an encounter with the former president, would be far better.

After the name is recorded, other facts relating to the individual can be easily added. For example, we could add the fact that George W. Bush was the 43rd president by linking *bush* to *rum* (*rum* representing 43 on the Numbers List). And the next fact of interest can be then linked to *rum*, and so forth using the Link System.

BERNARD MADOFF

The admitted mastermind behind what has been described as the largest Ponzi scheme in history.

Distinctive features: the large crooked nose and the thin lips.

The forename, Bernard, can be converted into *St. Bernard* (the breed of dog that features in the movie *Beethoven*).

The surname, Madoff, sounds similar to "mad-off", which can be visualised as a *mad off-button* (typically a red button consisting of a circle and a short vertical line). So perhaps picture an off-button in a straitjacket.

To combine the above, peg *St. Bernard* to *large crooked nose*; then link *St. Bernard* and *mad off-button*. Visualise a St. Bernard dog with Mr. Madoff's distinctive nose in place of a snout. Blow it out of proportion—perhaps by making it so large and heavy that the dog is finding it difficult to get up. Then picture a St. Bernard dog drooling billions of off-buttons in straitjackets.

PRESIDENTS AND RULERS

To memorise lists of presidents, rulers, or even dynasties for that matter, we employ the Peg System. It is up to the reader to decide which peg list is to be used for which task—in the examples below we will use the Effigy List. A long list of rulers would require a peg list equivalent in length. Where no such peg list is available, we can either extend one of the current peg lists to match the length of the new set of data, or we can utilise the Loci System (with markers) instead.

The preference for using the Peg System stems from the assumption that both the order of the information as well as the precise numerical position of each entry are important. The same can be achieved with the Loci System when markers are placed at fixed increments through the locus. But the Peg System is more efficient due to its ability to immediately provide the numerical position.

The procedure is as follows:

1. **Choose a peg list of sufficient length**. Ensure that there are enough items on the peg list to be able to memorise the entire set of new information.
2. **Convert the name** of the ruler into an image.
3. **Peg the image representing the ruler** to the item from the peg list that corresponds to the numerical position of the ruler in the list being memorised. If both the forename and the surname are required, peg the image representing

the forename, and then link the image representing the forename to the image representing the surname.

4. **Link any other information** of interest (such as, date elected, for example) to the image representing the ruler's surname.

5. **Use bundling**, where feasible, to reduce the number of images.

To illustrate the procedure, an example list containing the first five presidents of the United States will be utilised. It is left to the reader to continue with the rest of the presidents. (Note that the peg list chosen here would have to be extended in order to memorise all the presidents. Alternatively, you could use the Numbers List, which has 101 pegs available within it—more than enough for the count of presidents at the time of writing.)

№	President	Year elected
1	George Washington	1789
2	John Adams	1797
3	Thomas Jefferson	1801
4	James Madison	1809
5	James Monroe	1817

We proceed by using the Effigy List. Starting with George Washington, the image for George is *gorge* (as was the case for George W. Bush in the previous section). We therefore peg *gorge* to *tree* (which is the peg that represents *1* on the Effigy List). Visualise a tree that has a long vertical gorge instead of a trunk.

Notice how the unique identifier for George is applied consistently here. As mentioned (and reiterated) in earlier sections, this has a significant effect on efficiency.

Washington sounds similar to "washing-town", so link *gorge* with *washing-town*. Perhaps a gorge full of water is standing over a town, carefully scrubbing the town centre.

Next, to memorise the year in which the president was elected, we use the higher-dimensional technique with the **VWYZ** convention. For 1789, this results in the image of a *brown duck that is exploding*. So link *washing-town* to *brown duck that is exploding*. Visualise a brown duck being washed in the town centre whilst gradually becoming larger and larger until, to a thundering sound, it explodes, leaving the town gruesomely decorated.

Note that familiarity with the topic would allow the user to infer the century and millennium during which the president was elected, thus omitting the need to memorise the *17* portion of the above year.

Continuing to the next president, John Adams. John sounds similar to "yawn", and the name Adams can be represented by an *Adam's apple*. Using bundling, the image of an *Adam's apple yawning* can therefore represent the president's full name. We thus peg this image to the second item on the Effigy List, *swan*. Perhaps visualise a beautiful swan with a gigantic Adam's apple; all of a sudden, the enormous Adam's apple begins to yawn with a long diminuendoing sound—try to both see the image and hear the sound.

To memorise the year elected, we proceed by linking *pig* to *Adam's apple yawning*. Imagine that you are standing in the middle of a pigsty, but, instead of pigs, there are hundreds of yawning Adam's apples. Mentally hear the cacophony of strange yawns.

The reader will have noticed that in this example we only used the last two digits of the date, *97*, instead of its full form, 1797. It is only necessary to memorise that which you do not know. Since we already know that George Washington was elected in 1789, it is not necessary to memorise the *17* portion of the year for the president that succeeded Washington. Such tricks and shortcuts, where available, should always be employed when memorising. They all amount to the same principle that, used akin to a mantra throughout this text, should be becoming familiar by now: **only memorise that which is unknown,** and infer the rest from what you already know.

Next we have Thomas Jefferson. To visualise the first name, we could use the image of *Thomas the Tank Engine*. To peg the name to the Effigy List, locate the object that represents number three, *ant*, and then peg *Thomas* to it. Visualise a large ant with a wide Thomas-like smile pulling the carriages of a train.

The surname, Jefferson, sounds similar "chef-fussing". So to memorise the surname, we link *Thomas the Tank Engine* with *chef fussing*. Visualise Thomas the Tank Engine wearing a chef's toque, fussing over the pot in the kitchen.

Finally, to remember the year elected, 1801, and continuing to leverage upon prior knowledge, we use *suit* to represent *01*. So link *chef fussing* to *suit*. Proceed, therefore, by visualising that the toque atop the fussing chef's head is wearing a designer suit.

If, instead of opting to rely on previous knowledge, the practitioner wishes to continue with the application of the **VWYZ** convention, 1801 would be memorised by linking *chef fussing* to *grey dove showering*. In that case, visualise a chef fussing over the pot, as he notices that the grey dove is having a shower inside instead of getting cooked.

It is simple to then extend this procedure to the rest of the presidents:

- James Madison, 1809: Peg *jams* to *sail*; link *jams* with *medicine*; then link *medicine* with *soup*.
- James Monroe, 1817: Peg *jams* to *hook;* link *jams* with *moon row*; then link *moon row* with *duck*.
- And so forth with the rest of the presidents.

CALENDAR

To plan the day, we frequently use a physical or a digital calendar to assist in the process of memorising our appointments. Instead of this approach, or to complement it, one could dedicate a peg list in order to store the day's appointments. The example below will use the Rhyme List. The procedure is as follows:

1. **Assign the zero hour** of the day to the first item on the chosen peg list. Thereafter, do not change this mapping. Every period of the day is then uniquely defined by the distance it is away from the zero hour. Using the Rhyme List as an example, and assuming one's day always begins at 8 a.m. (the zero hour), we thus assign *Zorro* to represent the period starting at 8 a.m. and ending at 9 a.m. Thereafter, *Zorro* will always represent this period.

2. **Each item on the peg list represents a period of an hour.** The starting time of the period is determined by the distance of the item from the zero hour. In the Rhyme List, *zoo,* which represents *2,* thus two steps away from *Zorro,* which represents *0,* covers the period starting at 10 a.m.

3. **Peg each appointment** to the corresponding period on the peg list.

4. **For events that occur at half past the hour,** add a *machete* to the image. The *machete* represents division,

and, added to an image, it is used to indicate that the hour is being divided.

5. **For events that last for longer than one hour,** simply peg the same appointment to the multiple items, corresponding to the multiple periods, on the peg list.

For example, say one wanted to remember a day's schedule that consisted of:

Time	Appointment
08:00-09:00	Read the morning papers
09:00-10:00	Staff meeting
10:00-11:00	Inspect factory
11:00-12:00	Read the sales report
12:00-14:00	Lunch at Chez Septime
14:00-15:00	Interview candidates for a secretarial role
15:00-16:00	Meet with the bank manager
16:00-17:00	Pick up the kids from school
17:00-18:00	Read the evening paper
18:00-19:00	Prepare dinner

Using the Rhyme List, we assign to each of the 11 items on the peg list one hour of the working day (starting at 8 a.m. and ending at 7 p.m.).

To remember the first appointment, *read the morning papers*, we simply peg an image of it, *newspaper*, to the corresponding item on the Rhyme List, *Zorro*. Perhaps visualise a gigantic newspaper, with a mask encircling its eyes, riding on the back of a black Andalusian horse to rescue a damsel in distress.

Next, peg the second appointment, *staff meeting*, to the corresponding item on the Rhyme List, *gun*. Perhaps you enter the boardroom and see that around the conference table, instead of your company's directors, large shiny guns—dressed in suits—are sat waiting, ready for the meeting to begin. Feel the shock and fear, and smell the gunpowder residue diffusing through the air.

Continue by pegging each appointment to the corresponding item on Rhyme List.

In order to recall the time of an appointment, simply add the number of the item on the Rhyme List to your zero hour—which in the example above was 8 a.m. For example, after memorising the appointments above, your partner calls to ask at what time you will be having lunch that day. A nonsensical image involving *lunch* and *door* will come to mind. *Door* represents *4* on the Rhyme List; hence, added to 8 a.m., the lunch appointment must be at 12 noon.

In the example above, the zero hour was chosen to be 8 a.m. This should be modified to reflect the starting time of the practitioner's day. The key point is to then stay consistent and never change the zero hour, for all the other periods of the day are inferred from their distance to this hour.

For those who wish to incorporate more hours of the day, all that is required is to either utilise one of the longer peg lists or to extend the Rhyme List.

However, to plan one's schedule for the month or even the whole year, it is advisable to use a different system. For instance, planning for the month could be performed via the Grid System: each cell corresponds to one day of the month. To each cell's image the appointments are then pegged. To achieve this, peg the first appointment on that day's schedule to the cell's image, and then link the rest of the appointments in their order of occurrence.

Planning for the entire year, on the other hand, could be achieved by using the phonetic alphabet to create an image for each hour of every day in the year. We could use a **UVWXYZ** convention, where **UVW** is represented by an image created using the phonetic alphabet, and **XYZ** is represented by the added dimensions.

For example, say you had a doctor's appointment scheduled for May 12th, at 10 a.m. Numerically, the date and time combination could be represented as 120510 (using a dd/mm/hh date and time convention).

To memorise the appointment, we begin by employing the phonetic alphabet to create an image for 120—which is represented phonetically by (T or D)(N)(S or Z). A possible choice could be *TeNniS*—perhaps use a *tennis ball* as the object to represent 120.

Each of the next three numbers, 510, represents a property from the dimensions of Location, Colour and Action respectively. So ultimately, for 120510, we would visualise a *red tennis ball parachuting in outer space*. All that remains is to link this image to the appointment: *doctor*. Perhaps visualise a red tennis ball parachuting in outer space, injuring itself by landing on a pointy corner of a star, and then rushing quickly to seek the doctor for help.

Similarly, birthdays can be memorised in the same manner but using the **VWYZ** convention instead (to represent the day and month as dd/mm). **VW** is represented by the corresponding object from the Numbers List, whilst **YZ** is represented by the two added dimensions.

As an aside: A powerful combination of the techniques presented thus far would be to memorise a person's name and then link their birthday to the image representing their surname. The sequence would be as follows:

1. *Distinctive feature* image linked to
2. *Forename* image, which is linked to
3. *Surname* image, which is linked to
4. *Birthday* image.

Please note that, as always, if bundling is possible the steps above can be reduced to:

1. *Distinctive feature* image linked to
2. *Full name* image, which is linked to
3. *Birthday* image.

THE HUMAN ORGANISER

The techniques presented thus far allow us to introduce a powerful tool to structure one's thinking and interactions when access to one's notes is restricted. It is particularly useful when there is a need to project a certain degree of intellectual ability[12] and professionalism—e.g., in an interview or in meetings with senior members of an organisation.

The tool is merely a collection of the ideas presented thus far. When applied together, they remove any necessity of having a writing instrument at hand.

The Human Organiser is the totality of the individual instruments detailed in the subsections that follow. It is called the Human

---

[12] The protagonist in the novel *Rain Fund* employs this exact technique to eschew the use of a notebook or a tablet—albeit to a mild show-off effect.

Organiser, for it functions as a regular organiser while being fully contained within the practitioner.

In the subsections below, the abstract thoughts and concepts are converted into images in the same manner as presented thus far in the book. The images are then pegged to the relevant instrument in the Human Organiser.

THE LIGHTBULB

The Lightbulb is used to peg ideas that come to mind during conversations, in the shower, while resting, while driving, while playing sports, while exercising, etc. In sum, when note-taking is not feasible or when note-taking is simply not desirable,

Any time a worthy idea comes to mind, peg the image that represents it to the image of a *lightbulb*. Any further ideas that follow can then be linked to the first idea that was pegged. (That is, peg *idea1* to *lightbulb,* then link *idea2* to *idea1*, then link *idea3* to *idea2*, … , and so forth up to the latest idea by linking *idea[N]* to *idea[N-1]*.)

THE TROLLEY

The Trolley is used to memorise items that need to be purchased—typically items on a shopping list. Whenever you become aware of an item that should be added to the shopping list, simply peg it to *trolley* [*shopping cart*, for non-British readers]. Any other items to be purchased can then be linked to the first item that was pegged.

THE MEGAPHONE

During a conversation, especially while another party is speaking, if you become aware of a crucial point you would like to mention, simply peg an image representative of the thought to *megaphone*. All other points to discuss can then be linked to the first point that was pegged.

THE HAMMER

While occupied in whatever activities that typically comprise your day, if you become aware of a task that needs to be performed, add it on to your to-do list by pegging its representative image to *hammer*. Other to-do items that follow can then be linked to the first item that was pegged.

THE NOTEBOOK

During a meeting, a lecture or a conversation, if valuable information becomes available, you can memorise it by pegging the first piece of information to *notebook*. Thereafter, link all the other pieces of information to the first piece that was pegged.

The idea is to quickly capture the information without spending time or thought on where it should be filed. It is performed in this manner in order to ensure that the meeting, lecture or conversation proceeds without interruption. A pause or an interruption would defeat the purpose of using this system.

If The Notebook is to be utilised extensively, especially if long lectures will be involved, it is advisable to create (well in advance of applying the tool) an imaginary locus—perhaps a house built in the shape of a notebook. All the new information can then be pegged to the items within the locus. Furthermore, different rooms within the locus can be used to compartmentalise the separate topics into which the lecture/conversation may be divided.

Note, however, that if you are aware of the topic of conversation, meeting or lecture prior to it taking place, it is preferable to memorise the information and file it in its long-term location, rather than use the temporary *notebook.*

CALENDAR

The Calendar, presented separately in the previous section, is used to memorise birthdays and organise appointments.

CONTACTS

Contacts are recorded using the technique introduced for memorising names and faces. Important information is linked to the individual's surname (e.g., birthday, profession, telephone number, etc.).

CLEAR THE IMAGES EVERY DAY

At the end of each day, it is advisable to clear each of the instruments that together make up the Human Organiser. This way, the next day the tool is available to optimally perform its intended role.

To clear the instruments, each important piece of information should either be noted down physically or filed away in a mental location that is dedicated to the genre of information to which it belongs. Information of lesser importance can be disregarded or jotted down in a notebook of miscellanea for future reference.

Tasks yet to be performed (i.e., relating to items on the shopping list or on the to-do list) should be re-linked and reviewed at the end of the day. The next day, new items can be added by simply linking them to the last item on the relevant instrument of the Human Organiser.

VARIATIONS

Instead of using a single peg (*lightbulb, trolley, megaphone, hammer,* and *notebook)* for each instrument of the Human Organiser, it is possible to dedicate to each an entire peg list or a locus. For example, The Lightbulb could be a locus instead of a single peg, *lightbulb*. Ideas that come to mind would then be pegged to the items within the locus.

Using a peg list or a locus is particularly advantageous for the to-do list or the shopping list, since it may happen that at the end of some days not all tasks were completed. The original approach involves re-linking the items that remain uncompleted. In contrast, with a peg list or a locus, tasks that have been completed are cleared, and tasks still outstanding are merely reviewed using their original pegs.

Since there is no cross-dependency between the pegs, there is no need to reorganise the list. Old (and uncompleted) items remain pegged to their original pegs, and new items are pegged where no information is presently stored. For example, in a to-do list that initially consists of seven items, if the third and fifth items were to be cleared at the end of Day1, on Day2 new items would be added by pegging them to the third and fifth positions in the locus, and then continuing from the eighth position onwards.

The disadvantage of this alternative approach is that it limits the scope of the tool: the links that can be mounted are theoretically infinite, whereas the peg list and the locus are finite and must be predetermined prior to their use.

OENOPHILES AND "UISGEOPHILES"

Oenophiles, "uisgeophile"[13], and other smell and taste aficionados, derive much pleasure from the complex notes that certain wines and spirits have to offer.

There are two technique that could be utilised to memorise the tasting notes—which of the two to apply depends on the depth of the endeavour. If the purpose it to memorise only the main tasting notes, and only for a few bottles, the Link System should be used. If, on the other hand, the purpose is to memorise every subtle tasting note, and to do so for an entire collection, the Loci System is the preferred approach.

LINK SYSTEM APPROACH

When the purpose is to memorise only the key tasting notes, the Link System offers a simple solution. A key note is first selected from each of the standard categories, being COLOUR (the colour

---

[13] [Note that the term "uisgeophile" is not an established word. It is formed from the Gaelic *uisge beatha*, meaning "water of life", with the Greek suffix -*phile*, meaning "lover of". Among whisky enthusiasts, it is used, for lack of a better term, to describe themselves—though even then rather infrequently.]

of the wine or spirit), NOSE (the aromas of the wine or spirit while in the glass), BODY (the texture of the wine or spirit), PALATE (the taste of the wine or spirit while in the mouth), and FINISH (the impression that lingers after the wine or spirit was consumed). Each such key note is then linked in a specific order to the name of the bottle. The specific order allows us to later recall which note belongs to which category.

The procedure when using the Link System is as follows:

1. (Ideally, memorise the bottle while experiencing it. This will promote subtle—yet powerful—neurological connections between the abstract depictions and the actual experience.)
2. **Name.** Convert the name of the bottle into an image. Use bundling to include the year or the age in the image.
3. COLOUR. Convert the COLOUR into an image.
4. **Link** the image for the bottle's name to the image for the COLOUR.
5. NOSE. Convert the NOSE into an image.
6. **Link** the image for the COLOUR to the image for the NOSE.
7. **BODY.** Convert the BODY into an image.
8. **Link** the image for the NOSE to the image for the BODY.
9. PALATE. Convert the PALATE into an image.
10. **Link** the image for the BODY to the image for the PALATE.
11. FINISH. Convert the FINISH into an image.
12. **Link** the image for the PALATE to the image for the FINISH.
13. **Review.**

As an example, let us use Michael Jackson's (the late British writer, journalist, and beer and whisky guru, not the late pop star) Scotch whisky tasting notes. Picking a high-scoring Islay single malt, the Laphroaig 18-year-old, as it appears in *Michael Jackson's Complete Guide to Single Malt Scotch*, 6th edition:

Laphroaig 18-year-old

- COLOUR: Bright golden orange.
- NOSE: Brine and sea spray. Greasy rope. Hot road tar in the rain.
- BODY: Full and oily.
- PALATE: Industrial steam engine. Red liquorice. Peppered steak cooked on a hickory barbecue. Big and brooding.
- FINISH: Long, with peat coating the mouth and liquorice and hickory lingering.

When using the Link System, we are restricted to memorising only a single note from each category. The crux is to use the key note. In most professional tasting notes, the author usually writes the key ones first.

For the Laphroaig 18-year-old, we begin by converting the name into an image. Laphroaig sound similar to "la-frog", so picture a frog—perhaps one with a francophone accent. To incorporate the age—18-year-old—use the Numbers List to convert 18 into *dove*. So, overall, the name of the bottle is represented by *frog with a dove's head*.

Next, for the COLOUR category, we have *bright golden orange*. So link *frog with a dove's head* with *bright golden orange*. Perhaps visualise a frog with a dove's head carefully peeling an orange, only to find that a gigantic block of gold sits within it.

Proceeding to the NOSE category, we have *brine and sea spray*. We thus need to link *bright golden orange* to *brine and sea spray*. Visualise the sea crashing against the rocks near the shore, producing a spray of bright golden oranges.

For the BODY category, we have *full and oily*. So link *brine and sea spray* with *full and oily*. Perhaps visualise a barrel of oil sitting at the dinner table about to eat the last portion of its meal;

once full, it begins to belch, splashing the other guests with sea spray. Visualise the sea spray as weltering and whelming, and out of proportion when compared to the small barrel of oil that generated it.

For the PALATE category, we have *industrial steam engine*. So link *full and oily* with *industrial steam engine*. Picture a steam engine ejecting billions of sated barrels of oil.

Lastly, for the FINISH category, we have *long, with peat coating the mouth*. We must therefore link *industrial steam engine* with *long, with peat coating the mouth*. Visualise a steam engine ejecting billions of long, vertically stretched, mouths full of peat.

LOCI SYSTEM APPROACH

The above Link System example allowed us to capture the main characteristics of a single malt Scotch. If, however, the intention is to capture the subtle notes too, as well as to contain the topic within an easily accessible domain, the Loci System is the approach that should be used.

When applying the Loci System to this task, it is recommended to use a palace, a large house or a museum as the locus. The procedure is then as follows:

1. (Ideally, memorise the bottle while experiencing it. This will promote subtle—yet powerful—neurological connections between the abstract depictions and the actual experience.)
2. **Assign rooms**. To each bottle assign a room in the palace.
3. **Peg the name** of the bottle to the room's entrance.

4. **Peg the year or the age** of the bottle to the first item in the room.
5. **Peg the tasting notes** of the bottle to the rest of the items in the room.
    a. Begin by pegging the image of the category to the next item in the room (using *crayon* for COLOUR; *nose hair* for NOSE; *cadaver* for BODY; *tongue* for PALATE; and *chequered finish line* for FINISH).
    b. Then peg to the items that follow in the room the tasting notes under that category. This way, all the items that follow the image of the category are understood to belong to that category.
    c. Repeat for each of the categories.
6. **Travel clockwise through the palace**, from the bottom upwards.
7. **Travel clockwise through each room.**
8. **Review.**

For illustration purposes, we will use a palace that has the following rooms and items at its entrance:

1. Entrance hall: *Chandelier, fountain, vase, portrait, golden statue, knight's armour, mirror, umbrella stand, carpet* and *stairs*.
2. Dining room and kitchen: *serving table, long dining table, balcony, coat hangers, sink, stove, preparation table, pots and pans hanging from a rack, microwave* and *fridge*.

To demonstrate the technique, we will memorise a couple of famous wines. Note that the technique can be applied to whisky or other spirits too; wine is used below to add variety—the technique is not specific to it.

Romanée Conti 1929

- COLOUR: Red/orange.
- NOSE: Earth and spice.
- BODY: Full and fat.
- PALATE: Nutty and coffee.
- FINISH: Long and earthy.

Petrus 1961

- COLOUR: Purple.
- NOSE: Chocolate, plum, and subtle smoke.
- BODY: Fleshy.
- PALATE: Fruits, earth, and garden herbs.
- FINISH: Long coffee and spice.

We begin the journey at the locus's entrance hall. Romanée Conti sounds similar to "Roman counting". We thus peg *Roman counting*, to *entrance hall*. Visualise the hall's door counting Roman soldiers as they march through it.

We then proceed to the first item within the entrance hall, *chandelier*. We peg to *chandelier* the year of the wine, 1929. Using the **VWYZ** convention, 1929 is represented by *black toilet paper exploding*. Perhaps imagine that the chandelier is constructed out of lots of black toilet rolls that explode to produce the incandescent effect.

To the rest of the items in the room we then peg the characteristics of the wine. We start by pegging *crayon* (to indicate that the items which follow are part of the COLOUR category) to *fountain*. Visualise a fountain flowing with gigantic crayons instead of water.

Next in the locus we have *vase*. To it we peg the characteristics under the COLOUR category: *red/orange*. So peg *red orange* to *vase*. Picture a vase from which extend gigantic, fragrant red oranges.

Proceeding to the tasting notes under the NOSE category, we begin by pegging *nose hair* to *portrait*. Visualise nose hair in a serious pose depicted in the portrait.

When pegging the tasting notes under NOSE, to improve efficiency, we will use bundling. So, for *earth and spice*, peg *spice jar full of Earths* to *golden statue*. Imagine a hungry visitor shaking a spice jar full of Earths over the golden statue, to improve its flavour, before attempting to bite a tasty morsel.

Next, for the characteristics under BODY, utilising bundling again, we combine the characteristics, *full and fat*, and the category, *cadaver* (for BODY), into a single image. We thus peg *full and fat cadaver* to *knight's armour*. Perhaps the sated, fat cadaver is trying, to no avail, to put on the knight's armour.

Next, for the tasting notes under PALATE, we start by pegging *nutty tongue* (bundling *tongue*, which represents PALATE, and *nutty*, the primary tasting note) to *mirror*. Imagine that, as you walk in front of the mirror, your reflection is flashing you its gigantic nutty tongue.

Then, for the secondary tasting note under PALATE, peg *coffee* to *umbrella stand*. Perhaps the umbrella stand is loudly sipping a cup of coffee.

Next, for FINISH, we first peg *chequered finish line* to *carpet*. Visualise an immense chequered finish line walking on the carpet, savouring the softness of its fabric.

Lastly, for the tasting notes under FINISH, *long and earthy*: peg *long Earth* to *stairs*. Imagine a vertically-stretched planet Earth walking up the stairs.

Using the same approach for the second wine, we begin at the entrance to the second room.

- Peg *pet wrestling* (to represent Petrus) to the room's entrance.
- Then peg

  o *Green toilet paper showering* (to represent 1961) to *serving table.*
  o *Purple crayon* to *long dining table.*
  o *Chocolate nose hair* to *balcony.*
  o *Plum* to *coat hangers.*
  o *Smoke* to *sink.*
  o *Fleshy cadaver* to *stove.*
  o *Tongue made out of fruits* to *preparation table.*
  o *Earths and herbs* to *pots and pans rack.*
  o *Chequered finish line* to *microwave.*
  o *Long coffee bean inside a spice jar* to *fridge.*

Then proceed onwards through the palace with other wines.

VARIATIONS

Mixing the two approaches presented above makes for a powerful combination. The principle behind this hybrid is to use the Loci System, but to only memorise one key characteristic from each category. This circumvents the need to peg the categories (*crayon* for COLOUR; *nose hair* for NOSE; *cadaver* for BODY; *tongue* for PALATE; *chequered finish line* for FINISH), as their order of appearance is predetermined and only a single characteristic is recorded from each. This reduces the number of images required while still capturing the main tasting notes of the wine or spirit.

OTHER CONSIDERATIONS

As detailed in the Loci System section, it is recommended to use a location you are familiar with. Nonetheless, after following the journey through the locus provided above, and after reviewing the images created, the reader may begin to sense a degree of familiarity with the locus. This is an excellent illustration of how to build an imaginary locus. For those who wish to experiment with imaginary loci, and perhaps wish to extend the imaginary palace that was started above, simply create a new room before memorising the next wine or spirit.

Once the construction of such an imaginary palace is complete, reviewing the material can be almost as pleasurable as experiencing the wine/spirit in real life. Travelling through each room in the palace should elicit the aromas, textures and tastes of the wine/spirit that the room contains (the effect would be even more noticeable if the concentration techniques introduced in Part 1 of the book have been diligently practised). The learning experience and revision are thus no longer boring rote procedures but actually pleasurable events to look forward to.

OTHER APPLICATIONS

Grouped below are other common learning tasks that are similar in nature to the ones already covered in detail above. For each learning task, we outline how the material should be broken down into unique identifiers and which system should be utilised.

CHESS OPENINGS

To memorise chess openings, we use either the algebraic notation or the figurine algebraic notation of the moves. To transform these into unique identifiers, we perform the following:

1. Visualise each chess piece as its three-dimensional representation.
2. Each column's letter (or, more formally, each file's letter) is transformed into its numerical equivalent. For example, *e* would be represented by 5; *f* would be represented by 6.
3. Convert the notation for the move into an image using the Numbers List. For example, **e4** would be represented by 54, which is *lorry* on the Numbers List.
4. Bundle the image that represents the piece into the image that represents the move. For example, **Nf3** would be *jam made out of knights* (**N** is the notation for Knight; **f3** is converted into 63, which is represented by *jam*).
5. Other notation (e.g. pawn promotion or capture) can be bundled further into the image.

With the unique identifiers established above, the procedure for memorising the openings is as follows:

1. (Use the Loci System.)

2. **Assign a locus**. Assign a palace to represent all chess openings.
3. **Room per opening**. Each room in the palace will contain the details of a single opening.
4. **Peg the name**. The name of the opening is to be pegged to the room's entrance.
5. **Peg the moves**. The moves that together form the opening are to be pegged to the items in that room of the palace.
6. **Travel clockwise through the palace**, from the bottom upwards.
7. **Travel clockwise through each room**.

CORPORATE HIERARCHY

Use the Grid System with the CEO/President placed in the top row, and work your way downwards by pegging each person's name to the grid point in which he is placed.

DIRECTIONS

Using the Loci System, to each item in the locus peg the elements that together form the directions.

The directions will mostly consist of names of roads and which orientation to take. It is important, therefore, to have unique identifiers for left and right (perhaps *wristwatch* for left and *boxing glove* for right). Bundle the unique identifier for left/right with the name of the road at which the next turn is to be made. Then peg that image to the corresponding item on the locus.

If no unique identifier for left/right is bundled into an image, the interpretation is that the direction to be maintained is straight.

MAPS

Use either the Standard Grid or the Circular Grid, depending on the shape of the city or the country being memorised. At each grid point identify the main road, street, or place name that is most dominant in that cell, and then peg it to the image the represents the grid point.

Then use the Link System to connect to the abovementioned dominant element the rest of the cell's contents. Travel systematically through each grid point, completing one before moving on to the next grid point: journey from left to right and from the bottom upwards (west to east and south to north).

MORSE CODE

Use the phonetic alphabet.

1. Represent *dash* with the letters *T* or *D*.
2. Represent *dot* with the letters *R, P* or *B*.
3. Any vowel sound can be used to connect the above letters together.
4. Then create a unique identifier for each letter in the alphabet by finding a word that is formed by the dots and dashes that represent the letter in Morse code.

For example, the letter A in Morse code is ● ▬ (*dot* followed by *dash*).

Using the system above, the letter A can thus be converted into *RaT, RoD, PaD, BaT, etc.* Choose one.

Proceed by creating unique identifiers for the rest of the letters. To remember these unique identifiers, simply peg the Morse image to the corresponding image from the Alphabet List.

OPTION VOLATILITY SURFACE

Use the Grid System, which can be modified for this task by using the option strikes as the first row, option maturities as the first column and the option volatility as the entry in each cell. Peg each image for the volatility (convert the number into an image using the Numbers List) to the image of the corresponding grid point.

PAINTINGS

Use the Link System.

1. Pick a distinctive feature of the painting or use the painting itself as the setting for your image.
2. Link the distinctive feature or the painting itself to the name of the painting.
3. Link the name of the painting to the name of the artist.

PERFUMES

Use the Loci System in the same manner that was applied to wines and spirits in the Oenophiles and "Uisgeophiles" section.

PHILATELISTS

Use the Link System.

1. Pick a distinctive feature of the stamp or the stamp image itself.
2. Link the distinctive feature or the image of the stamp to the name of the stamp.
3. Link the name of the stamp to the year in which it was issued (using the **VWYZ** convention).

POETRY

Use the Link System.

1. **Read through the entire poem slowly**, preferably aloud, and make sure that its main theme is understood.
2. **Link the name of the poet** to the name of the poem.
3. **Link the name of the poem** to the first word in the poem.
4. **Link the first word to the next key word in the poem**—especially a word to which another would rhyme in the next line.
5. **Link the key words**. Proceed by linking each key word to the next.
6. **Memorise two lines at a time**. As you form the links, cover two lines at a time and attempt to recall the rest of the words (i.e., those that were not linked). Repeat this step until you are able to recite all the words contained within the two lines.
7. **Recall and review**. Move to the next two lines. Link the key words together. Attempt to recall the two lines. Recite the previous two lines and then attempt to recall the current two lines again.

8. **Review four lines at a time**. Continue with the rest of the poem by working in groups of four lines: reciting the two lines that are already known while attempting to recall the two lines that follow.
9. **Page review**. Once a full page of the poem is memorised, attempt to recall the entire page before beginning to memorise the next.
10. **Review** the entire poem.

Note that it is feasible to link together every word in the poem, but that, in general, is cumbersome and less enjoyable. In contrast, linking just the key words is short and efficient, and creates a structure onto which the rest of the poem is ensconced.

RECIPES

Use the Link System.

1. Link the name of the recipe to the first step in the recipe.
2. Link the first step in the recipe to the succeeding steps.
3. When linking the steps of the recipe, bundle to the images that you create the quantities, ratios, measurements and temperatures that appear in the recipe.

Alternatively, the Loci System could be utilised, assigning a room to each recipe—thus creating a palace of recipes.

TUBE/TRAIN/UNDERGROUND MAP

Either use the Grid System for the entire map, as was detailing in the Maps subsection above, or use the Link System to link together the stations along each route.

The Link System approach would simply involve taking the name of the underground/train line and linking to it the names of the stations in their order of appearance.

BUILDING YOUR OWN SYSTEM

After following the applications and examples presented above, the pattern in the allocation of system to memory task should be becoming familiar. New applications, that is, applications not covered above, should be designated a system using the same logic. If in doubt, look for the application above that most resembles the memory task you are facing, and adapt the procedure therein.

After practising with memory systems for a while, your personal preferences and unique style will emerge. However, certain key principles should be maintained:

1. **Distil from the data the key components** that make up the topic.
2. **Provide an image—a unique identifier—for each component**. Ensure that there are no conflicts between the identifiers—both internally within the topic as well as with other topics you have already covered.
3. **Apply the unique identifiers consistently**: neither alter them nor make exceptions.
4. **Choose the system that is most appropriate for each task**. Personal preferences will have an influence on this choice.
5. **The more absurd the links or pegs are, the stronger— and longer—the memory will persist**. You will eventually settle on a unique style of imagery to which your brain reacts most loudly.

6. **Most importantly, and to reiterate an earlier emphasis of this point, for long-term retention of the information, you must review the data**. Revision should be performed according to the schedule detailed in the Importance of Revision section. If the review step is skipped, the information will only be available for a short period of time.

TRAINING PLAN

I n order to master the techniques presented in this part of the book, the reader is recommended to follow the schedule presented below. The key point to note is that the optimal approach to mastering the memory principles is through their incorporation into daily activities. The schedule is therefore designed to gradually integrate the techniques into daily life.

WEEKS 1 TO 4: BECOMING FAMILIAR WITH THE SYSTEMS

The purpose of the first four weeks is to establish the tools that will thereafter be applied to all memory tasks. The objectives are therefore as follows:

1. **If you have not done so already, commit to memory at the very least the following information:**
   a. The phonetic alphabet.
   b. The Numbers List: this can be achieved by memorising ten numbers and their corresponding objects from the list every day. At the start of each session, revise the numbers that were memorised on the preceding days, and then memorise the next ten.
   c. The Alphabet List.
   d. The Effigy List.
   e. The Rhyme List.
   f. The Body List.
   g. The Standard Grid.
2. **Create at least three loci** (based on real locations, not imaginary loci): one locus with at least 100

monuments/items, and two loci with at least 20 monuments/items in each.

3. **Learn five new words every day:** these can be unfamiliar words encountered while reading, in conversation, on TV, etc. Simply note the words down, look up their meaning and memorise them using the technique presented in this part of the book. Make sure you review these words as instructed. If you cannot serendipitously locate five new words a day, simply search the internet (word-a-day websites are a good option) or work systematically through the dictionary.

4. **Memorise the name of every new person you encounter**—be it an encounter in person, a spokesman on the news, a character on a TV show, an avatar on the internet, etc.

5. **Memorise numbers you encounter during the day.** It could be a stock index, a price of a product, an extension number, a measurement, etc. Get into the habit of converting such numerical data into images and memorising them.

6. **Note that revision is not necessary for items you do not wish to store in long-term memory.** The objective is to provide convenient and relevant opportunities to practise the techniques; whether the information is worthy of long-term storage is then for you to choose.

WEEKS 5 TO 8: INTRODUCING THE TECHNIQUES TO DAILY LIFE

Weeks 5 to 8 are designed to apply the tools you now possess to common daily memory tasks.

1. **Increase the daily vocabulary intake**: Learn ten new words every day.
2. **Memorise your shopping list** and try to conduct your shopping without looking at the written version.
3. **Memorise phone numbers as you dial them.** Then, the next time you need to contact the same individuals, try dialling without consulting your phonebook.
4. **Memorise your day's schedule** and try to think about your appointments without referring to the written version.
5. **Continue with the habit of memorising the name of every person you encounter**
6. **Employ the Human Organiser.** If you are not sufficiently confident with applying this tool, use your regular organiser, but only consult it after first attempting to retrieve the information from the Human Organiser. With time, proficiency—and thus confidence—will emerge.
7. **Memorise the map or directions before travelling to a new location.** Carry a navigation device or map with you, but attempt to travel to your destination from memory alone—consulting the navigation device/map as a backup or if an alternative route is required.
8. **Regularly drive, cycle or walk through new places.** This will increase the loci available to you. After each visit, mentally review the journey several times and select the monuments that will be utilised. In order to gradually build expansive loci, it is advisable to be systematic in the coverage of the territory.

WEEK 8 ONWARDS

Continue with the habits formed above but also add the following:

1. **Learn a new language.** Use the techniques from this part of the book to memorise the grammar and vocabulary.
2. **Commit to memory every new fact and figure** you come across.
3. **Read three articles/entries (of interest) from your preferred encyclopaedia** every day and memorise the key facts contained in each.
4. **Create a palace** of wines or whiskies or cognacs, or, if wines and spirits are low in favour, perhaps a palace of perfumes or recipes.
5. **Memorise one short poem every week.**
6. **Create a (locus) town of knowledge**: encompassing the contents of an entire field of study.
7. **Extend the peg lists** to provide you with more pegs and to allow for more possibilities.
8. **Extend your current loci** and add new loci as you travel to new locations. (Especially locations visited while on holiday: the positive associations formed while in a peaceful state of mind will be felt each time the locus is employed.)
9. **Ensure that you are spending an adequate amount of time on revision**—it is crucial for long-term storage. Ideally, allocate a regular slot in your daily schedule.
10. **If you are interested in memory championships,** start charting your progress. The list below contains key measurements that together will provide a reasonable snapshot of your progress:
    a. Time how long it takes you to memorise a pack of cards.

b. Time how long it takes you to recall the pack of cards and note how many errors (if any) you made.

c. How many cards can you memorise in ten minutes?

d. How many binary digits can you memorise in a single minute?

e. How many digits of a long number can you memorise in five minutes? (Use a number worthy of the time spent; pi and phi are common choices.)

f. How many names and faces can you memorise in five minutes? (Use the yearbooks of schools, universities and associations to which you do not belong; or, worthier still, use the portraits of famous historical figures from an era or nation you are not familiar with.)

g. How long does it take you to memorise a list of ten historical events and the dates on which they occurred? (Work systematically through a history book, preferably of a culture/civilization with which you are unfamiliar.)

h. Chart your progress on a spreadsheet by noting the memory tasks above and the result achieved on each attempt. The tasks have to remain the same for the measurements to be consistent and meaningful.

i. Once you are getting close to the records held on the cards and numbers memory tasks, start practising the specific memory events of the competition in which you intend to enrol.

j. Note that using the memory techniques in competition differs to using them to accumulate knowledge. The focus in the former is speed; in the latter, it is long-term storage. Furthermore, in the above tasks to measure your progress, an attempt was made to utilise information that has some value while still ensuring it is new, so as not to bias the measurement. Training for a competition, however, involves much time spent memorising information that is of absolutely no value—the only value is in the training. Therefore, it is advisable to be sure that your goals are aligned accordingly.

SUMMARY AND REVISION MAP

KEY POINTS

- All memory systems rely on deconstructing new information and designing an approach through which each element can be uniquely represented by an object/image.
- The resulting objects/images are either glued together in the desired order or glued to designated mental locations.
- The gluing mechanism employed in memory techniques involves vivid and exaggerated imagery, ludicrous and nonsensical action, plenty of colours and contrasts, as well the involvement of as many senses and emotions as possible.
- The Link System involves gluing each new piece of information to the last—forming a chain of images, each connected to both its antecedent and its succedent.
- The Peg System involves gluing each new piece of information to an item that is already known from previously established lists.
- The Loci System involves gluing new information to items that are already known, whose order and structure correspond to a physical location familiar to the practitioner.
- The Grid System is used to memorise visual data by gluing the information to the item that represents the corresponding cell.
- The purpose of having ready-made peg lists and loci is to put at the practitioner's disposal an efficient way of filing

data—in particular if recall of numerical positions is required.

- Dimensions can be added and bundling can be utilised to incorporate more data into each image, as well as to reduce the repetitions of single units of information.
- Revision should be performed within the optimal windows. It is absolutely essential for long-term storage.

REVISION MAP

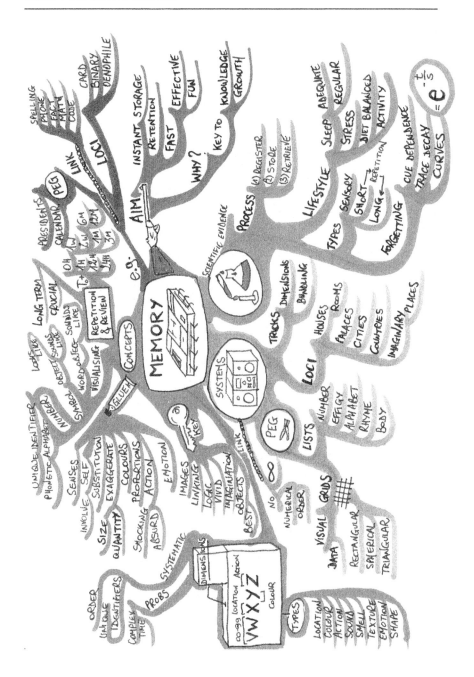

Part 3

SPEED READING

I took a speed reading course and read 'War and Peace' in twenty minutes. It involves Russia.

—Woody Allen

THE AIMS OF PART 3

- To increase your reading speed.
- And, at the same time, to either maintain the level of comprehension or improve it.

INTRODUCTION

There is a great deal of controversy about speed reading. It may have originated from unverified—and sometimes fantastical—claims by purveyors of courses on the topic. Suspicion may have then further expanded with the pseudo-scientific treatment of the next evolution of speed reading: that of subconscious or photographic reading. The purported reading speeds in this latter form of speed reading are even more difficult to accept. Woody Allen's famous joke on the subject sums up the arguments.

There is a large number of different speed reading courses available; however, these can generally be split into two genres:

1. **Traditional speed reading**: mechanical, systematic, and with a focus on drills to improve reading speeds.
2. **Subconscious (or photographic) reading**: utilising deep meditative states to absorb the reading material, with hunch-based follow-up reading to further the level of comprehension.

Traditional speed reading focuses on improving the mechanics of reading. The areas of focus are: minimising regressions while reading, usually through the use of a guide; reducing sub-vocalisation, and capturing more words with each glance. This type of speed reading involves performing drills daily in order to improve (and, eventually, to maintain) the skill.

The second genre of speed reading involves utilising the subconscious mind in order to capture the information. It offers a very different approach to reading when compared to the traditional route. The key theme is to enter into deeper levels of consciousness—levels at which the subconscious mind is able to capture the information desired at rates that are faster than those possible using the conscious mind alone.

Each of the two genres above has a wide range of advertised attainable reading speeds. Traditional speed reading courses commonly claim that practitioners can achieve reading speeds of up to 5,000 wpm[14], whilst subconscious reading systems often claim that speeds of over 25,000 wpm (together with high rates of comprehension) are easily attainable.

The author's experience suggests that there are merits to both genres, but that advertised reading rates are not as pervasive among practitioners as commonly marketed. Additionally, it is difficult to reconcile how 25,000 wpm could be attained by the masses if the six-time world record holder, Anne Jones, can only read at a glacial 4,200 wpm. Such inconsistencies are most likely a result of overzealous marketing, which can be attributed to operating in a fiercely competitive industry. Distasteful, perhaps, but it should not discourage one from using the techniques if value can be derived.

There are clear advantages to using both types of speed reading. The aim of this part of the book is to provide a simple system that combines the best of each type, but with a strong emphasis on traditional training drills. The ultimate goal is to have a powerful and pragmatic reading technique that maximises both speed and comprehension.

Fantastical claims around the reading speeds feasible with the system below would likely lead the practitioner on a path filled with distracting anticipation. The simplistic target of reading faster and understanding more should be the only goal in mind—

---

[14] *wpm* stands for Words Per Minute.

anything else that is attained on top of that should be viewed as a bonus.

The key to the system is **regular** practice. The best analogy is that of competitive sports or, better still, bodybuilding: any gains made through hard work and diligent training can be lost if the same level of training is not maintained.

The analogy, however, is only partially similar, since, with reading drills, one is able to choose the topic on which to practise. Therefore, one can, in essence, spend drill time on reading that would have had to be completed regardless. Training time, if wisely planned, can be costless.

Lastly, it is important to recognise that different reading materials require different reading speeds. This is a point that is largely ignored in the propaganda of reading rates. To be able to read at 1,000 wpm does not mean that such speeds are applicable to reading an advanced mathematics textbook to which the reader has had no previous exposure. Some topics require logical reasoning that cannot be performed by simply reading the material (a mathematical proof that uses novel concepts to arrive at the proof's conclusion is the quintessential example). It is therefore unrealistic to expect high reading speeds through such topics.

As a consequence, in order to accurately measure your reading speed, it is necessary to perform the test with a consistent genre. A modern work of fiction appears to be the best candidate and will be the medium used below.

SCIENTIFIC EVIDENCE

Reading is considered to be a complex cognitive process during which symbols are decoded to extract the meaning and feeling that the author attempted to portray. A certain degree of proficiency with the cognitive processes involved is required for the decoding procedure to be automatic. The automation, in turn, is necessary for the attention to be dedicated to understanding the concepts being relayed.

The physical mechanics of reading involves a series of eye fixations. These fixations can be either on individual words or on groups of words. Research has shown that fast readers tend to have less fixations, but that each fixation encompasses a larger proportion of the text.

More specifically, studies designed to evaluate the differences between fast and slow readers revealed that slow readers tend to read with more fixations, tend to have longer fixations, and experience a larger number of regressions. The cause and effect in this evidence, however, remains unclear. Nonetheless, what has been established is that with continued practice of speed reading techniques involving less fixations and few regressions, a higher reading speed without a decrease in comprehension is achieved.

Research on speed reading dates back as far as 1897, when John O. Quantz conducted an extensive study of the factors that contribute to rapid reading. In 1925, William S. Gray consolidated the available literature on speed reading (within a larger literature review about reading) and concluded that speed can be increased using various techniques without hindering comprehension. Studies published between the 1930s and the 1950s generally confirmed this, and are together thought to be the contributing factor for the profusion of speed reading courses developed during that period (and their persistence to date). Unfortunately, ensuing peer review and analysis pointed to weaknesses and faults in the aforementioned studies.

Subsequent research was more structured and controlled; it also focused on quantifying the maximum possible speed. These studies suggested that reading—defined here as capturing and decoding all the words on every page—faster than 900 wpm is not possible. This speed limit was derived from the following measurements:

1. The shortest recorded fixation period (approximately a sixth of a second).
2. The shortest recorded period between fixations (approximately one-thirtieth of a second).
3. The maximum recorded number of words that the eye can see in a single fixation (approximately three words[15]).

Utilising the above three measurements together, it was established that a ten-word line of four inches could be processed, as defined above, at a rate of at most 900 wpm.

Even though through regular training the perception speed and perception span can improve, there are limits set by the anatomy of the eye. The figure of 900 wpm is the ceiling derived based on these limits. Furthermore, studies involving exceptional readers—in particular, those trained in speed reading

---

[15] Note that more than three words may be processed with each fixation. Nevertheless, the methodology used in the scientific literature relied on the range at which all words are seen with an acuity greater than 50 percent. At lower acuity levels, words may be understood through a process of context-based deduction. However, incorporating this factor would have, in turn, increased the required length of the fixation, would have affected comprehension, and thus would have complicated the derivation of the speed limit.

techniques—found that their perception speed and perception span are within the normal ranges—reinforcing the validity of the ceiling.

Reading at speeds higher than 900 wpm is therefore considered as skimming. And, consequently, comprehension levels associated with such reading rates are considered to be weaker.

The most recent evidence and meta-analysis seem to confirm that reading with high comprehension is limited to below 1,000 wpm. Effective skimming, on the other hand, can occur at very high rates, and may be useful when searching for information, reviewing previously-read material or reading content with which the reader is intimately familiar. Nonetheless, based on the scientific evidence available, a clear distinction needs to be made between the two types of reading.

In terms of the neurological mechanics of speed reading, studies employing fMRI[16] found that those trained in speed reading showed lower activation during reading in the left superior and middle temporal gyri (or near Wernicke's area) as well as in Broca's area—two regions that are linked to the processing of speech. The results suggest that speed reading involves fewer phonological processes as well as fewer semantic and syntactic processes—yet, and significantly so, without hindrance to comprehension. In consequence, the findings indicate that speed reading involves processing the information in a fundamentally different manner.

In other research, studies focusing on the benefits of speed reading for foreign language acquisition found that speed reading instruction improved reading speed while maintaining comprehension. The result was first noted to occur during the

---

[16] *fMRI* stands for functional Magnetic Resonance Imaging.

course period and using known-vocabulary texts, and subsequent research confirmed that the results were transferrable to other texts. It was also found that regular practice after the course's completion maintained the higher reading rate that was initially attained. And, in addition, it was found that, even without practice, those who undertook the speed reading training read faster and with higher comprehension than the control group after the course's completion.

Along with Extensive Reading, a technique that essentially involves reading voluminously through texts with mostly familiar vocabulary, and Repeated Reading, a technique that involves repeatedly reading through the same material (varying between reading aloud and reading silently), Speed Reading is considered a principal approach to increasing the reading speed in a foreign language.

In terms of research into the second type of speed reading—that is, subconscious reading—the available literature suggests that the reading speeds attained by practitioners are substantially lower than the rates being marketed, and appear to actually be close to normal reading speeds.

In summary, the scientific literature is mostly filled with scepticism towards the high reading speeds being marketed and professed by some practitioners. And the studies involved have mostly discredited such claims. More importantly though, the scientific literature is also populated with evidence pointing to the efficacy of speed reading, albeit at more realistic speeds. The main points to take are:

- Reading at around 900 wpm with full comprehension is feasible. It is, however, the established limit.
- Reading at higher speeds (higher than 900 wpm) can be employed in a sophisticated form of skimming, where

irrelevant/known information is skipped (or not processed).

- Attaining high comprehension levels while processing at speeds greater than 900 wpm requires reading and skimming to be treated complementarily. In this approach, skimming is used to build a foundation, to survey for new/relevant information, and to perform a review, while reading is used to process new information.
- Speed reading involves a neurologically different approach to processing information.

THE SPEED READING SYSTEM

It is important to view speed reading as a medium, a means to an end—focusing very little on the method of reading and much more on the reading itself. It is common for practitioners to obsess about their progress and whether their technique is correct, searching for nuanced variations that will improve their speed. This often results in confusion and poor performance. For this reason, it is important for the technique to be simple to understand, to be logical and to be easy to implement—requiring the least possible attention while being deployed.

The concepts that form the system presented below are utterly simple. Therefore, the reader is urged not to try to extract hidden ideas or deeper meanings—since there are none. The reader should instead follow the procedure as instructed, allowing the mind to focus principally on the reading.

Self-doubt as described above is of particular concern when performing subconscious reading. The effects of subconscious reading—especially to the neophyte—are not very noticeable, which often leads the practitioner to believe that he may be applying the technique incorrectly. This, in turn, leads to unnecessary focus on the technique and thus lack of focus on the actual reading. Furthermore, when deluged with fantastical claims about reading speeds that cannot possibly materialise (see the Scientific Evidence chapter above), this diverted focus is all but certain to set in. **The reader is therefore urged to note this point and keep it in mind.**

To circumvent this obstacle as well as to increase speed, the system below relies heavily on performing daily reading drills. Regularly performing such reading workouts provides ample opportunity and a no-pressure setting in which one can perfect the skill. And doing so daily without fail will certainly yield measurable improvements—the ultimate confirmation of progress. Regular measurement is therefore another key theme: plotting one's performance will indicate beyond any doubt whether the technique is producing the desired effect.

In terms of prerequisites, the first and most obvious one is the ability to see the words clearly (using glasses or contact lenses if so prescribed).

Secondly, for optimal results it is necessary for the reader to be proficient in the language of the written material. Speed reading was shown to be effective in the acquisition of a foreign language, but the speed level that was being targeted was that of a native reader. So non-native readers should curtail their expectations accordingly; speed reading will be effective, but other aspects of the language (vocabulary, grammar, idioms, etc.) will require diligent study to break through to higher speeds.

Thirdly, vocabulary and technical terms also impose a limitation on speed. Some unfamiliar words can be inferred from the context; but if this approach is relied upon too frequently, speed will suffer. Expanding one's vocabulary should therefore be an ongoing endeavour—and an easy one to perform with the memory techniques from Part 2 of the book.

With the warnings and caveats securely in place, we can introduce the key ingredients of the speed reading system:

1. **Concentration.** Attention should be dedicated exclusively to the reading, blocking out all other distractions. The concentration techniques from Part 1 of the book—and their regular practice!—were designed to fulfil this paramount requirement.

2. **Avoiding regressions**. *Regressions* occur when a word, a phrase, a sentence, a paragraph, a page or more requires repeated reading to clarify a point or to improve comprehension. Frequent regressions are caused by lack of concentration and by not having a tool (or mental control) with which to pace the reading.

3. **Reducing sub-vocalisation**. Sub-vocalisation, much like reading aloud, sets a barrier on the reading speed. Reducing this habit allows one to break through to higher reading rates, and doing so is particularly important for effective skimming.

4. **Capturing more words with each fixation**. Reading fast relies on using the least amount of fixations possible while capturing the maximum amount of words possible with each fixation.

5. **Using layered reading.** As indicated in the previous chapter, the maximum speed at which all the words on a page can be read is around 900 wpm. However, not every word needs to be read; incorporating skimming to get an overview and to identify the portions that require a deeper reading will increase the overall reading speed without hindering comprehension. Furthermore, using skimming to survey the material, to identify significant portions, as well as to review the content, will provide several angles of coverage that, applied together, will actually aid comprehension.

6. **Using subconscious reading.** Similarly to skimming, subconscious reading is used as an additional step in the layered reading. Though the scientific evidence on its contribution to speed is not flattering, its effect on comprehension has received positive anecdotal support— mostly from practitioners reporting increased familiarity with the topic being studied.

The above concepts will become clearer in the next sections and will be distilled into an easy-to-deploy procedure.

As with the acquisition of any skill, regular practice is necessary. For speedier results, it is recommended to incorporate the skill into daily activities. Therefore, the reader is recommended to develop the habit of including all of the above concepts when reading—irrespective of the subject matter. After following the instructions below and performing the drills for a while—that is, after becoming familiar with the concepts involved—incorporating the system into daily reading should be straightforward.

CONCENTRATION

The subject of concentration was covered in Part 1 of the book because it is the single most crucial element involved in any learning experience. Since reading is perhaps the ultimate knowledge acquisition tool, concentration is naturally a key component of any reading system.

Succumbing to the mind's eccentricities and wandering ways while reading leads to frustration—mostly from having to repeatedly read the same sentence or page. Such fitful read-repeat cycles make the whole reading process less efficient as well as less pleasurable.

For the speed-reader, allowing the mind to drift is even more detrimental. At the high rates at which a speed-reader typically travels through the reading material, a distracting thought not only quashes momentum but also results in a high number of words being missed. At 900 wpm, the reader covers 15 words per second; a two-second lapse in attention thus results in three lines being skipped—necessitating either a second read of said lines or accepting the loss in comprehension. The higher the speed, the more severe the consequences of the mind wandering away.

Regular practice of the concentration techniques introduced in Part 1 of the book is crucial for the implementation of the reading system presented herein. So continue with the practice as indicated in Part 1.

In addition to the regular practice, **every reading session should begin with a five-minute concentration exercise** (ten minutes would be better, so do so whenever possible; five minutes was chosen to keep the procedure practical). The concentration exercise acts as a centring mechanism for the learning experience that follows. It also promotes the alpha brainwave frequency, which will aid in the understanding of the material while reading as well as its later recall.

REGRESSION

Regression is the term used to describe a situation in which the reader has to stop the flow of the reading in order to repeat a previously read portion of the text. Although this frequently occurs when studying complex topics, the cause is seldom due to the complexity of the material. Most regressions are actually caused by a lapse in concentration as well as not having a tool with which to pace the reading.

Even for the most complex of topics (say, mathematics, quantum physics, or ancient polysemous poetry), the reading should flow smoothly at a comfortable pace without any regressions. If a portion of the text is still not fully understood after having performed all the steps in the layered reading, a deep and slow analytical reading of the section can be undertaken. The point is to move smoothly through the whole text and leave the abstruse pieces to the end—at which point some of the earlier confusion may have already been answered by information that followed. This type of gradually increasing comprehension is more efficient and longer-lasting than a painstaking analysis of every word in a single read-through.

There are two commonly used approaches to avoid regressions: the first is to improve concentration, as was discussed above and in Part 1 of the book. The second is to use a *guide*, which is essentially a mechanism to pace the reading. Since the topic of concentration was already covered in great detail, this section will focus on using a guide.

Utilising a guide refers to employing an aid that would lead the reader through the passage without having to stop or repeat any of the material. The guide is there to set the rhythm and pace of the reading according to the practitioner's skill.

Most traditional speed reading systems lay great emphasis on using one's hand as a guide, and some even specify the different hand motions that the user should apply to different reading materials. The author's experience suggests that focusing on matching hand motions to different texts puts too much focus on the technique and insufficient focus on the reading. Therefore, the system below is centred around two simple hand motions: one for skimming and one for reading. Additionally, in order to help the practitioner during the early stages of training, an optional hand motion that does not require wide fixations is also provided.

The key principles behind using the hand as a guide are as follows:

1. **The hand should be moving in a rhythmic pace that matches your present reading abilities.** Skimming should be performed at a fast pace, and the goal should be to garner an overview of the topic. Reading, on the other hand, should be performed at a slower pace, and the goal should be high comprehension.

2. **Adapt the speed.** If the general ideas are not being picked up while skimming, the hand motion's pace is too fast and should be reduced accordingly. If too many words are being missed/skipped while reading, so much so that comprehension is jeopardised, the hand motion's pace should be reduced.

3. **Follow the hand with your eyes and stay ahead of it: never fall behind it and never regress.** If a bunch of words or a concept is missed, or is not fully understood, a question mark can be pencilled in the margin to indicate that the section should be read again once the full read through the material has been completed. This is a much better approach to learning: the simple concepts and the basics are captured in the first reading, whereas the more complex details and subtle ideas are added on subsequent reading. Gradually building comprehension in this manner results in a better structural understanding of the topic.

4. **Do not focus on the hand or pay too much attention to its motion.** The goal is to move rhythmically, without regression, through the text while focusing only on the reading. The hand, merely a guide, is there to help set the pace—do not allow it to become a distraction.

The idea of reading smoothly at a continuous pace obviously extends to flipping the pages: make it quick and efficient. A simple approach is to have the hand that is not being used as a guide ready to turn the page as you near its bottom.

SKIMMING

Skimming is performed with an S-shaped motion. This hand motion is designed for rapid reading, so it is commonly used for initial survey and later review of the material.

The procedure for this hand motion is as follows:

1. (Place your hand comfortably on the page.)
2. **Perform the motion with the tip of the middle finger** tracing the shape presented in the diagram below.
3. **Start and end each horizontal movement approximately one third of a line away from the respective margin**. There is no need to travel from one extremity of the written material to the other—the words contained therein are within the catchment area of the fixation.
4. **Capture approximately three lines with each loop of the motion**. That is, you will be reading three lines at a time.
5. **Keep up with the hand: do not regress**. Low comprehension is not a concern at this stage; comprehension will be developed further in the next steps of the layered reading.
6. **Do not focus on the hand motion itself: all the attention should be centred on the reading**. The hand is only utilised to guide you rhythmically at your skimming pace and to ensure no regression takes place.

The diagram below illustrates the hand motion for skimming.

XXXXXXXXXXXXXXXXXXXXXXXXXXXXXXXXXXXXX
XXXXXXXXXXXXXXXXXXXXXXXXXXXXXXXXXXXXX
XXXXXXXXXXXXXXXXXXXXXXXXXXXXXXXXXXXXX
XXXXXXXXXXXXXXXXXXXXXXXXXXXXXXXXXXXXX
XXXXXXXXXXXXXXXXXXXXXXXXXXXXXXXXXXXXX
XXXXXXXXXXXXXXXXXXXXXXXXXXXXXXXXXXXXX
XXXXXXXXXXXXXXXXXXXXXXXXXXXXXXXXXXXXX
XXXXXXXXXXXXXXXXXXXXXXXXXXXXXXXXXXXXX
XXXXXXXXXXXXXXXXXXXXXXXXXXXXXXXXXXXXX
XXXXXXXXXXXXXXXXXXXXXXXXXXXXXXXXXXXXX
XXXXXXXXXXXXXXXXXXXXXXXXXXXXXXXXXXXXX
XXXXXXXXXXXXXXXXXXXXXXXXXXXXXXXXXXXXX
XXXXXXXXXXXXXXXXXXXXXXXXXXXXXXXXXXXXX
XXXXXXXXXXXXXXXXXXXXXXXXXXXXXXXXXXXXX
XXXXXXXXXXXXXXXXXXXXXXXXXXXXXXXXXXXXX
XXXXXXXXXXXXXXXXXXXXXXXXXXXXXXXXXXXXX
XXXXXXXXXXXXXXXXXXXXXXXXXXXXXXXXXXXXX

READING: VERTICAL LINE

The hand motion for regular reading is simply a vertical line that runs down the middle of the text. The procedure is as follows:

1. (Place your hand comfortably on the page.)
2. **Perform the motion with the tip of the middle finger** drawing the shape depicted below.
3. **Keep up with the hand: do not regress**. If, while reading, a section of the text proves problematic, pencil a question mark in the margin. The question-marked sections will be captured in subsequent reading/analysis.

4. **Do not focus on the hand motion itself: all the attention should be centred on the reading.** The hand is only utilised to guide you rhythmically at your reading pace and to ensure no regression takes place.

The diagram below illustrates the hand motion for reading.

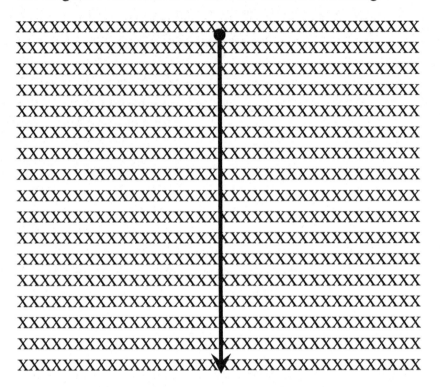

READING: TEXT TRACING (OPTIONAL)

An alternative hand motion for reading involves tracing each line of text. For some practitioners, it may be necessary to use this approach at the beginning—at least until the perception speed and the perception span are increased to the level at which comprehension is high while employing the Vertical Line approach. The perception speed and span will improve with the training provided below, so the Text Tracing approach may be viewed as a transitional tool.

It is recommended to use the Text Tracing approach both for training as well as actual reading until high comprehension can be attained with the Vertical Line approach. Nonetheless, some practitioners prefer, and thus stay with, the Text Tracing approach indefinitely, for the continuous rapid movement provides more flexibility in rhythm and pace. It is also advantageous for non-standard text formats, where a line cannot be read in two fixations (rendering the Vertical Line approach impractical).

For the abovementioned reasons, this hand motion is included in the system but is classified as optional, as the practitioner's preferences and circumstances will ultimately determine its deployment.

The procedure is as follows:

1. (Place your hand comfortably on the page.)
2. **Perform the motion with the tip of the middle finger** drawing the shape depicted below.
3. **Start and end each horizontal movement approximately one third of a line away from the respective margin**. There is no need to travel from one extremity of the written material to the other—the words contained therein are within the catchment area of the fixation.
4. **Keep up with the hand: do not regress**. If, while reading, a section of the text proves problematic, pencil a question mark in the margin. The question-marked sections will be captured in subsequent reading/analysis.
5. **Do not focus on the hand motion itself: all the attention should be centred on the reading**. The hand is

only utilised to guide you rhythmically at your reading pace and to ensure no regression takes place.

The diagram below illustrates the alternative (optional) hand motion for reading.

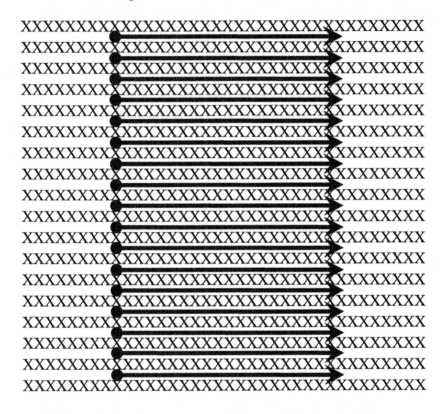

In sum, when using a guide it is important to maintain a comfortable pace and travel through the material without stopping for anything. Consequently, it is necessary to mark portions that have not been fully understood for further focus in subsequent reading. Performing this adequately requires discipline and confidence in the technique—which will develop with practice.

SUB-VOCALISATION

Sub-vocalisation is the term used to describe the process of internally pronouncing each word while reading. In some cases, this may result in subtle movements of the muscles associated with speech, and, in more extreme cases, it may even result in movement of the lips. Such an approach to reading essentially takes a visual input and converts it into an audio output that is then decoded into a concept.

There is some evidence to suggest that non-observable sub-vocalisation is a natural part of the reading process, and that it helps the reader evaluate meanings, comprehend the ideas and remember what is being read. However, fMRI studies comparing fast and slow readers (during a reading task) indicate that between the two groups there are significant differences in the brain areas being activated. In particular, it was found that rapid readers show lower activation in the brain regions associated with speech, which indicates that the higher speeds were attained, in part, by the reduction in sub-vocalisation. The difference between the separate scientific findings can be reconciled by viewing speed reading as a different—faster yet equal in comprehension—way of processing information.

Among speed readers, and supported by scientific evidence, it is generally accepted that reading at higher speeds requires some control over the step in which words are translated into sounds. Speed reading relies primarily on decoding visual inputs directly into the concept that they represent.

Being able to transform a block of words directly into the concept that they represent—without the need to sub-vocalise the individual components—becomes necessary when breaking through speed limits that are set by physical barriers. The "sound barrier" is estimated to be placed at approximately 650 wpm;

reading faster than this is not possible while sub-vocalising. This estimate was derived from records attained by the world's fastest speakers. At the time of writing, the world's fastest speaker, Sean Shannon, was officially recorded speaking at a rate of 655 wpm. (For comparison, the previous *Guinness Book of World Records* titles were awarded to, Steve Woodmore and John Moschitta., Jr, who could speak at 637 wpm and 586 wpm respectively.)

There is some disagreement among practitioners about whether sub-vocalisation should be eliminated completely, but there is clear agreement that it should be reduced in order to achieve higher reading speeds.

Deliberate use of full sub-vocalisation, or even reading aloud, is left for tasks that involve learning text verbatim. In such situations, the act of reading aloud reinforces the visual representation, which together result in a stronger memory imprint.

In summary, when speed reading, the frequency of sub-vocalisation must be reduced. The approach utilised to achieve this is as follows:

>**Perform a specific training routine to increase the number of words that can be read during the sub-vocalisation of a single word.** Exercise 3 (detailed in the next chapter) provides the specific training necessary to improve peripheral vision and to reduce sub-vocalisation. It involves a gradual widening of the fixation span while, with each fixation, only a single word is sub-vocalised. Regular practice will improve the skill of deliberately sub-vocalising a single word while reading multiple words.
>
>**Habit formation.** Once you can read multiple words while sub-vocalising only a single word, it is important to

incorporate this into your daily reading activities. Ultimately, the goal is for the procedure to occur subconsciously, so that full attention could be dedicated to understanding the content being read.

When controlled sub-vocalisation is applied outside of the training sessions, it is important to ensure that the number of words captured in each fixation is within your level of competence—do not allow this new habit to hinder comprehension. Begin with a fixation that encompasses two words while sub-vocalising (to be clear: pronouncing mentally, not aloud) only one of them; once comfortable with two-word fixations, move to three words, and so forth one additional word at a time.

The underlying principle is simple: force a slow sub-vocalisation while capturing multiple words. In doing so, it becomes impossible to sub-vocalise anything else. This approach controls the amount of sub-vocalisation by applying it consciously. It does not, however, eliminate sub-vocalisation—controlled sub-vocalisation is considered a desirable component of the system.

For the sake of clarity, let us use a brief example. The sentence *once upon a time in a land far, far away...* should be, at least at first, sub-vocalised as "once, time, in, land, far". With practice, this can be reduced to "time, far".

At this point, a pertinent question frequently follows: "Which word should I choose to sub-vocalise?"

The answer is that it does not matter. Furthermore, with practice, a certain degree of intuition will take over, at which point, the decision process around what to sub-vocalise will drift beyond the grasp of conscious thought. **In practical terms: try not to think about it. Sub-vocalise the first word that comes to**

mind; most often, one of the words will stand out as more significant.

In terms of interaction with the hand motions, when using the skimming technique, each fixation captures three half-lines while the practitioner sub-vocalises only one of the words within the said half-lines. For the Vertical Line reading motion, each fixation captures half a line while only one word within the half-line is sub-vocalised. With the Text Tracing reading motion, the practitioner can choose the size of the fixation, but the principle remains the same: multiple words are read while sub-vocalising only a single word.

FIXATIONS

When we read, we generally do not flow through the material smoothly. Instead, we perform numerous mini-pauses—that is, fixations—which, for most readers, involve gazing at one or two words at a time, recognising their meaning, and then moving on to the next one or two words—and so forth through the text. Reading is essentially a series of jumps between fixations.

The inefficient reader tends to read one word at a time. This, in turn, increases the number of fixations required to complete the entire text. Each fixation involves a pause, and travelling from one fixation to the next also involves an expenditure of time. Ergo, the higher the number of fixations, the slower the reading rate becomes.

Therefore, the goal is to increase the number of words that are read at every such pause; that is, the number of words captured in each fixation. Covering the same text with less fixations will increase the overall reading speed. The other, more subtle, benefit is that the stringing of individual words into a concept is replaced with capturing an entire concept with each fixation. And concept-per-fixation carries an advantage in terms of comprehension: since it is no longer necessary to track and connect the words that together make up a concept, more attention can be dedicated to understanding the concept itself.

The approach utilised to increase the number of words contained in each fixation is similar to the approach that was proposed to gain control over sub-vocalisation: the crux being specific training and habit formation. The set of drills in the next chapter involve specific training to increase peripheral vision, as well as comprehension training to promote the understanding of a concept through a group of words (instead of reading one word at a time and building the concept along the way).

Habit formation follows the same lines of instruction as described for sub-vocalisation. The key is to incorporate this habit into daily reading activities. Again, it is important to ensure that this is executed at your current level of competency: begin with a fixation that encompasses two words, and, as you become more proficient with the system, move to three words, and so forth one additional word at a time.

In terms of interaction with the hand motions: **the hand motions pace and organise the sequence of fixations.**

To synchronise the fixations with the hand motion, it is important to note the following:

- **Each fixation should typically last less than a quarter of a second.** However, and depending on the individual, achieving this may require practice. Begin with a period length with which you can read comfortably with high comprehension—commonly around half a second—and, as you gain confidence through practice, reduce the length of the period gradually.

- **The hand motion sets the pace.** The fixations should coincide with the position of the hand (as illustrated earlier, the hand traces the thick black line in the diagrams below). If a shorter fixation period is desired, all that is necessary is to increase the speed with which the hand travels through the text.
- **The eyes should not move during the fixation period.** The eyes should focus only on the point of fixation, which, in the diagrams below, is illustrated as an inner circle within the ellipse.
- **The eyes should focus on the point of fixation but should also capture everything else in the region of fixation using peripheral vision.** In the diagrams below, each region of fixation is depicted by an ellipse.
- **Regular practice is required to increase the span of the region of fixation.** The drills in the next chapter are a necessary component of such practice.
- **Wider fixations.** Although the scientific literature is centred on regions of fixation that contain words at greater than 50 percent acuity (that is, fixations containing approximately three words), with practice, **wider fixations can be utilised without hindering comprehension.** The reason for this is as follows: firstly, not all words need to be read for high comprehension to be attained. And, secondly, words with lower acuity can be inferred from nearby words and the overall context.

To better elucidate the concepts above, let us look at the reading process when the hand motion and the fixations are combined.

SKIMMING

Starting with the hand motion for skimming, in the diagram below, each ellipse illustrates a region of fixation. The circle within the fourth ellipse provides an example of a point of fixation, whilst the numbered boxes depict the sequence of fixations. Scilicet, the first region of fixation is the ellipse below Box 1; the second region of fixation is the ellipse below Box 2; the third region of fixation is the ellipse next to Box 3, etc.

As should be apparent from the diagram, the sequence of fixations follows the path that the hand traces through the text.

Note that the process for skimming involves regions of fixation that each contains three half-lines. The eyes should focus in the middle of the region of fixation—i.e., in the middle of each ellipse—while peripherally capturing the entire region (i.e. the three half-lines contained in said ellipse).

Also note that, when skimming, the sequence of fixations is not the standard left-to-right, but rather it is left-to-right followed by right-to-left, then left-to-right again, and so on in alternation. It is not a natural sequence to perform, but it is efficient and effective for skimming.

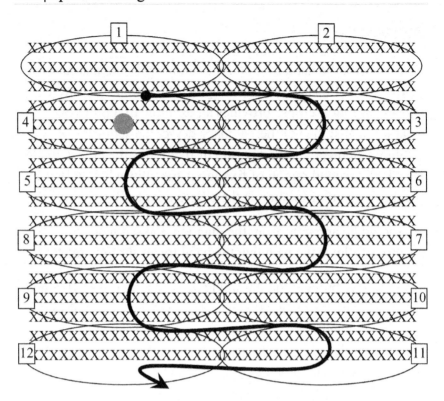

READING: VERTICAL LINE

In the main hand motion for reading, the Vertical Line approach, the sequence of fixations follows the natural left-to-right path. In the diagram below, each ellipse illustrates a region of fixation. The circle within the third ellipse provides an example of a point of fixation, whilst the numbered boxes depict the sequence of fixations. Scilicet, the first region of fixation is the ellipse below Box 1; the second region of fixation is the ellipse below Box 2; the third region of fixation is the ellipse next to Box 3, etc.

As should be apparent from the diagram, the sequence of fixations follows the path that the hand traces through the text.

Note that the process for Vertical Line reading involves regions of fixation that each contains half a line. The eyes should focus in the middle of the region of fixation—i.e., in the middle of each ellipse—while peripherally capturing the entire region (i.e. the half-line contained in said ellipse).

READING: TEXT TRACING (OPTIONAL)

In the Text Tracing hand motion, the sequence of fixations follows the natural left-to-right path. The size of each fixation, however, depends on the practitioner's level of competency. At the beginning, each fixation will likely encompass just two words (the region of fixation), with the point of fixation placed between the two words. With practice, the region of fixation will expand, and the ability to read a regular-sized line of text in two fixations will be within reach. At that stage, the Vertical Line approach usually becomes the preferred hand motion for reading.

As with the other hand motions, when using Text Tracing, the sequence of fixations follows the path that the hand traces through the text.

(In order present a comprehensible diagram, the numbered boxes indicating the sequence of fixations were restricted to the margins.)

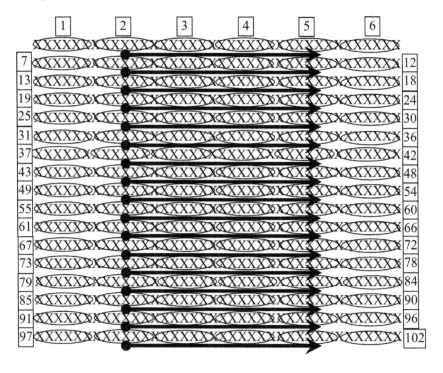

LAYERED READING

Layered reading is the process of breaking the study of a text into several layers of coverage. With each layer, the level of analysis and the resulting understanding of the topic deepens.

The advantage of layered reading is that if a concept is not fully understood during the initial poring over the text—i.e., in the initial layers—it can, if dimmed significant, become the point of focus in subsequent layers. **This is a noteworthy advantage because it allows the reader to flow through the material in a relaxed manner— knowing that if anything is missed it can be recovered later.** Hence, in addition to the benefits stemming from reading with a relaxed and confident state of mind, layered reading also promotes a minimisation of any tendency to regress.

The second advantage is that such a layering of the learning experience results in a more effective assimilation of the information. Learning the basics and the fundamental ideas first provides a firm structure onto which more complicated, nuanced concepts can be placed. And such an incremental progression results in the nuanced concepts being understood in congruence with the fundamentals.

The third advantage is that the overall reading speed that results from layered reading is higher than the speed that could be attained with a single read-through that targets the same level of comprehension. This occurs for the following reasons:

- Skimming occurs at extremely high rates; it provides a foundation while contributing to a higher overall reading speed. It also identifies the areas that require more focus: thus subsequent time is not wasted on areas that do not require further attention.
- The relaxation and confidence that result from knowing that anything that is currently unclear will be better understood in subsequent layers also promote higher speeds. This is partly due to the state of mind and partly due to the synergies produced by flowing without regression (even while some words/portions are being missed) through the text.

Layered reading is therefore recommended for any protracted reading sessions—especially those involving the formal study of a subject. The types of material for which layered reading is not recommended are short texts, fiction and other leisure reading—e.g., news reports/headlines and novels. For these, only the speed reading step is required.

The steps of the layered reading process are as follows:

1. **Preview**. The Preview step should be brief—lasting at most five minutes. It involves reading the back cover, the table of contents and having a quick glance at the structure and format of the text. If available, information about the author(s) should also be perused.

2. **Skim**. The Skim step involves processing the entire text using the skimming hand motion. The focus should be on extracting the general themes, the fundamental concepts and the basic ideas. This step will set the structural foundation of the topic; onto the ideas and concepts understood at this stage, a more nuanced understanding will be moulded. During this step, place single dots along the way to flag portions of interest, to mark areas that contain information with which you are not familiar, or simply to signal sections that require further analysis. Using an asterisk may be more appropriate than a dot, but physically marking it requires more time. And time is a critical factor: the longer the distraction the further the attention will drift, and the slower and less smooth the skimming process will become.

3. **Speed Read**. The Speed Read step involves reading through the entire book using the Vertical Line hand motion. The aim should be to understand the deeper aspects of the ideas developed in the text. Particular attention should be dedicated to portions of the text

marked with single dots (which were placed during the Skim step). During the Speed Read step, place question marks next to portions of the text that still require further analysis. (The question marks are thus distinct from the dots deposited while skimming.)

4. **Review**. The Review step involves going through the material once more mainly using the skimming hand motion. The purpose of this step is twofold: firstly, it allows the practitioner to review all the information covered—thus further reinforcing the ideas therein. And, secondly, it provides an additional opportunity to perform a deeper analysis of the concepts that were not fully understood during the Speed Read step. For these reasons, the skimming hand motion is applied, but at sections annotated with a question mark, the reading rate is reduced—preferably using the Vertical Line approach (or the Text Tracing approach)—to a pace that allows the practitioner to understand the complex ideas involved. In sum, the purpose of this step is to review the entire text and to fill any remaining gaps in understanding.

If properly performed, the time spent on layered reading should be less than the time that would have been spent using a standard reading approach, and the level of comprehension with layered reading should be higher.

For expansive texts—especially those that are unlikely to be completed in a single sitting—it is recommended to apply the layered reading process to each chapter (or section or subsection, depending on how the text is structured.) in isolation. It is advisable to perform Step 1 and Step 2 on the entire text, and then apply Steps 2 to 4 on each chapter in isolation, followed by Step 4 for the entire text. Note that Skim and Review steps are performed twice: once for the entire text and once for each chapter as it becomes the focus of study.

In the interest of clarity, the steps of the procedure are repeated below in adaptation to the length of the text.

For a text that can/will be read in a single sitting:

1. Preview the entire text.
2. Skim through the entire text.
3. Speed read through the entire text.
4. Review the entire text.

Examples: a case study, an academic paper, an article analysing current events, a long e-mail, an encyclopaedic article, etc.

For a text that will require multiple sittings:

1. Preview the entire text.
2. Skim through the entire text.
3. Then, one chapter at a time:
    a. Skim through the entire chapter.
    b. Speed read through the entire chapter.
    c. Review the entire chapter.
4. Review the entire text.

Examples: a textbook (irrespective of the subject matter), a biography, a how-to book, an instruction manual, etc.

It is recommended to form the habit of following the layered reading approach with all appropriate texts encountered in your daily life.

SUBCONSCIOUS READING (OPTIONAL)

The author's experience with the various subconscious reading systems available suggests that, even though the fantastic reading rates claimed by such courses are not truly attainable (see the Scientific Evidence chapter), the ability to understand a new topic appears to be enhanced by an initial subconscious read through the material. To reiterate an earlier mention of this point: This comprehension phenomenon is anecdotal and not backed by scientific evidence [at least to the author's knowledge].

For the purported benefit of higher comprehension, this technique has been included in the system herein. However, given the lack of scientific evidence to support this claim, subconscious reading is considered as an optional step in the procedure.

The main principle behind subconscious reading is the assertion that the subconscious mind is able to process information at higher rates than the conscious, analytical mind.

Accessing the subconscious mind for the purpose of reading is achieved by first entering into a meditative state. The meditative state is then maintained while processing the text at extremely high speed. To maintain the deeper state of mind, the eyes must remain unfocused. Focusing on any word would immediately trigger the analytical mind, which, in turn, would herald the exit from the deeper state.

Alas, the information captured during subconscious reading, being subconscious in its nature, is not immediately available to the conscious mind. Most systems then rely on "activating" the information using various methods. The approach utilised in the system herein simply relies on the rest of the steps in the layered reading to trigger conscious associations with that which has been subconsciously reasoned.

Proponents of subconscious reading suggest that the effectiveness of the process relies on the belief in its success. It is commonly agreed that the subconscious mind is highly suggestible. By that trait, disbelief in subconscious reading is the self-fulfilling cause of failure, whereas pure conviction is the driving force that bears its fruit.

Given the lack of scientific evidence to support the claim, pure conviction is difficult to implement, and, by definition, it can be neither forced nor faked. Nonetheless, a practitioner interested in the optional step of the system herein should attempt to control his scepticism. One way to achieve this is by logically deducing that, since this step is an optional addition to the process, nothing is lost in return for the possibility of being pleasantly surprised.

The procedure for subconscious reading is as follows:

1. **Sit with the book placed on the table in front of you.**
2. **Close your eyes.**
3. **Spend five minutes using your favourite concentration technique to enter into a deeper state of mind.**
   Buddhist breathing (Technique 3 from Part 1 of the book) is the recommended approach. It is preferable to spend ten minutes instead of five, if time permits; this can count towards your daily concentration training (as detailed in Part 1 of the book).
4. **Mentally state the name of the book and your purpose for reading it.**
5. **Focus your attention on the top back of your head** until your eyes feel relaxed and your peripheral vision is expanded. (Spend one to two minutes.) Given that your eyes are closed, you will not be able to visually discern

whether your peripheral vision has expanded, but you will be able to feel it.

6. **Open your eyes but do not focus them** (that is, do not focus on any object). Open the book on the first page and ensure that your field of vision covers the entire two-page spread—i.e., you should be able to see (peripherally) the four corners of the book. The main point to note is that the eyes should not be focused at any point during subconscious reading. You should not be able to read the words on the pages; you only need to capture the graphic representation of the words within the two pages in your gaze, not their meaning. To reiterate this crucial principle: **do not try to read!** The aim is for your subconscious mind to capture (to photograph and later assimilate) the information. Your gaze will seem blurry—but that is the desired state. Just capture two pages with each glance and do not focus on any word, phrase or figure.

7. **Flip through the pages at a rhythmic pace**. With every turn of the page, ensure that you maintain your unfocused gaze. Aim for a rate of one flip per second—i.e., subconsciously capture 120 pages per minute.

8. **Ensure that the meditative state is preserved while you flip through the pages.** If your mind begins to wander, simply let go (as you have done in the concentration exercises of Part 1) and continue flipping through the pages. The whole experience should feel more akin to meditating than to reading.

9. **Once finished, close the book and affirm to yourself that your mind has absorbed all the information contained therein.** Furthermore, state firmly to yourself that, as you follow the rest of the steps in the layered reading, the subconscious reasoning will activate and combine with the conscious reading that ensues.

10. **Close your eyes and spend another five minutes with your favourite concentration technique.**
11. **Take a break of at least one hour to allow for the information to be processed.** The ideal waiting period is 24 hours: the aim is to permit a night's sleep to assist in the assimilation of the information that was captured during subconscious reading.

The subconscious reading procedure should be performed before skimming. The goal is for the subconscious mind to capture and assimilate the topic, and then allow the rest of the steps in the layered reading to trigger, and consciously connect to, knowledge reasoned by the subconscious mind.

As stated earlier, this process alone does not produce high reading speeds. It is applied here as an addition to the layered reading procedure, with the goal of extracting a firmer structural foundation of the topic. With a sound structural foundation, the whole reading process becomes easier and more intuitive, and results in higher comprehension.

In the interest of clarity, the overall layered reading procedure is repeated below with the addition of the subconscious reading step.

For a text that can/will be read in a single sitting:

1. Preview the entire text.
2. Subconsciously read through the entire text (optional).
3. Skim through the entire text.
4. Speed read through the entire text.
5. Review the entire text.

Examples: a case study, an academic paper, an article analysing current events, a long e-mail, an encyclopaedic article, etc.

<u>For a text that will require multiple sittings:</u>

1. Preview the entire text.
2. Subconsciously read through the entire text (optional).
3. Skim through the entire text.
4. Then, one chapter at a time:
    a. Skim through the entire chapter.
    b. Speed read through the entire chapter.
    c. Review the entire chapter.
5. Review the entire text.

Examples: a textbook (irrespective of the subject matter), a biography, a how-to book, an instruction manual, etc.

(For the interested reader, an excellent exposition of subconscious reading [at least in the opinion of the author of *The Manual*] is Paul R. Scheele's *PhotoReading* book. This well-presented resource contains some thought-provoking ideas. It should, however, be read while keeping in mind the scientific evidence presented herein.)

VARYING READING SPEEDS

As mentioned in the Regression section, the reading speed should be adjusted according to the complexity of, and familiarity with, the subject of study. It is therefore important to set the hand motion's pace at the speed that is most appropriate for the given topic. The general rule is: read as fast as possible without compromising comprehension.

Novels will generally permit a faster pace; unfamiliar technical texts—say, starting a new topic in chemistry—will require a substantially slower pace.

Furthermore, the reading speed applied to a given text is generally not applied uniformly. Some pages will require more time for reasoning, especially if they have been annotated for further analysis (dots from skimming or question marks from speed reading). Other pages, perhaps through previous exposure to the concepts discussed therein, will require a less thorough read, so the speed can be increased. There are exceptions, of course, with novels being one—where the speed is generally uniform through the text.

Slowing down at a difficult section is not considered as a regression. The two are significantly unalike. In the former, the speed is reduced, but a momentum is maintained; whereas, in the latter, the direction of travel is reversed and the momentum is lost.

Irrespective of the speed that is being used, it is important to always apply the reading principles of: concentration, avoiding regressions, controlling sub-vocalisation, capturing multiple words with each fixation and using layered reading. At the beginning, applying these principles may not feel natural; but, with time **and training**, it will eventually become the only way you would feel comfortable reading.

TRAINING PLAN

A daily training routine is the deciding factor between a successful—and fruitful—implementation of speed reading and an ineffective one. Without training on a daily basis, it is simply not possible to maintain a high reading speed, nor is it possible to develop it in the first place.

For the reading drills contained herein, it is recommended to use simple reading materials (novels are a good choice) rather than complicated technical texts. That is because, in the latter, the reading speed and its uniformity may vary from one session to another depending on your familiarity with the topics. Whereas, in the former, the speed is uniform and is at its maximum, which makes it a more conducive environment in which to push your limits.

To, idiomatically at least, kill two birds with one stone, the practitioner may choose to train with texts that are on his compulsory reading list (e.g., academic papers, textbooks, biographies, reports, analytical articles, etc.). However, the abovementioned consideration regarding difficult/unfamiliar texts should be kept in mind.

Training with technical texts aside, for the measurement of progress, the practitioner is strongly recommended to use a modern novel. The rationale for this is as follows: a modern novel's complexity is likely to stay consistent, whereas other reading materials are likely to contain varying degrees of complexity. Such inconsistent and non-uniform complexity hinders the ability to accurately chart progress. Accurate charting thus relies on the complexity variable being controlled.

When calculating your reading speed through a physical text (or, generally, where a word-count is not available), it is not necessary to count the number of words on every page that you read. A simple approximation of the number of words on a typical page is sufficient to arrive at an estimate. One such approach involves counting the number of words in a typical row and multiplying it by the number of rows on a typical page. The reading speed is then the number of pages read multiplied by the number of words on a typical page, all divided by the time taken to complete the reading (time in minutes). This would provide your reading speed in wpm. The formula is as follows:

$$Speed = \frac{Number\ of\ Pages\ Read \times Words\ on\ a\ Typical\ Page}{Reading\ Time}$$

It is recommended to chart your progress once a week. Doing so more frequently may detract from the purity of training, and doing so less frequently does not generate a sufficiently granular measure of progress.

When performing the exercises, it is important to remove any worry or anxiety linked to comprehension. At times you will be reading at speeds that, given your current degree of proficiency, will result in low levels of comprehension. But that is absolutely necessary if breaking through to higher reading speeds with high comprehension is to be accomplished. The key is to let go of any worries or concerns and follow the exercise instructions.

The main point of the training is to feel free to push against your current limits in order to improve the speed at which you can read with high comprehension.

You must stay concentrated while training, with your attention focused exclusively on the reading—even if the speed is too fast to fully comprehend the ideas and concepts therein.

At the early stages of training, when you are still trying to combine the mechanical steps of the process, you may feel the urge to contemplate whether the steps are being executed correctly. Avoid such contemplation during practice at all costs. The time for contemplation is before reading or after reading— but never while reading. This is an important habit to maintain. If necessary, give yourself a minute at the beginning and a minute at the end of each workout to allow you to reflect. Keep a diary to note down your thoughts and ideas; review these ideas prior to the workout, and add to them at the end of the workout.

On a practical note: in order to measure the time elapsed (as instructed in each exercise), it is advisable to use a stopwatch when performing the exercises below. To avoid having to check the time left in each step of the exercise, a countdown function is the ideal tool to use.

EXERCISE 1: SPEED AND COMPREHENSION

The purpose of this exercise is to improve both speed and comprehension. In this drill, a fixed portion of the text is read several times—each time at a faster pace. The procedure is as follows:

1. Take the reading material chosen for the practice and note the page from which you will start reading.
2. Begin reading at a comfortable speed for **five minutes** using the Vertical Line hand motion. The aim is to read

with full comprehension; this is a critical requirement, so, in this step, do not attempt to read faster than your level of proficiency permits.

3. After the five minutes have elapsed, note your position in the book.

4. Read through the same passage again (using the Vertical Line hand motion) but increase your speed so that you arrive to the same end point (noted in Step 3 above) in **four minutes**.

5. Repeat again, but this time complete the reading in **three minutes**.

6. Repeat again, but this time complete the reading in **two minutes**.

7. Repeat once more, but this time use the **skimming hand motion** and complete the reading in **one minute**.

8. Finally, starting from the end point noted in Step 3 above, read at your comfortable reading speed for **one minute**.

9. Once a week note down the reading speed attained in Step 8 above. That is, note the number of words read in that one minute period (use the formula above).

EXERCISE 2: SPEED

The purpose of this exercise is to break through to higher speeds. In this drill, the length of the text is increased multiplicatively with each reading while the time allocated to completing the task remains fixed. The procedure is as follows:

1. Take the reading material chosen for the practice and note the page from which you will start reading.

2. Begin reading at a comfortable speed for **three minutes** using the Vertical Line hand motion. The aim is to read with full comprehension; this is a critical requirement, so,

in this step, do not attempt to read faster than your level of proficiency permits.

3. After the three minutes have elapsed, note your position in the book.

4. Count the number of pages you have read and add this number to the end point noted in Step 3 above—this is your target end point, Target 1. For example, say you read from page 103 to page 106 (inclusively)—a total of four pages. You would add four pages to the end point—i.e., the end of page 106—to arrive at your target end point (Target 1) of page 110. In total there are now eight pages to read.

5. Starting from the same page noted in Step 1, read through the material again (using the Vertical Line hand motion) but increase your speed so that you **reach Target 1 (noted in Step 4 above) in three minutes**.

6. Increment the end point again by adding the original number of pages read (the amount read in Step 2) to the end point from Step 4 above. This is the new end point—Target 2. To continue with the previous example, you would add four pages to page 110, the end point from Step 4, to arrive at the new target of page 114. In total there are now 12 pages to read.

7. Starting from the same page noted in Step 1, read through the material again (using the Vertical Line hand motion) but increase your speed so that you **reach Target 2 (noted in Step 6 above) in 3 minutes**.

8. Increment the length of the text one last time—this is Target 3. So, continuing with the previous example, add another four pages to yield the final target of page 118. In total there are now 16 pages to read. (For clarity, note that the size of the increment is always equal to the number of pages read in Step 2.)

9. Starting from the same page noted in Step 1, read through the material again, but this time **use the skimming hand motion** and increase your speed so that you **reach Target 3 (noted in Step 8 above) in three minutes**.
10. Finally, starting from the end point noted in Step 3 above, read at your comfortable reading speed for **one minute**.
11. Once a week note down the reading speed attained in Step 10 above. That is, note the number of words read in that one minute period (use the formula above).

EXERCISE 3: PERIPHERAL VISION AND SUB-VOCALISATION

The purpose of this exercise is to expand the fixation span while controlling sub-vocalisation. In this drill, the fixation span is gradually increased while the amount of words being sub-vocalised remains constant. The procedure is as follows:

1. **Using the Vertical Line hand motion**:
2. Take the reading material chosen for the practice and note the page from which you will start reading.
3. Read through the text by capturing **two words** with each fixation while mentally pronouncing only one of the words. Read in this manner for two pages (or, equivalently, approximately 700 words).
4. Starting from the same page noted in Step 2, read through the text again, but this time capture **three words** with each fixation while mentally pronouncing only one of the words. Read in this manner for two pages (or, equivalently, approximately 700 words).
5. Starting from the same page noted in Step 2, read through the text again, but this time capture **half a line** with each

fixation while mentally pronouncing only one of the words therein. Read in this manner for two pages (or, equivalently, approximately 700 words).

6. **Now, using the skimming hand motion**:

7. Starting from the same page noted in Step 2, read through the text again, but this time capture **two half-lines** with each fixation while mentally pronouncing only one of the words therein. Read in this manner for four pages (or, equivalently, approximately 1400 words).

8. Starting from the same page noted in Step 2, read through the text again, but this time capture **three half-lines** with each fixation while mentally pronouncing only one of the words therein. Read in this manner for six pages (or, equivalently, approximately 2100 words).

9. Starting from the same page noted in Step 2, read through the text again, but this time capture **half a paragraph** with each fixation while mentally pronouncing only one of the words therein. (The length of a paragraph will likely vary across the text; this does not affect the exercise.) Read in this manner for ten pages.

Throughout this exercise, maintain a uniform, rhythmic pace. Comprehension in Steps 2 to 5 should be high; if this is not the case, you are going too fast. Fixation speed is not the focus of the exercise: the aim is to expand the fixation span while controlling sub-vocalisation.

EXERCISE 4: COMPREHENSION

The purpose of this exercise is to improve comprehension. In this drill, a passage is read several times, each time at a slower pace. With each repetition, the level of comprehension is tested. The procedure is as follows:

1. Take the reading material chosen for the practice and note the page from which you will start reading.

2. Begin reading using the skimming hand motion for **one minute**. The aim is to get an overview of the topic—the pace should therefore be fast. However, if you are not absorbing any of the ideas therein, you are going too fast. Therefore, adapt the pace to your level of proficiency.

3. After the one minute has elapsed, note your position in the book.

4. On a blank piece of paper, note down your understanding of the passage you have just read. This should ideally be done in a Revision Map format (see Part 4 of the book).

5. Read through the same passage again (using the skimming hand motion), but reduce your speed so that you arrive to the same end point (noted in Step 3 above) in **two minutes**.

6. On a blank piece of paper, note down your (improved) understanding of the passage you have just read (for the second time). This should ideally be done in a Revision Map format.

7. Using the **Vertical Line** hand motion, read through the same passage again, but reduce your speed so that you arrive to the same end point (noted in Step 3 above) in **three minutes**.

8. On a blank piece of paper, note down your improved understanding of the passage you have just read (for the third time). This should ideally be done in a Revision Map format.

9. Using the Vertical Line hand motion, read through the same passage again, but reduce your speed so that you arrive to the same end point (noted in Step 3 above) in **four minutes**.

10. On a blank piece of paper, note down your improved understanding of the passage you have just read (for the

fourth time). This should ideally be done in a Revision Map format.

11. Using the Vertical Line hand motion one last time, read through the same passage again, but reduce your speed so that you arrive to the same end point (noted in Step 3 above) in **five minutes**.

12. On a blank piece of paper, note down your improved understanding of the passage you have just read (for the fifth time). This should ideally be done in a Revision Map format.

When noting down your understanding of the topic, the focus should be speed rather than neatness and presentability. Therefore, complete the notes (or Revision Map) as quickly as possible. Furthermore, the recall should be unaided—so do not look at the text as you note down your understanding.

The act of noting down one's understanding of the text has a powerful effect on how the brain captures information in subsequent reading. Regular practice improves the ability to comprehend at the high reading speeds.

EXERCISE 5: FIXATION SPAN AND COMPREHENSION

The purpose of this exercise is to improve comprehension when wide fixations are being used. In this drill, each fixation is projected onto a blank piece of paper before moving to the next fixation. And, as the exercise progresses, the fixation span is gradually increased. The procedure is as follows:

1. **Preparation:** fold (or cut) a blank piece of paper (or, preferably, a blank piece of cardboard) so that it has the

same width as half a typical line in the chosen reading material. Then fold (or cut) again so that its length is equal to the height of a page in the chosen reading material.

2. Using the text chosen for this drill, capture in a single fixation the first half a line of text on the first page. Then, quickly cover that half a line of text with the blank piece of paper (from Step 1) and try to picture the words on the blank surface. Essentially, you are to project the contents of the fixation onto the blank surface that covers the very same half a line of text.

3. Proceed to the second half of the same line; glance at it and then quickly cover it. Then, try to picture the contents of the second half of the line on the blank surface that covers it.

4. Continue in the same manner (fixate   cover   project) for subsequent lines in the text (half a line at a time) until you have completed **three pages**.

5. Then, for the **next five pages**, repeat the procedure but capture **two half-lines** with each fixation. That is, first capture two half-lines of text, and then visualise those two half-lines on the blank surface that now covers them.

6. Then, for the **next ten pages**, repeat the procedure but capture **three half-lines** with each fixation. That is, first capture three half-lines of text, and then visualise those same three half-lines on the blank surface that now covers them.

It is important to perform this exercise rhythmically: maintain a uniform, smooth pace throughout.

It is not necessary to visualise the hidden contents perfectly. The act of attempting to project them is the mechanism through which comprehension is trained. Therefore, do not spend time memorising the words so that they could be better projected.

The time spent on each fixation should equal to your typical fixation period—not a moment longer. Similarly, the time spent on projecting the words onto the blank surface should, at most, equal to twice your typical fixation period. For example, if your typical fixation period is half a second long, spend half a second on the fixation and, at most, a second on projecting it, then immediately shift to the next fixation and repeat the process.

This drill does not require the involvement of any hand motions. The training is solely focused on the interaction between fixation span and comprehension.

TRAINING SCHEDULE

The system presented in this part of the book initially relies on drills to improve the reading speed and later relies on the same drills to maintain the speed at a high level. Rather than employ a large number of exercises that are marginal variations of the same theme, the system herein focuses on five fundamental exercises that together train every element necessary for effective speed reading.

The key, as with the development of any skill, is regular practice. For speed reading, it is necessary to practise daily. The table below provides the recommended schedule. The schedule involves all five exercises presented in this part of the book, with a greater emphasis on Exercises 1 and 3.

Day	Exercise
Monday	Ex. 1: Speed and Comprehension
Tuesday	Ex. 2: Speed
Wednesday	Ex. 3: Peripheral Vision and Sub-Vocalisation
Thursday	Ex. 1: Speed and Comprehension
Friday	Ex. 4: Comprehension
Saturday	Ex. 3: Peripheral Vision and Sub-Vocalisation
Sunday	Ex. 5: Fixation Span and Comprehension

Each exercise can be extended in length simply by multiplying each step by a suitable factor. For example, in Exercise 1 we can multiply each step by a factor of five. This results in the first read-through being 25 minutes long (instead of 5 minutes); the second read-through being 20 minutes (instead of 4); the third being 15 minutes (instead of 3), and so on.

For the sake of clarity, note that for Exercises 1, 2, and 4 it is the **time** element that should be multiplied by the factor, whereas for Exercises 3 and 5 it is the **number of pages to be read** that should be multiplied by the factor. Crucially, note that the number of words and the number of half-lines should **not** be modified by the factor. These should remain as detailed in the instructions irrespective of any extension made to the length of the exercise.

The extension factor you ultimately choose will depend on the time you have available to perform the exercise. **Performing the exercises in the schedule without extending them is sufficient to make measurable progress.** Thus, extending the exercises is not a necessity. However, it is important to note that the longer you are able to exercise at a time (and, assuming you can do so regularly), the faster your progress will be. The acceleration in progress is commonly proportional to the magnitude of the extension factor.

INCORPORATING SPEED READING INTO DAILY LIFE (CRUCIAL)

The ultimate way to master a skill is through its incorporation into daily life. For speed reading, this could be achieved in the following ways:

1. **Employ the speed reading principles whenever you read**.
2. **Develop a book-a-week habit**. Those who read more, become faster readers naturally. Once you become proficient with the system herein, a book-a-day habit becomes feasible.
3. **Use layered reading at every appropriate opportunity**.
4. **Read multiple genres of interest concurrently**. That is, on any given day, progress through multiple texts. For example, in the morning read a technical text (be it work-related, study-related or just a technical text of interest); at noon read classic literature, and in the evening read a novel.
5. **If you are multilingual, apply the speed reading principles regardless of the language you are reading in**. Furthermore, read regularly in each language. For example, if you are trilingual, in the morning read a technical text in the first language, at noon read literature in the second language, and in the evening read a novel in the third language.
6. **Always carry a book with you (a physical book or an e-reader)**. Use every idle moment to read: it could be while waiting in line, while commuting, on a lunch break, etc.
7. **Continue expanding your vocabulary with the memory techniques from Part 2**. It is essential for optimal speed reading results.

8. (Optional) Use subconscious reading at least once a week.

9. **Most importantly: practise the drills daily**.

SUMMARY AND REVISION MAP

KEY POINTS

- Concentration is crucial to faster reading. Hence regular practice of the concentration techniques from Part 1 is important.
- Regressions should be eliminated. This can be achieved by centring your attention prior to reading as well as employing a guide (hand motion techniques) to set an appropriate pace.
- There are two main hand motion techniques: the skimming hand motion and the Vertical Line hand motion for reading. Text Tracing is an optional hand motion for reading; it is especially useful in the early stages of training.
- Sub-vocalisation must be minimised in order to break through to higher reading speeds.
- The number of words contained in each fixation should be expanded while the time spent on each fixation should either be maintained or further reduced.
- Layered reading should be applied to all subjects of study. This will reduce the overall time required to complete the reading task, enhance comprehension, increase long-term recall, and, in general, require less effort—thus making studying the subject easier.
- Subconscious reading can be added to the layered reading procedure for a further improvement in comprehension.
- Attention must always be focused on the reading. It is appropriate to reflect on one's progress and one's application of the speed reading principles, but such

analysis must be performed either before or after the reading session—never while reading.

REVISION MAP

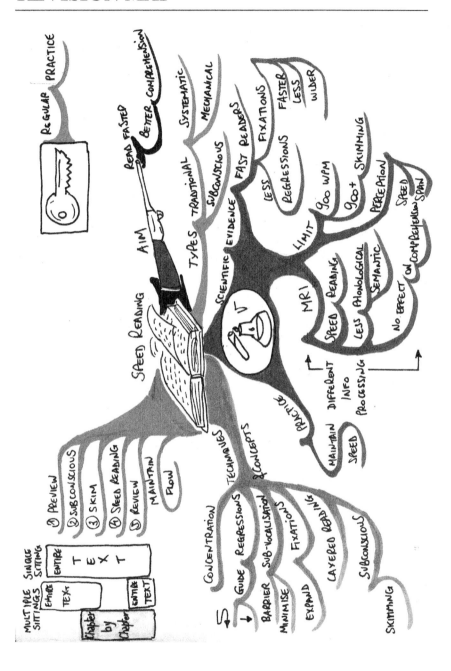

Part 4

THE ULTIMATE STUDY METHOD

What we learn with pleasure we never forget.

—Alfred Mercier

THE AIMS OF PART 4

- To combine the techniques presented thus far into an efficient and effective structured approach to learning.
- To optimise note-taking and revision.
- To understand the principles behind learning and assimilation, and to employ them in your studies.
- To retain all that you learn.

INTRODUCTION

The Ultimate Study Method (USM) is the combination of all the topics presented thus far in the book. They are applied together in an easy-to-follow procedure to produce an optimal, enjoyable, efficient and effective approach to learning anything.

The sequence of steps that generally occur when learning something new are as follows:

1. **Exploring** the topic.
2. **Understanding** the topic.
3. **Memorising** the understanding—that is, memorising your interpretation of the concepts that together form the topic.
4. **Reviewing** the memorised information to keep it fresh and to promote its long-term retention.
5. **Reinforcing** the information and **integrating** it to other ideas/concepts that are already known by answering questions, solving problems, completing puzzles and playing content-related games.
6. **Expanding** your knowledge by building on what you already know: learning a new or related topic that employs what you have already learnt as its foundation.

In order to arrive at Step 6 in the list above, it is necessary to have diligently gone through the previous steps on the same list. It then becomes apparent that to truly expand one's knowledge, it is necessary to have an effective method to accumulate what has already been learnt, and to have it available in easily-accessible—yet long-tern—storage. Without Steps 3 to 5, any further learning would be met with impeding limitations due to a lack of necessary foundation.

The general aim should be to keep anything that is of even mild importance in long-term storage. This is feasible with the system illustrated below. As you progress with such application of the USM, you will come to realise that, the more you know and retain, the more easily you can learn new concepts. With ever-accelerating accumulation of knowledge, you will also come to appreciate the vast resources that you can now leverage upon for the creation of new ideas as well as for solving harder problems.

It has recently been argued that the need to maintain vast amounts of data in the brain had become redundant with the advent of easily accessible stores of digital data, which can be accessed almost instantaneously through powerful search engines. This argument misses a crucial point: information is of limited use when it is not reasoned out, imprinted in the mind, intimately connected to related topics, and applied in practice. For example, it would be very difficult for one to solve a problem whose concepts are so alien that he would not even know which search criteria to impose. Even if the necessary information were to be found, the individual's background knowledge would not be sufficient to formulate the steps that lead to the solution.

When information is reasoned out and then imprinted in the brain, it begins to overlap and interconnect with previously established knowledge. The same process also brings about creative ideas and new concepts. Having the same information reside in a digital ether does not allow for these results to transpire.

Perhaps the reader should ponder over how many truly revolutionary ideas have come about following the invention of the internet and compare them to the feats of the human mind that were attained prior to it. It may hap that when we can train computers to connect between concepts (Artificial Intelligence, in common parlance, which is already here yet still in its infancy) and to integrate these concepts to create new ones, knowledge accumulation would become redundant. Unless there is a subsequent shift to greater truths that only the human mind (perhaps assisted by an intelligent computer) can explore, the redundancy of knowledge accumulation and creative thinking would rob humanity of the joy of learning and creating. It would be the antithesis to every scholar's Faustian predilection, and likely go against the naturally selected traits of our species.

Futile future predictions aside, while we remain in the present knowledge-based, novelty-rewarding society, a system for efficient and effective accumulation of knowledge is invaluable.

KEY CONCEPTS

The USM is easy to learn and comes naturally after very little practice. The overall procedure is as follows:

1. **Gather all the materials** necessary for the completion of the study.
2. **Enter a relaxed state of mind** using your preferred concentration technique from Part 1. Buddhist breathing (Technique 3 from Part 1) is the recommended approach, but stick to whichever technique works best for you (while also considering what your environment and circumstances permit).
3. **Apply layered reading** in order to process the reading materials:
    a. **Preview.**
    b. **Subconsciously read** through the study texts (optional).
    c. **Skim:**
        i. Mark difficult sections with a dot.
        ii. Highlight, underline or mark with the letter V the key points.
        iii. Once you finished skimming, complete the main branches of the Revision Map.
    d. **Speed read:**
        i. Slow down at sections marked with a dot.
        ii. Mark difficult sections with a question mark.
        iii. Highlight, underline or mark with the letter V the key points.
        iv. Once you finished reading, add to the Revision Map the key concepts that were identified and annotated in this step of the procedure.

e. **Review:**
  i. Slow down at sections marked with a question mark.
  ii. Highlight, underline or mark with the letter V additional key points if necessary.
  iii. Once you finished reviewing, add to the Revision Map the key concepts that were identified and annotated in this step of the procedure.

4. **Note-taking:**
  a. Reason clearly in your mind every aspect of the topic. And, as you do so:
  b. Complete a set of linear notes.
  c. Complete the Revision Map.

5. **Memorise:**
  a. (Create/maintain a list of unique identifiers.)
  b. Memorise the Revision Map.
  c. Memorise the linear notes.
  d. Revision: Review according to the optimal revision schedule.

6. **Reinforce:**
  a. Solve problems and puzzles or answer open questions that involve the concepts of the topic.
  b. If you are studying for a specific exam, practise, under timed conditions, previous exam papers. And continue to practise until you are able to score full marks on each such paper.
  c. Apply the concepts of the topic in different contexts, and where possible, to unrelated fields (i.e., stimulating transferability).
  d. Play content-related games (if available).
  e. Put the knowledge to practical use.

The entire procedure above forms the USM: no step should be skipped! It works best when it is followed according to the above prescription.

In the sections below, each step of the procedure will be elucidated in more detail.

STUDY MATERIALS

Gather all the materials necessary for the completion of the study. This may include textbooks, study aids, supplementary papers/books, class notes, class exercises, problem sets, previous exam papers, content-related games, content-related videos, etc.

STATE OF MIND

Regular practice of the concentration techniques introduced in Part 1 of the book is crucial for the implementation of the USM. So continue with the practice as indicated in Part 1. A solid grasp of the concentration techniques is a key requirement of this system. It is why concentration features in the first part of the book: everything follows from it.

In addition to the regular practice from Part 1, **every study session should begin with a five-minute concentration exercise** (ten minutes would be better, so do so whenever possible; five minutes was chosen to keep the procedure practical). The concentration exercise acts as a centring mechanism for the learning experience that follows. The motivation behind this step is to centre the mind and ensure that the entire study period is spent focused on the task at hand. It also promotes the alpha brainwave frequency, which will aid in the understanding of the material while reading and while reasoning, and it will overall improve its later recall. This enhanced retention also occurs because, through heightened concentration, you are focusing your attention—and attention is the key to memory.

Buddhist breathing (Technique 3 from Part 1) is the recommended technique, but choose whichever technique works best for you and whichever is most appropriate for the environment you are situated in while studying.

REVISION MAP

A Revision Map is a pictorial representation of the topic. It is an extremely versatile tool to capture the structure of a topic as well as its key facts.

Diagrammatic representations of topics and ideas have been used for centuries, with notable examples including Porphyry of Tyros, Ramon Llull, Leonardo da Vinci, and, centuries later, Evelyn Wood. Most recently, Tony Buzan's system of Mind Mapping® has refined diagrammatic representation with a precise methodology—transforming this general concept into an effective tool for studying, brainstorming, lecturing, thinking, organising information, problem solving, decision making, and more.

The pictorial representation of a topic has taken many names over the years: Concept map, Mind map, Mental map, Spider diagram, Recall pattern (e.g., Slash recall pattern), to name but a few. However, in this book we will refer to such a representation as a Revision Map. This is because the USM applies the technique primarily as a revision tool for long-term memory storage.

Revision mapping forms a key component in the Ultimate Study Method. Such a succinct representation of the topic offers a route through which a rapid review of what has been learnt can be performed. It is therefore the conduit through which long-term memory storage is stimulated. Apart from its advantages when reviewing a topic, creating a Revision Map forces the user to think critically about the overall structure of the topic and how different elements are related—this in itself improves the understanding and imposes a structural order on the assimilated concepts.

To spur one's motivation further, below is the list of key advantages of using a Revision Map.

1. **Succinct representation**, which offers an efficient route for stimulating long-term memory storage.
2. **Forces one to think about how the different concepts are related**. This improves the understanding of the topic and imposes structural order when the concepts are assimilated.
3. **Synoptic representation** of the topic.
4. **Utilises both brain hemispheres and multiple modalities.** This increases the number of regions involved when processing the topic, which further improves understanding and retention. Furthermore, it also enhances the topic's integration and association with related concepts.
5. **Permits organising large amounts of information** into a form that facilitates reasoning.
6. **A natural process** that emulates the way in which the brain links information together.

7. **Seeing the big picture.** The pictorial form that fits on a page can encompass within it the contents of an entire book. Such a representation permits one to form an all-encompassing impression of the topic that is not generally attainable by other means.

8. **Enhances creativity**.

The Ultimate Study Method employs Revision Maps in a very specific manner. And Revision Maps are not the only form of notes being created in this study method—linear notes are composed as well. The Revision Maps are used to provide a structural representation that is easy to review for the purpose of long-term memory storage, whereas the linear notes provide a more complete coverage of all the key elements of the topic.

Linear notes are absolutely necessary, since, on its own, a Revision Map cannot capture some of the subtleties that need to be explained fully in words. Having a set of linear notes ensures that there is a lasting record of your understanding, which can be referred to and reviewed for long-term storage.

Neither a set of linear notes nor a Revision Map is necessarily better than the other: they complement each other. Both must be used, as the purpose that each serves is different.

PROCEDURE

The procedure for the creation of a Revision Map is as follows:

1. **Begin at the centre** of a blank page; there draw an image representing the topic.

2. **From the main image draw branches** that represent the key divisions of the topic.

3. **On each branch write the key word** that represents the division.
   a. A branch should only be as long as its key word.
   b. Use only a key word, nothing else—do not write full sentences or explanations.
   c. If there is an image that represents the key word well, use that image instead of the key word. **In general, in a Revision Map, images are preferred to words.**
   d. If the image only mildly reminds you of the key word, then put both on the branch to avoid confusion when reviewing.
   e. An excellent combination of the above ideas is to use the image for the key word as the branch—i.e., the image itself is the branch—and to place the key word on top of it (for examples, see the Revision Maps included in this book).

4. **You can then further divide the topic into its subdivisions** by drawing branches from each (division's) key word.
   a. The branches should be thickest near the centre and become thinner as they extend outwards. So the main divisions of the topic will have thick branches whilst the subdivisions will have thinner branches, and so on.
   b. Proceed in the same manner as with the topic's divisions. Continue using key words exclusively: one key word per branch.
   c. Use an image instead of a key word where the image interpretation is obvious; otherwise, use both. If there is no image that comes to mind for a particular key word, then do not place an image—it is not compulsory, but it is preferable where feasible.

5. **Use boxes to contain items that are not key words**. For example, an important formula should be placed in a box next to the key word that describes it.
6. **Proceed in this manner, possibly through further subdivisions**, until the main themes and concepts have been exposed on a single page.

GENERAL CONSIDERATIONS

1. **Do not spend time on making the images perfect**. It is not necessary. Simply ensure that each image represents—to you—the concept you wanted to portray and then move on. Aesthetics, fine details and a form pleasing to others are of no added value.
2. **Use a colouring scheme**. Each main branch sets the colour for that entire division of the topic. So, for example, if the topic can be divided into five main divisions, you will use five colours. Each division will employ one colour; that is, the main branch and all the sub-branches (for subdivisions) of a particular division will be of the same colour.
3. **Use black ink for writing the key words**. Irrespective of the colour of the branch, key words and formulae should all be written in black ink.
4. **Use capital letters for the key words**. This requires marginal extra effort but makes the review process much faster.
5. **Use arrows to connect related concepts** that are on different branches.
6. **Ensure the Revision Map is clear, concise and well organised.**
7. **Create (and review) the Revision Map in clockwise order.**

8. **Spend some time looking at others' Revision-Maps.** Especially at the beginning, this provides useful examples and imparts ideas you can explore further in your own Revision Maps. Note, however, that it is not necessary to do so, and it is certainly not advisable to spend much time viewing others' creations. It is merely a suggestion to explore other art forms and to seek inspiration and new ideas.

9. **With time, practice, and experimentation, you will develop your own personal style.** Artistic freedom notwithstanding, it is important that the main guidelines above are adhered to.

This book is divided into five parts; at the end of each part there is a Revision Map summarising the concepts discussed within that part of the book. These should serve as examples of how a Revision Map should look like.

Remember, the emphasis is not on artistic prowess but on synoptic exposition of the main concepts. You should not compete with others in making better, nicer or awe-inspiring Revision Maps. The true goal is to develop an effective mechanism for recording, organising, reasoning and quickly reviewing learnt information.

LINEAR NOTES

Linear notes are the traditional way in which a topic is summarised. With the recent popularity of non-linear notes (e.g., Mind Maps®), fewer people are relying on linear note-taking. Such an approach is flawed, since non-linear notes are, in general, not sufficient for covering all the concepts in a topic. In particular, any subtle point—i.e., a concept whose very definition must involve a detailed explanation—can easily lose its intended meaning when presented with key words alone.

The aim of the set of linear notes is to capture, in your own words, all the concepts in a given topic. For example, when reading through a textbook, the linear notes should cover all the concepts detailed in the textbook, but with brief personally-worded explanations rather than the full analysis and views of the author.

The general theme is to reason through the ideas in the topic and then put that understanding in your own words in the linear notes. There are differences beyond measure and reason between one's personally-worded understanding and the very same idea outlined in a textbook by its author.

This understanding that you form while the topic is still fresh in your mind can quickly dissipate if it is not subsequently reviewed in a timely manner. If much time has elapsed and only a vestige of the understanding remains, another read through the same text becomes necessary, with another round of reasoning also likely required. Such an approach is inefficient. The linear notes are therefore used to record your understanding: to form a permanent record of what you had reasoned and understood.

PROCEDURE

The procedure for linear note-taking is as follows:

1. **All the concepts in the topic should be captured**. Every concept developed in the text should be captured in the linear notes. Taking notes and summarising does not mean omitting content.

2. **Use your own words.** Each concept should be summarised using your own words. This first requires reasoning through the ideas developed in the text and then articulating this understanding in your own words.

3. **Keep it brief.** Try to explain each concept in a single paragraph—ideally less than three lines in length. Your explanation should be as brief as possible. The key motivation is to have a concise record to which you can later refer in order to immediately regain the understanding you had already arrived at in the past.

4. **Hierarchical structure.** Stick to the following hierarchical structure:

   a. Each main division heading should be double underlined.

   b. Each subdivision heading (subheading) should be single underlined.

   c. For each concept:

      i. The concept should be preceded by a bullet point.

      ii. The key word (preferably written in capital letters) describing the concept should follow the bullet point.

      iii. The explanation (in your own words) of the concept should follow the key word.

      iv. Each subsidiary concept (if there are any) should indent a new line and be preceded by a hyphen—or be preceded by roman numerals if order is important.

      v. Include diagrams and formulae (if there are any) with the concept. Each diagram or formula should be surrounded by a box.

GENERAL CONSIDERATIONS

1. **Handwritten notes are superior to typed notes**[17].
   Typing and organising one's notes using computer software is substantially easier: you can copy and paste formulae, diagrams, tables, important quotes, key extracts, etc., and you can easily reorganise at a later date if new information is encountered. However, the physical act of writing fortifies the knowledge of the ideas being studied and stimulates multiple memory pathways that are absent when typing on a computer. And these pathways are further reinforced with each review of the physical set of notes.

2. **Use black ink for the explanations**. Headings and subheading should also be written in black ink.

3. **Use a different colour for the key words**.
   a. Any colour that you find pleasing is suitable, but ensure that it is sufficiently contrasted to be visible— if it is an effort to discern the word, it fails to serve its purpose.
   b. Some practitioners find that alternating between several pleasing colours for the key words improves retention. So, for example, the first key word would be in blue, the second key word would be in red, the third in green, the fourth in purple, and so forth.
   c. Other practitioners prefer to use a different colour for each division: so the key words in the first division would be in one colour while the key words in the second division would be in a different colour.

---

[17] In "The Pen is Mightier Than the Keyboard", *Psychological Science,* April 2014, the study authors, Pam A. Mueller and Daniel M. Oppenheimer, have found that students who took handwritten notes performed better on conceptual questions and were more successful in integrating, retaining and applying their knowledge than those who used computer software to take notes.

    d. Whichever key word colouring scheme you ultimately choose, the explanations should always be written with the same strong colour contrast—thus black ink on a white background is highly recommended.

    e. The alternating colours can also be used when drawing the boxes around diagrams and formulae.

    f. Employing colours for the key words in the linear notes is not a requirement—it is a common preference. Moreover, the novelty of alternating colours has favourable effects on the memories created.

4. **Underline important words within your explanations**. But do not overdo this: underline only one or two words at a time.

5. **The organisation of the ideas should be in whichever order you think is best**. It does not necessarily have to be in the order chosen by the author of the text. If in your mind a more logical categorisation exists, let your notes take that form.

The linear notes should initially be relied upon to reason, integrate and fully understand the topic. **It is necessary to read through these notes several times until the topic is absolutely clear in the mind.** Once the topic is clearly understood and all the facts have been memorised, it is only necessary to go through the linear notes again during the specified review periods (as detailed in Part 2 and repeated in the Memorising section below).

EXAMPLE

Included below is a generic example for linear notes:

Book/Topic Title

Division heading 1

Subdivision heading 1

    KEY WORD 1: explanation
    KEY WORD 2: explanation

          | Formula |

    KEY WORD 3: explanation

     -Subsidiary concept/explanation 1

     -Subsidiary concept/explanation 2

    KEY WORD 4: explanation

    i.   Ordered concept/explanation 1
    ii.   Ordered concept/explanation 2
    iii.   Ordered concept/explanation 3

Subdivision heading 2

    KEY WORD 5: explanation
    KEY WORD 6: explanation
    KEY WORD 7: explanation

Division heading 2

Subdivision heading 3
    KEY WORD 8: explanation
    KEY WORD 9: explanation

Diagram

Subdivision heading 4

Etc.

UNIQUE IDENTIFIERS

To recapitulate from Part 2: The term *unique identifier* is used to describe an object that can be interpreted as only a single piece of information (be it a word, a number, a symbol or other).

The term *building blocks* is used to describe the most basic components from which the abovementioned unique identifiers are constructed. For words it is the syllable sounds or the word itself; for numbers it is the phonetic alphabet. Building blocks should themselves be uniquely identified; and, vice versa, unique identifiers larger than the basic building blocks can, as progress is made in a given topic, act as building blocks themselves.

Lastly, the term *consistent unique identifier* is used to indicate that the unique identifier is applied consistently—that is, whenever a certain piece of information is encountered, the same object is used to represent it. For unique identifiers to become building blocks, they must be applied consistently.

A system then consists of a set of building blocks and a set of rules with which they are to be applied so that each piece of information is uniquely identified—and consistently so.

The steps to achieving this are as follows:

1. **Building blocks**. Before memorising a major topic, break down the information into building blocks that can be uniquely identified by easy-to-visualise objects. For example, each letter, symbol, number, syllable, sound, smell, radical, etc., should have a unique identifier.
2. **Unique identifiers**. The building blocks can then be used to construct unique identifiers for the pieces of information contained in the topic.
3. **Consistency**. The unique identifiers should thereafter be applied consistently.
4. **No conflict**. Any building block or unique identifier should neither conflict nor present an ambiguity across topics. **To that end, it is advisable to use a notebook to write down the list of building blocks, and, where feasible, the list of key unique identifiers.** The phonetic alphabet presented in Part 2 of the book is an archetypical example for a list of building blocks. The table listing unique identifiers for the numbers 0 to 100 is a quintessential example for a list of key unique identifiers.

The crux is to break down the topic into its most basic building blocks. For each such building block, a unique identifier should be assigned. Through this approach, any complex piece of information that is a combination of these building blocks can easily be visualised and thus memorised. Thereafter, the unique identifier for the complex piece of information can be used as a building block for pieces of information that are more complex still (and so forth).

To eliminate any confusion around this principle (as presented in Part 2 of the book), note that it is absolutely not necessary to tabulate each item being memorised and the unique identifier to represent it. The idea is to generate a set of building blocks of which there are far less than data in the entire topic. This far smaller set of elements is then tabulated and used to organise the entire topic and to systematically derive other unique identifiers. For example, the phonetic alphabet was the set of building blocks for any topic involving numbers. It is finite in size and easy to tabulate, yet it is able to transform any number into a unique identifier.

As explained in Part 2 of the book, employing building blocks and consistent unique identifiers allows the user to systematically decompose the subject into its constituent components. All data in the topic are then memorised in congruence with each other. This avoids the confusion that commonly arises from multiple interpretations of identifiers, it reduces the inefficiency of having multiple identifiers for the same piece of data, it speeds up the process of memorising, and it facilitates later recall.

As an example of what to tabulate, let us use the list of unique identifiers from the Mathematical Formulae section in Part 2 of the book:

Symbol	Unique Identifier	Reason/Logic Behind the Choice
+	Pus	*Plus* sounds similar to "pus"
-	Dennis the Menace	*Minus* sounds similar to "menace"
=	Eagle	*Equal* sounds similar to "eagle"
2π	Two pies	It is the Greek letter pi, and there are two
μ	Cow	The letter is pronounced "mu"
$\sqrt{}$	Root	It is the square root symbol
( )	Twin Towers	Visually it looks like two leaning towers
σ	Sigmund Freud (visualise a white beard)	The letter is pronounced "sigma", which sounds similar to "Sigmund"
Division ($\div$)	Machete	Division is associated with cutting
Power ($\wedge$ or x^y)	Bodybuilder	Physical power is associated with muscles and size
Integration ($\int$)	Interrogation light	*Integration* sounds like "interrogation"
Differentiation (∂)	Sock	Differentiating between the pairs of socks when the clean laundry returns.

These symbols appear in a large variety of mathematical formulae; hence, setting a unique identifier for each in advance makes the process of memorising formulae quicker, easier and without conflict or confusion. The list should then be extended as and when new symbols are encountered.

At its current state, the list only contains basic building blocks. As new formulae are memorised, each can be given a unique identifier. For formulae that often appear within other more complex formulae—e.g., the normal density function—it is advisable to add their unique identifiers to the table above.

It is essential to be consistent across topics. So, for example, if you were studying physics as well as mathematics, you would be using the same table above for both and only adding to the list components that are not already present.

The list tabulating the building blocks and unique identifiers is considered as part of your set of notes.

LAYERED READING

The layered reading procedure should be performed as instructed in Part 3 of the book. There are, however, a few points that should be elucidated further: the annotation of the material as you read through it, the stages of reasoning through the topic, and the interaction between reading and note-taking.

The key to the reading step in the USM is to maintain a continuous flow through the reading material. It is crucial to avoid any pauses and regressions. This is especially significant for pauses and regressions that occur at the beginning of the reading session: these ultimately compound and lead to a reduced overall reading speed, reduced comprehension, and, quite frequently, frustration.

To ensure that a high level of comprehension is attained, the forgone pauses and regressions must be replaced with an additional read through the problematic sections at a later time. To remain efficient, this must be performed systematically without unnecessary repetition. A specific annotation procedure is therefore utilised to achieve this.

GENERAL CONSIDERATIONS

The general considerations for annotating and reasoning are as follows:

1. **Annotate at the margin.** When reading through difficult concepts that are not clearly understood as you initially encounter them, annotate at the margin of the line the concept is on. Mark a dot when skimming; mark a question mark when speed reading.
2. **Pull out the key concepts.** When reading through key concepts that should be included in the notes and later memorised, either underline (or highlight) the relevant words or mark the margin with the letter V. In general, underlining (or highlighting) takes longer, and, as every moment of concentration matters for efficient reading, marking the letter V at the margin is usually the better approach. It is certainly more efficient when more than a single line is to be marked. In such cases, a vertical line at the margin—to capture the length of the section— followed by the letter V is better than underlining the whole section.
3. **Reserve thorough reasoning for later.** Do not stop to reason any difficult point as you encounter it: the aim is to flow through the text smoothly and continuously. This way, the fundamental concepts are picked up first, and onto these further details are amalgamated as you fill the gaps in subsequent reading.
4. **Thorough reasoning is performed while composing the set of notes.** Reasoning through anything that

remains unclear can be done at the note-taking stage. While note-taking there are no requirements to pass through the text smoothly, continuously and without regression. Each point can thus be reasoned through fully, referring to alternative sources of information and other background reading where necessary. There are no time restrictions. Then, once a concept is fully understood, it can be added to the set of notes.

PROCEDURE

Combining the abovementioned general considerations with layered reading, we arrive at the following procedure for the reading stage in the USM:

1. **Preview.**
2. **Subconsciously read** through the study texts (optional).
3. **Skim**:
   a. Mark difficult sections with a dot.
   b. Highlight or underline key points—the concepts that together form the topic. Or if a whole paragraph is of interest, mark a vertical line at the margin and add the letter V next to it.
   c. Once you finished skimming, complete the main branches of the Revision Map.
4. **Speed read**:
   a. Slow down at sections marked with a dot.
   b. Mark difficult sections with a question mark.
   c. Highlight or underline key points—the concepts that together form the topic. Or if a whole paragraph is of interest, mark a vertical line at the margin and add the letter V next to it.

d. Once you finished reading, add to the Revision Map the key concepts that were identified and annotated in this step of the procedure.

5. **Review:**
   a. Slow down at sections marked with a question mark.
   b. Highlight, underline or mark with the letter V additional key points if necessary.
   c. Once you finished reviewing, add to the Revision Map the key concepts that were identified and annotated in this step of the procedure.

6. **Note-Taking:**
   a. Begin writing your linear notes. These should contain all the key concepts of the topic in your own words. Therefore, go through the text again and add to your linear notes every concept that was annotated. **When writing these notes, spend whatever time is necessary to reason through the topic**. It is at this stage that you can stop at sections that have not been clearly understood in earlier reading. Reason through the topic until it is fully understood—and it is this understanding that is to be contained in the linear notes.
   b. Add to the Revision Map all additional concepts and connections gleaned while writing the linear notes.

A neat variation to the above procedure involves annotating the material with the letter that represents the step in the procedure instead of the generic V. That is, annotating M when skimming, S when speed reading, and R when reviewing. This saves time when filling the Revision Map after each step, as annotation from previous steps can be easily identified and skipped.

MEMORISING

Once the topic is fully understood and the set of notes is complete, the next step involves memorising the topic.

The preparatory step for memorising is to set the unique identifiers. It is advisable to create a basic table of unique identifiers (as detailed in the Unique Identifiers section). It can be expanded where necessary as you memorise the topic.

Memorising the topic then consists of three steps:

1. **Memorising the Revision Map**. The Revision Map is memorised in order to anchor an overall understanding of the topic and to establish a structure on to which you can attach further knowledge.
2. **Memorising the linear notes**. Adding on to the structure established by memorising the Revision Map, this procedure appends the finer details and subtle points.
3. **Revision**.
    a. Review the linear notes using the optimal revision schedule.
    b. Review the set of Revision Maps every other day.

Out of the three steps above, it is usually the last step (Revision) that tends to be neglected. Long-term retention of the concepts and lucid understanding of their interconnected structure relies on periodic review: if this step is omitted, all efforts expended on learning and memorising will have been in vain.

In order to be efficient, one should review according to the optimal revision schedule (as detailed in The Importance of Revision, in Part 2 of the book). This way we only perform what is sufficient for long-term retention—without exceeding the requirements and wasting time.

When memorising the Revision Map and the linear notes, the most appropriate memory technique should be applied to each portion of the notes. For example, every formula should be memorised with the approach demonstrated in the Mathematical Formulae section in Part 2 of the book, whilst every definition should be memorised with the technique presented in the Non-Foreign Vocabulary section in Part 2 of the book.

The overall aim should be to memorise the Revision Map in its entirety and to memorise only the key facts and subtle points from the linear notes. That is, only memorise from the linear notes information that cannot be immediately discerned from the Revision Map.

Note that the linear notes are there to provide a full coverage of the topic, but presented in a terser form and in your own words. It is there to allow you to reason through the topic, to have a concise yet complete source of information, and to contain your understanding and interpretation. It is not necessary to memorise it verbatim.

THE VALUE OF TESTING

Performing a revision does not mean simply rereading the set of notes. This is a significant misconception. Such approach is suboptimal[18]. **Performing an effective revision involves testing your knowledge.**

The present day culture and its commonly accepted approach to learning means that testing is viewed as an evaluation tool. It is rarely viewed as a learning tool. This is unfortunate, for testing,

---

[18] See the scientific journal references provided in the References and Extra Reading chapter.

if performed under stress-free conditions, and if timed appropriately, can produce better recall of facts—as well as a deeper and more nuanced understanding—than can be achieved by learning without testing.

When testing is applied as a learning tool, it is commonly called *retrieval practice*. The premise for using this tool is that every time a piece of information is recollected from memory, the memory itself changes. The neurological structure of the memory become stronger, more stable and requires less energy and effort when accessed in the future.

Furthermore, fMRI studies have shown that recalling information from memory, as compared with simply rereading it, generates significantly higher levels of activity in areas of the brain associated with consolidation. And it was shown that high activation in these areas while learning results in superior long-term retention.

Some experts would venture so far as to say that recalling what we already know is a more powerful learning event than storing that same information in the first place.

Interestingly, testing not only improves retention for the information being retrieved, but also stimulates and improves retention for related information—i.e., information that was not specifically tested but is somehow connected.

Moreover, the act of testing—of consciously calling to mind information from memory—also promotes what is commonly referred to as *deep learning*. Practitioners immersed in deep learning are able to understand the underlying principles of a topic and to draw inferences from these; they are able to connect the individual pieces of information, and they are able to apply this understanding in different contexts and circumstances (which is commonly referred to as *transfer*).

For all the abovementioned reasons, you should make testing a central part of your learning process. As a first step (more testing will take place when you reinforce), when you review your notes you should try and call to mind the concepts of the topic as they appear in the notes, rather than simply read through the notes. This should be performed as follows:

- **For a Revision Map,**
  - o **When reviewing as part of the optimal revision schedule:** start with a blank piece of paper and try to replicate the Revision Map (without looking at the original). You should <u>not</u> use multiple colours or draw any images, nor should it be neat. It should be rough and quick—even if the result is largely illegible. Once completed, glance at the original to ensure that you have not missed anything.
  - o **When reviewing the set of Revision Maps every other day:** repeat the procedure above, but, instead of redrawing the map physically, review it mentally. Then read through the original to ensure that all concepts had been captured.
- **For the linear notes:** read through the set of linear notes while using your hand to cover sections, formulae, definitions, etc., that you have memorised and would like to test yourself on. Then call to mind the information; once the information is reviewed mentally, uncover the portion of the notes and verify whether you were correct.

In sum, revision in the USM is performed through testing.

MEMORISING THE REVISION MAP

The procedure for memorising the Revision Map is as follows:

1. **Link or Loci.** The recommended approach is to use either the Link System or the Loci System, and to do so under the following considerations:

   a. If the Link System is the chosen approach, each key concept is linked in clockwise order to the concepts that are connected to it. You begin with the innermost concept—the topic's name—and link the key concepts on its branches in clockwise order. You then repeat the procedure for each of the aforementioned key concepts and the ideas on their respective sub-branches, and so forth until the entire Revision Map has been memorised. For example, link the topic's name to KEY WORD 1, link KEY WORD 1 to KEY WORD 2, and link KEY WORD 2 to KEY WORD 3. Then, for the sub-branches, link KEY WORD 1 to KEY WORD 1.1, link KEY WORD 1.1 to KEY WORD 1.2; then link KEY WORD 2 to KEY WORD 2.1, link KEY WORD 2.1 to KEY WORD 2.2, link KEY WORD 2.2 to KEY WORD 2.3, etc.

   b. If the Loci System is the chosen approach, some preparatory work is required: using the Loci System involves dedicating a town (real or imaginary) to your studies. Each building and location (e.g., house, shop, office, tower block, shopping mall, road, junction, park, etc.) in the town can store information. If, for example, you create an imaginary town, each road can contain a field of study, each house can then contain a topic, each room in the house can store one of the concepts on the main branches, and each item in the room can store one of the concepts on the sub-branches. You would then peg the concepts from the Revision Map in clockwise order to the corresponding elements of the locus.

2. Revision.

    a. Review, at the very least, using the optimal revision schedule. Given that the linear notes are also reviewed according to the optimal revision schedule, you should review the Revision Map every time you review the linear notes (see next subsection). The review should involve calling the information to mind unaided by the Revision Map—not simply rereading it.

    b. In addition, and since the Revision Map is so short and concise, it is recommended to review it every other day.

With time, as you study and accumulate more topics, you will come to have many such Revision Maps. By that time, you will have grown so comfortable with the old ones that it would take less than a minute to go through each one. That would mean that you could easily keep, say, 30 topics fresh in the mind whilst spending less than 30 minutes every other day.

Once you have accumulated more than 30 topics, forgo the alternate-day recommendation and split the revision over several days—so that there are at most 30 topics to review on any given day. If, for example, there are 90 topics, the revision of each should recur every three days—with 30 topics reviewed each day.

It is strongly recommended to include the alternate-day (or, for a large number of topics, the multiday split) revision. The extra exposure will ensure that the topics you have spent much time and effort learning remain fresh at all times. To be clear: the optimal revision schedule is sufficient for long-term storage, but reviewing the Revision Maps every other day will, at a marginal cost, result in substantially more accessible memories.

The few minutes spent every other day are worth it. And since you would be going through the ludicrous images you had created when you memorised the topic, this should actually be a pleasurable experience.

MEMORISING THE LINEAR NOTES

1. **Read and understand.** Read through the linear notes a few times to make sure that the topic has been clearly understood.
2. **Do not memorise verbatim.** It is not necessary to memorise the linear notes word for word: only the key facts and subtle points should be memorised.
3. **Use the memory techniques.** Memorise the key facts and subtle points using the techniques introduced in the Part 2 of the book. Note, however, that it is **not necessary** to memorise the structure of the linear notes (i.e. the order of the headings and subheading, or in which section each fact resides). As the structure was already memorised with the Revision Map, all that remains is to memorise the key facts and subtle points: in general, to memorise information in the linear notes that cannot be discerned from the Revision Map.
4. **Revision.** This is of utmost importance:
   a. Immediately after memorising each piece of data in the linear notes (calling the time at which this occurs T_0), call to mind the scene or image, to ensure that the data has been absorbed.
   b. An hour later, that is, $T_0 + 1$ hour, review your linear notes by reading them again and testing yourself on

the data you memorised. For each such piece of data, unaided by the linear notes (i.e., cover the relevant data with your hand), attempt to recall the information and review the scene/image.

c. Ideally, a couple of hours before going to bed, that is, $T_0 + 12$ hours (assuming that the data was learnt in the morning; otherwise, simply perform 12 hours after T_0), review again.

d. Review again the next day, i.e., $T_0 + 24$ hours.

e. Review once more a week later, i.e., $T_0 + 1$ week.

f. Review once more two weeks later, i.e., $T_0 + 2$ weeks.

g. Review once more a month later, i.e., $T_0 + 1$ month.

h. Review once more three months later, i.e., $T_0 + 3$ months.

i. Review once more six months later, i.e., $T_0 + 6$ months.

j. Review once more twelve months later, i.e., $T_0 + 12$ months.

Note that it is not necessary to connect the information from the linear notes to the link or the locus that was created when you memorised the Revision Map. For example, if a name of a formula appears in the Revision Map, and that name is therefore pegged to an item in the locus, it is not necessary to then peg the contents of the formula (from the linear notes) to other items in the locus. Instead, the contents of the formula should be memorised as was instructed in the Mathematical Formulae section in Part 2 of the book. This essentially means that the name of the formula is associated with the topic, but the formula itself is memorised as an independent fact.

REINFORCING

We learn best by doing! And, in the USM, *doing* is administered in several layers. Testing is one layer, which forms part of the revision process that was explained in the previous section. But it is merely the first layer: for testing knowledge of facts only stimulates a superficial level of understanding. Deeper levels are accessed by solving problems and answering questions, by applying the knowledge to other fields, and, ultimately, by using the current knowledge to solve unsolved problems and to derive new ideas. That is, in general, moving away from being a receiver of knowledge to being a creator of knowledge.

The level of reinforcement should be commensurate with your purpose. If you are learning a topic in preparation for an exam that evaluates your knowledge of the facts—e.g., in multiple-choice form—then deeper learning is not necessary, and the Reinforce step can be curtailed. However, for problem-solving and lateral-thinking based evaluations, or for job-related applications of a topic's ideas, the Reinforce step is vital.

PROCEDURE

The Reinforce step should include, where available, the following components:

1. (Test yourself on the contents of the topic—i.e., revision.)
2. **Solve basic problems** or answer open questions that involve the concepts of the topic.
3. **Complete puzzles and more advanced problems** that involve (or partially involve) the concepts of the topic.
4. **If you are studying for a specific exam, practise, under timed conditions, previous exam papers.** And continue

to practise until you are able to score full marks on each such paper.

5. **Apply the concepts of the topic in different contexts**, and where possible, to unrelated fields (i.e., stimulating transferability).
6. **Play content-related games** (if available).
7. **Put the knowledge to practical use.** For example, say you were studying the mathematics of neural networks: try to code such an algorithm on a computer. If you were learning organic chemistry: experiment in a laboratory. Etc.

GENERAL CONSIDERATIONS

The secret to success in the Reinforce step is to make it diversified and fun. This can be achieved by performing the additional activities listed above in a playful manner. Here are some suggestions:

- **Challenge yourself.** Challenge yourself on either the time you take to solve a problem or the level of difficulty you are able to unravel.
- **Keep it stress free.** You should maintain a stress-free environment while you test and challenge yourself. Espouse a mentality of nonchalance—of not caring about the result, just enjoying the process. Only when you feel that you are ready to demonstrate your knowledge in formal testing, debate or discussion, do so. Until then, covertly build your knowledge and confidence in your ability.
- **Introduce rewards.** When you test yourself, reward good results—or improved scores—with a gourmet meal, a tasty snack, or some other pleasurable event. For

example, an ice cream or a favourite chocolate bar (if diet permits). Essentially, reward yourself with whatever you find pleasurable. However, do not overdo this: only reward significant improvements (too frequent a reward loses its value).

- **Vary the surroundings.** For example, solve physics problems on the beach; trek through a forest, stop for a picnic and write a poem; or go fishing and analyse a piece of literature while waiting for the fish to bite.
- **Watch movies or read other books related to the topic.** In particular, documentaries about the topic; or, even better, works of fiction that stretch the ideas of the topic in thought-provoking ways, if any exist.
- **Join forums.** Join forums to debate the topic.

The above suggestions and examples are there to provide direction. Use your imagination and come up with ideas that are pleasurable and fun for you.

In closing, let us expand on a crucial point alluded to above: Learning should be stress free. However, in a society where evaluation of knowledge is necessary, stress is quite often a principal factor. The key to avoiding this is to plan your study schedule carefully, so that stress is never part of the learning process—it then only remains a part, and a minor one at that, of the evaluation process.

To achieve this, if you are enrolled in formal study, attempt to learn the topic before the beginning of the academic year. Or, at least, find the order of instruction and learn each part of the topic ahead of the class. This way, there will be no stress during the learning period; there would be no stress if a pop quiz is given. In fact, pop quizzes will offer an excellent opportunity to reinforce your knowledge further. The classes themselves will form part of the Reinforce step, and would deepen your level of understanding further—and certainly further than other members of the class. Altogether, the added confidence and deeper exposure will remove stress completely, and the memory and the overall impact of the learning will be longer-lasting and more profound.

In sum, control stress by having a clear study plan that is ahead of the formal instruction schedule. And execute your plan assiduously, even as you find yourself light-years ahead of the class or others in the field.

USM

For completeness, consolidated below is the full USM procedure. And in the section that follows, a shorter version for quick reference is also available.

THE USM PROCEDURE IN FULL

STEP 1: STUDY MATERIALS

Gather all the materials necessary for the completion of the study. This may include textbooks, study aids, supplementary papers/books, class notes, class exercises, problem sets, previous exam papers, content-related games, content-related videos, etc.

STEP 2: STATE OF MIND

Enter a relaxed state of mind using your preferred concentration technique from Part 1 (spend at least five minutes, but preferably ten). Buddhist breathing (Technique 3 from Part 1) is the recommended approach, but stick to whichever technique works best for you (while also considering what your environment and circumstances permit).

STEP 3: LAYERED READING

Apply layered reading in order to process the reading materials:

1. **Preview.**
2. **Subconsciously read** through the study texts (optional).
3. **Skim:**
   a. Mark difficult sections with a dot.
   b. Highlight or underline key points—the concepts that together form the topic. Or if a whole paragraph is of interest, mark a vertical line at the margin and add the letter V next to it.
   c. Once you finished skimming, complete the main branches of the Revision Map.
4. **Speed read:**
   a. Slow down at sections marked with a dot.
   b. Mark difficult sections with a question mark.
   c. Highlight or underline key points—the concepts that together form the topic. Or if a whole paragraph is of interest, mark a vertical line at the margin and add the letter V next to it.
   d. Once you finished reading, add to the Revision Map the key concepts that were identified and annotated in this step of the procedure.
5. **Review:**
   a. Slow down at sections marked with a question mark.
   b. Highlight, underline or mark with the letter V additional key points if necessary.
   c. Once you finished reviewing, add to the Revision Map the key concepts that were identified and annotated in this step of the procedure.

STEP 4: NOTE-TAKING

Begin writing your linear notes. These should contain all the key concepts of the topic in your own words. Therefore, go through the text again and add to your linear notes every concept that was annotated. **When writing these notes, spend whatever time is necessary to reason through the topic.** It is at this stage that you can stop at sections that have not been clearly understood in earlier reading. Reason through the topic until it is fully understood—and it is this understanding that is to be contained in the linear notes.

LINEAR NOTES PROCEDURE:

1. **All the concepts in the topic should be captured.** Every concept developed in the text should be captured in the linear notes. Taking notes and summarising does not mean omitting content.

2. **Use your own words.** Each concept should be summarised using your own words. This first requires reasoning through the ideas developed in the text and then articulating this understanding in your own words.

3. **Keep it brief.** Try to explain each concept in a single paragraph—ideally less than three lines in length. Your explanation should be as brief as possible. The key motivation is to have a concise record to which you can later refer in order to immediately regain the understanding you had already arrived at in the past.

4. **Hierarchical structure.** Stick to the following hierarchical structure:
   a. Each main division heading should be double underlined.
   b. Each subdivision heading (subheading) should be single underlined.
   c. For each concept:
      i. The concept should be preceded by a bullet point.
      ii. The key word (preferably written in capital letters) describing the concept should follow the bullet point.

iii. The explanation (in your own words) of the concept should follow the key word.

iv. Each subsidiary concept (if there are any) should indent a new line and be preceded by a hyphen— or be preceded by roman numerals if order is important.

v. Include diagrams and formulae (if there are any) with the concept. Each diagram or formula should be surrounded by a box.

Then add to the Revision Map all additional concepts and connections gleaned while writing the linear notes.

REVISION MAP PROCEDURE:

1. **Begin at the centre** of a blank page; there draw an image representing the topic.

2. **From the main image draw branches** that represent the key divisions of the topic.

3. **On each branch write the key word** that represents the division.

   a. A branch should only be as long as its key word.

   b. Use only a key word, nothing else—do not write full sentences or explanations.

   c. If there is an image that represents the key word well, use that image instead of the key word. **In general, in a Revision Map, images are preferred to words.**

   d. If the image only mildly reminds you of the key word, then put both on the branch to avoid confusion when reviewing.

   e. An excellent combination of the above ideas is to use the image for the key word as the branch—i.e., the image itself is the branch—and to place the key word on top of it (for examples, see the Revision Maps included in this book).

4. **You can then further divide the topic into its subdivisions** by drawing branches from each (division's) key word.

   a. The branches should be thickest near the centre and become thinner as they extend outwards. So the main divisions of the topic will have thick branches whilst the subdivisions will have thinner branches, and so on.

   b. Proceed in the same manner as with the topic's divisions. Continue using key words exclusively: one key word per branch.

   c. Use an image instead of a key word where the image interpretation is obvious; otherwise, use both. If there is no image that comes to mind for a particular key word, then do not place an image—it is not compulsory, but it is preferable where feasible.

5. **Use boxes to contain items that are not key words.** For example, an important formula should be placed in a box next to the key word that describes it.

6. **Proceed in this manner, possibly through further subdivisions**, until the main themes and concepts have been exposed on a single page.

STEP 5: MEMORISE

(Create/maintain a list of unique identifiers.)

MEMORISE THE REVISION MAP:

1. **Link or Loci.** The recommended approach is to use either the Link System or the Loci System, and to do so under the following considerations:

   a. If the Link System is the chosen approach, each key concept is linked in clockwise order to the concepts that are connected to it. You begin with the innermost concept—the topic's name—and link the key concepts on its branches in clockwise order. You then repeat the procedure for each of the aforementioned key concepts and the ideas on their respective sub-branches, and so forth until the entire Revision Map has been memorised. For example, link the topic's name to KEY WORD 1, link KEY WORD 1 to KEY WORD 2, and link KEY WORD 2 to KEY WORD 3. Then, for the sub-branches, link KEY WORD 1 to KEY WORD 1.1, link KEY WORD 1.1 to KEY WORD 1.2; then link KEY WORD 2 to KEY WORD 2.1, link KEY WORD 2.1 to KEY WORD 2.2, link KEY WORD 2.2 to KEY WORD 2.3, etc.

b. If the Loci System is the chosen approach, some preparatory work is required: using the Loci System involves dedicating a town (real or imaginary) to your studies. Each building and location (e.g., house, shop, office, tower block, shopping mall, road, junction, park, etc.) in the town can store information. If, for example, you create an imaginary town, each road can contain a field of study, each house can then contain a topic, each room in the house can store one of the concepts on the main branches, and each item in the room can store one of the concepts on the sub-branches. You would then peg the concepts from the Revision Map in clockwise order to the corresponding elements of the locus.

2. **Revision.**

a. Review, at the very least, using the optimal revision schedule. Given that the linear notes are also reviewed according to the optimal revision schedule, you should review the Revision Map every time you review the linear notes (see next procedure). The review should involve calling the information to mind unaided by the Revision Map—not simply rereading it.

b. In addition, and since the Revision Map is so short and concise, it is recommended to review it every other day.

MEMORISE THE LINEAR NOTES:

1. **Read and understand.** Read through the linear notes a few times to make sure that the topic has been clearly understood.

2. **Do not memorise verbatim.** It is not necessary to memorise the linear notes word for word: only the key facts and subtle points should be memorised.

3. **Use the memory techniques.** Memorise the key facts and subtle points using the techniques introduced in the Part 2 of the book. Note, however, that it is **not necessary** to memorise the structure of the linear notes (i.e. the order of the headings and subheading, or in which section each fact resides). As the structure was already memorised with the Revision Map, all that remains is to memorise the key facts and subtle points: in general, to memorise information in the linear notes that cannot be discerned from the Revision Map.

4. **Revision.** This is of utmost importance:

a. Immediately after memorising each piece of data in the linear notes (calling the time at which this occurs T_0), call to mind the scene or image, to ensure that the data has been absorbed.

b. An hour later, that is, $T_0 + 1$ hour, review your linear notes by reading them again and testing yourself on the data you memorised. For each such piece of data, unaided by the linear notes (i.e., cover the relevant data with your hand), attempt to recall the information and review the scene/image.

c. Ideally, a couple of hours before going to bed, that is, $T_0 + 12$ hours (assuming that the data was learnt in the morning; otherwise, simply perform 12 hours after T_0), review again.

d. Review again the next day, i.e., $T_0 + 24$ hours.

e. Review once more a week later, i.e., $T_0 + 1$ week.

f. Review once more two weeks later, i.e., $T_0 + 2$ weeks.

g. Review once more a month later, i.e., $T_0 + 1$ month.

h. Review once more three months later, i.e., $T_0 + 3$ months.

i. Review once more six months later, i.e., $T_0 + 6$ months.

j. Review once more twelve months later, i.e., $T_0 + 12$ months.

STEP 6: REINFORCE

1. **Solve basic problems** or answer open questions that involve the concepts of the topic.

2. **Complete puzzles and more advanced problems** that involve (or partially involve) the concepts of the topic.

3. **If you are studying for a specific exam, practise, under timed conditions, previous exam papers.** And continue to practise until you are able to score full marks on each such paper.

4. **Apply the concepts of the topic in different contexts**, and where possible, to unrelated fields (i.e., stimulating transferability).

5. **Play content-related games** (if available).

6. **Put the knowledge to practical use.** For example, say you were studying the mathematics of neural networks:

try to code such an algorithm on a computer. If you were learning organic chemistry: experiment in a laboratory. Etc.

THE USM PROCEDURE (QUICK REFERENCE)

1. **Gather all the materials** necessary for the completion of the study.
2. **Enter a relaxed state of mind** using your preferred concentration technique from Part 1.
3. **Apply layered reading** in order to process the reading materials:
   a. Preview.
   b. Subconsciously read through the study texts (optional).
   c. Skim.
   d. Speed read.
   e. Review.
4. **Note-taking**.
   a. Reason clearly in your mind every aspect of the topic. And, as you do so:
   b. Complete a set of linear notes.
   c. Complete the Revision Map.
5. **Memorise**:
   a. (Create/maintain a list of unique identifiers.)
   b. Memorise the Revision Map.
   c. Memorise the linear notes.
   d. Revision: Review according to the optimal revision schedule.
6. **Reinforce**:
   a. Solve problems, puzzles, open questions and exams.

b. Apply the concepts of the topic in different contexts, and where possible, to unrelated fields.
c. Play content-related games (if available).
d. Put the knowledge to practical use.

SUMMARY AND REVISION MAP

KEY POINTS

- The USM builds on all the concepts introduced earlier in the book.
- A Revision Map provides a structural representation of the topic.
- Linear notes provide a terse, yet full, coverage of the topic in the practitioner's own words.
- Revision Maps and linear notes must be used together—neither is sufficient on its own.
- Revision is crucial for long-term retention.
- Stress-free testing is a critical part of the revision process.
- For superior results, all the Revision Maps—encompassing all previously studied topics—should be reviewed every other day.
- The Reinforce step is important for deeper levels of understanding.

REVISION MAP

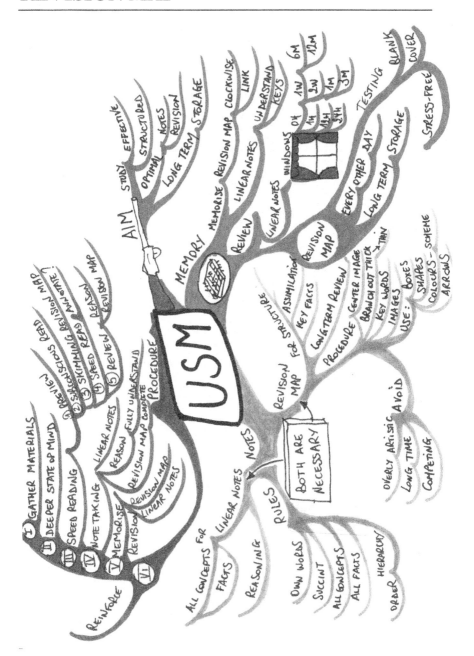

Part 5

RAPID MATH

Mathematics is the queen of sciences and arithmetic is the queen of mathematics.

—Carl Friedrich Gauss

THE AIMS OF PART 5

- To improve the ability to understand and use numbers in daily life.
- To reduce the need for a calculator or machine-assisted thinking that slows down the thought process.
- To improve problem-solving abilities.
- To provide a "power workout" for your memory skills.
- To challenge and exercise the brain.

INTRODUCTION

D irecting the mind to perform mental arithmetic is a powerful approach for keeping the mind sharp. Unfortunately, such a generalisation does not yield insight into the scale and scope of the benefits.

When one performs mental arithmetic, one first needs to be able to visualise the numbers in the mind's eye. Then there is the need to decide on the optimal technique for the calculation. This, in turn, is followed by performing the logical manipulations mentally, and doing so while simultaneously memorising each digit of the result. The whole process is then concluded by recalling the result from memory.

Dissecting the mental arithmetic process in this manner illustrates the faculties required—and thus exercised—during the calculation process. Mental calculations test one's memory and concentration abilities to their extremes: it is a superb all-round brain exercise.

Apart from keeping the mind sharp, another advantage of practising mental arithmetic is that, by being able to calculate mentally, the train of thought is rarely disrupted by the need to reach out for a calculator, a smartphone or a computer in order to find a result from which further thinking can follow. The ability to do so is significant for some jobs more than others; it is especially important where quick decision-making is a necessary skill for remaining profitable. A financial markets trader is a typical example, but market vendors for physical goods and other professional hagglers also tend to have excellent arithmetic skills.

Becoming proficient at mental arithmetic will open a gateway into the world of numbers and set a cornerstone upon which more abstract thinking can be placed on sounder footing. Moreover, such practice was also found to improve general problem-solving abilities and logical thinking (see the Scientific Evidence chapter for more information)—which are crucial in the evaluation and application of knowledge.

To be clear, rapid mental arithmetic is not a critical part of the USM. It is included with this manual for the abovementioned reasons, for they complement the effort of improving one's ability to understand, to learn, and to remember.

A note regarding the exposition in this part of the book: With arithmetic, as is the case with mathematics in general, examples are a fundamental part of learning process. Therefore, the exposition incorporates examples with every technique and variation. The reader is advised to follow the examples closely until the logic is clearly understood.

WORLD RECORDS

To provide some flavour (and motivation) of what can be achieved with a trained mind, below is a sample of recently recorded feats of mental arithmetic.

Category	Result	Record Holder	Year
Multiplying two 13-digit numbers.	28 seconds	Shakuntala Devi	1980
Adding ten 10-digit numbers.	10 correct results in 191 seconds	Naofumi Ogasawara	2012
Extracting the square root of a 6-digit number (to eight decimal places).	10 correct results in 135 seconds	Rhea Shah	2014
Multiplying two 8-digit numbers.	10 correct results in 295 seconds	Marc Jornet Sanz	2014

SCIENTIFIC EVIDENCE

Functional neuroimaging research suggests that the parietal brain circuits are the predominant areas involved during the performance of mental arithmetic. However, there are variations to this result, and these appear to be driven primarily by the individual's stage of development and proficiency level. It was shown that, in both children and adults, gaining arithmetic competence is reflected by a shift of activation from the frontal brain regions to the parietal regions.

Furthermore, with higher levels of proficiency in mental arithmetic, a shift in activation was also reported to occur within the parietal regions—with significant increases in angular gyrus activation. It was shown that the pattern of activation for "calculating prodigies"—those viewed as innately exceptional in their ability to perform mental arithmetic—was similar to the pattern observed for individuals who attained higher mathematical abilities through extensive training. Both of these groups displayed stronger activation of the left angular gyrus while solving arithmetic problems.

The immediate conclusion is that trained experts and calculating prodigies are able to tackle mathematical problems with a different toolkit. Most notable, however, is that the activation of such circuits was found to change with training. Research on the development of children as well as adult performance with training have shown that the activation of circuits of the brain that are crucial for mathematical skills can change with training, experience and developmental growth. In 2003, Delazer et al. have shown that adults who had received training in mental arithmetic have demonstrated higher activation of the left angular gyrus relative to adults who had not received such training.

Other research, focusing on abacus experts performing mental arithmetic (unaided by an abacus), has shown that, through intensive training and practice, solving simple and complex problems resulted in similar patterns of activation. Whereas, for non-experts the pattern of activation involved larger variations between simple and complex problems. In essence, the experts' neural pathways have connected more effectively for the purposes of mental arithmetic, thus resulting in exceptional—and effortless—calculation abilities.

The scientific literature to date suggests that, with training, mental arithmetic abilities can be improved in most cases. And this improvement is associated with the structural changes to the aforementioned parietal regions. Most remarkably, though, it was also found that the improvement and corresponding structural changes have significant spill-over effects. Specifically, it was shown that arithmetic training improves the ability to solve more complex mathematical problems and furthers general problem-solving skills.

In conclusion: practising mental arithmetic has several documented benefits. The immediate and obvious ones relate to the actual computational task and the supporting memory functions involved in the calculation. The less obvious, yet highly significant, are the transfer effects to other mathematical abilities and general problem-solving skills.

TECHNIQUES

This chapter introduces the techniques that together form the Rapid Math System. Only optimal methods are included: the focus is on efficiency and pragmatism, rather than a complete exposition of all the tricks and techniques available.

According to the author's experience, relying on a multitude of tricks that are each applicable under different circumstances, forces the practitioner to spend valuable time in search of the right tool. Instead, that valuable time is better put to use in actual computation. Familiarity with a few tricks that are frequently applicable, combined with a powerful general technique, is an approach that offers better performance overall. Furthermore, too frequent a reliance on tricks leads to a reduction in actual computation practice—with search-recall practice dominating. Such an approach would, in accordance with the scientific evidence detailed in the previous chapter, benefit less from the favourable effects of arithmetic training.

Therefore, for each arithmetic operation, the exposition of this chapter focuses on a principal technique as well as carefully selected complementary tricks. The system for each arithmetic operation is then completed by providing a strategy for when each element should be deployed.

ADDITION

The most natural place to start an exposition of mental arithmetic is with addition. For it is the simplest of arithmetic operations, and it forms a fundamental component of more complex operations.

For addition, the approach taken in the Rapid Math System is simple and requires no calculation tricks: the principal technique is applied equally to all addition problems.

PROCEDURE

1. **Preparation:** If the numbers to be added together are not in writing, memorise them as they are being read out (using either the Link System or the Loci System). However, once you become proficient with the technique, you can simply add the numbers along as each one is being read out to you. If, on the other hand, the numbers are written down, this step is not necessary.
2. **Mentally right-align all the numbers.** That is, ensure that the digits belonging to the *ones column* are vertically aligned with each other; the digits belonging to the *tens column* are vertically aligned with each other; and so forth.
3. **Begin with the rightmost column (the *ones column*) and add all its digits together.** If the result is greater than ten, reserve the rightmost digit for the answer and carry the rest to the next column.
4. **Working from right to left, proceed to the next column.** Start with any number carried over from the previous step and add to it the digits in the column. With the addition of each digit, mentally vocalise the digit from the previous step (Step 3) that was reserved for the answer. The mental vocalisation is there to ensure that this portion of the answer is not lost prior to the Memorise step.

5. **Memorise the two rightmost digits of the answer.** Use the Link System: link this first portion of the answer to *pus*.

6. **Repeat the procedure.** Proceed to subsequent columns by starting with the number carried over (if any) and adding to it the digits in the column.

7. **Continue by memorising two digits of the answer at a time.** Link each two new digits of the answer to the previous two digits. (Use the Numbers List to retrieve the unique identifier for each such pair of digits.) Alternatively, for added speed, in the final step, all the resulting digits can be memorised by linking them directly to the previous two digits.

EXAMPLE 1

Add 4,567 to 8,977:

$$\begin{array}{r} 4{,}567 \\ +\quad 8{,}977 \\ \hline \end{array}$$

- Begin by adding the rightmost digits together: $7 + 7 = 14$. Reserve the *4* for the answer and carry the *1*.
- Take the carried *1* and add to it the digits in the next column (second from the right): $1 + 6 + 7 = 14$. With the reserved *4* from the previous step, we now have *144*.
- Link *44* to *pus* and carry the *1* to the next column. The image could be that of a roaring lion (for *44*) made out of pus.
- Take the carried *1* and add to it the digits in the next column (third from the right): $1 + 5 + 9 = 15$. Carry the *1* and reserve the *5* for the answer.

- Proceed as before to the next column and add to the carried *1* the digits in the column: **1 + 4 + 8 = 13.** Combined together with the *5* reserved in the previous step, *135* is the final portion of the answer.
- Memorise *135* by linking its image/s to the previous image in the answer, *lion.* You can either link *mule* (for 35) to *lion* and then *tie* (for 1) to *mule,* or you can just link *tamale* (for 135) to *lion.*

To recall the answer, think of pus and you will receive the answer from right to left.

Answer: 13,544

EXAMPLE 2

Add together 135,897, 448,185, 399,407, 915,323, and 466:

$$
\begin{array}{r}
135,897 \\
448,185 \\
399,407 \\
915,323 \\
+ \quad 466 \\
\hline
\end{array}
$$

- Add together the digits in the rightmost column: **7 + 5 + 7 + 3 + 6 = 28.** Carry the *2* and reserve the *8.*
- Take the carried *2* and to it add the digits in the second column (second from the right): **2 + 9 + 8 + 0 + 2 + 6 = 27.** With the reserved *8* from the previous step, we now have *278.*
- Link *78* to *pus* and carry the *2* to the next column.
- To the carried *2* add the digits in the third column: **2 + 8 + 1 + 4 + 3 + 4 = 22.** Carry the *2* and reserve the other *2.*

- Proceed to the fourth column and to the carried *2* add the digits in this column: **2 + 5 + 8 + 9 + 5 = 29**. With the reserved *2* from the previous step, we now have *292*.
- Link *92* to *78* and carry the *2*.
- To the carried *2* add the digits in the fifth column: **2 + 3 + 4 + 9 + 1 = 19**. Carry the *1* and reserve the *9*.
- To the carried *1* add the digits in the final column: **1 + 1 + 4 + 3 + 9 = 18**. With the reserved *9* from the previous step, we now have *189*.
- Link *189* to *92*.

Answer: 1,899,278

EXAMPLE 3: NOTHING TO CARRY

In this example we demonstrate what to do when there is nothing to carry.

$$
\begin{array}{r}
1,234,501 \\
98,415,200 \\
874,521,898,700 \\
2,465,001 \\
+ \quad 54,877,775,600 \\
\hline
\end{array}
$$

- Add together the digits in the rightmost column: **1 + 0 + 0 + 1 + 0 = 2**. Nothing to carry; reserve the *2*.
- Nothing carried, so simply add the digits in the second column (second from the right): since all are zero, the sum is zero. With the reserved *2* from the previous step, we now have *02*.
- Link *02* to *pus*—i.e., link *sun* to *pus*. Perhaps think of the sun as emitting pus instead of rays.

- Nothing carried, so proceed to the third column and add the digits therein: **5 + 2 + 7 + 0 + 6 = 20**. Carry the *2* and reserve the *0*.
- Then, from the fourth column onwards, proceed as in the previous examples.

Answer: 929,501,789,002

LIMITS??

There really are no limits to the technique. You can, in fact, add up in your mind more than what your calculator or even Microsoft Excel can handle. For example, try adding the following numbers on your calculator or in Excel:

4,565,897,987,056,132,165,798 + 25,648,912,303,548,943,152

The operands will be rounded off (Excel has a precision of 15 significant figures), and the answer provided will not be accurate to the nearest integer. However, in your mind, you can perform this calculation quickly and precisely.

MULTIPLICATION TRICKS

Unlike addition, when performing multiplication, we first check whether simple tricks can simplify the calculation and, if so, we deploy them. If no simplification is offered, we proceed by applying the Principal Multiplication Technique, which can be used for any multiplication problem. The overall strategy is as follows:

1. Are both numbers reasonably close to the same 100?

    a.   Examples: **107 x 103**, both are marginally over 100; **89 x 92**, both are marginally below 100; **212 x 198**, one is marginally above 200 and the other is marginally below 200.

    b.   Examples where this is not the case: **152 x 154**, as both are too far from 100; **212 x 107**, as the two numbers are not near the same 100.

2. If so, use the tricks below.

3. If not, use the Principal Multiplication Technique.

PROCEDURE

If both numbers in the problem are close to the same 100, then the following tricks make the multiplication much simpler. The procedure is as follows:

1. **Are both numbers near and above the same 100?** If so,

    a.   Take the amount by which one of the numbers is over the nearest 100 and add it to the other number in the problem. This will form the **left part** of the answer. Link the image of this result to *multiplex* (multiplex cinema), which is the suggested unique identifier for the word multiply.

    b.   Take the amount by which each number is over the nearest 100 and multiply them together.

        i.   If the result consists of two digits, the two digits together form the **right part** of the answer.

        ii.   If the result consists of more than two digits, keep the two rightmost digits (now the **right part** of the answer) and add the rest to the result from Clause (1.a.). In this case, also link the updated **left part** of the answer to *multiplex*.

     iii.   If the result consists of a single digit, attach a zero to its left. The two digits together form the **right part** of the answer.

   c. Link the **left part** of the answer to the **right part** of the answer.

2. **Are both numbers near and below the same 100?** If so,

   a. Take the amount by which one of the numbers is under the nearest 100 and subtract it from the other number in the problem. This will form the **left part** of the answer. Link the image of this result to *multiplex*.

   b. Take the amount by which each number is under the nearest 100 and multiply them together.

     i.   If the result consists of two digits, the two digits together form the **right part** of the answer.

     ii. If the result consists of more than two digits, keep the two rightmost digits (now the **right part** of the answer) and add the rest to the result from Clause (2.a.). In this case, also link the updated **left part** of the answer to *multiplex*.

     iii. If the result consists of a single digit, attach a zero to its left. The two digits together form the **right part** of the answer.

   c. Link the **left part** of the answer to the **right part** of the answer.

3. **Is one number near and below, and the other number near and above, the same 100?** If so,

   a. Take the amount by which one of the numbers is over the nearest 100 and add it to the other number in the problem. Then multiply by 100. Link the image of this result to *multiplex*.

   b. Take the amount by which each number is away from the nearest 100 and multiply them together. Subtract this from the result in Clause (3.a.). This gives you the answer.

    c. Link the answer to *multiplex*.

(Note carefully that both numbers have to be near and above/below the **same** 100.)

Also note that, in the procedure above, certain instances require an update to the portion of the answer that is linked to *multiplex* (e.g., Clause [1.b.ii]). An alternative approach is to have two objects to which we can link the answer: one for the possibly temporary portion, and one for the final answer.

For example, we could use *multitemp*, a made-up word that consists of *multiply* and *temporary*. This can then be converted into an easy-to-visualise object as before: Perhaps think of an old Mayan temple (temple for *temp*) that is being used as a multiplex cinema. Any items linked to this unique identifier will be considered as temporary. The final answer is then linked to *multiplex*.

Nevertheless, given that the answer is rarely required for long periods of time, using *multiplex* several times in succession does not commonly result in confusion. The choice of which approach to deploy is left to the reader.

EXAMPLE 1

Multiply 104 by 103:

$$\begin{array}{r} 104 \\ \times\ \underline{103} \end{array}$$

- Both numbers are near and above the same 100, so we can apply this technique.

- The amounts by which the numbers are over 100 are 4 and 3.
- Perform either **3 + 104 = 107** or **4 + 103 = 107**, in both cases the result is 107. This is the left part of the answer. Link *107* to *multiplex*. In the case of 107, either use *desk* (using the phonetic alphabet: **DeSK** = 1-0-7), or link the *1* to *multiplex* and then link the *07* to *1* (using the Numbers List). Or, alternatively, you could use a **VWY** convention, where **VW** is represented by an object from the Numbers List, and **Y** is the *colour* dimension. In the case of 107, we have *pink Taz*—so link *pink Taz* to *multiplex*.
- Now, multiply together the amount by which each number is over 100—i.e., **4 x 3 = 12**. This is the right part of the answer. Since it is only two digits in length, no further calculation is required. Link *12* to *desk*.
- Therefore, the answer is **107 & 12 = 10,712**.

EXAMPLE 2

Multiply 111 by 112:

$$
\begin{array}{r}
111 \\
\times \ \underline{112}
\end{array}
$$

- The amounts by which the numbers are over 100 are 11 and 12.
- Perform either **12 + 111 = 123** or **11 + 112 = 123**. This is the left part of the answer. Link *123* to *multiplex*.
- Now, multiply together the amount by which each number is over 100—i.e., **11 x 12 = 132**. This is the right part of the answer. Since it is three digits in length, we

need to add to the number that was linked to *multiplex* any digits beyond the two rightmost digits of the above result. Therefore, in the case of 132, split the number into *1 & 32*. Add the *1* to the left part of the answer and keep the *32* as the right part of the answer.

- That is, perform **123 + 1 = 124**—this is the updated left part of the answer. Link *124* to *multiplex*. Then link *32* to *124*.
- Therefore, the answer is **124 & 32 = 12,432**.

EXAMPLE 3

Multiply 98 by 91:

$$
\begin{array}{r}
98 \\
\times\ \ 91 \\
\hline
\end{array}
$$

- The amounts by which the numbers are below 100 are 2 and 9.
- Perform either **91 – 2 = 89** or **98 – 9 = 89**. This is the left part of the answer. Link *89* to *multiplex*.
- Now, multiply together the amount by which each number is below 100—i.e., **2 x 9 = 18**. This is the right part of the answer. Since it is only two digits in length, no further calculation is required. Link *18* to *89*.
- Therefore, the answer is **89 & 18 = 8,918**.

EXAMPLE 4

Multiply 87 by 89:

x 89

- The amounts by which the numbers are below 100 are 13 and 11.
- Perform either **89 – 13 = 76** or **87 - 11 = 76**. This is the left part of the answer. Link *76* to *multiplex*.
- Now, multiply together the amount by which each number is below 100—i.e., **11 x 13 = 143**. Since it is three digits in length, add the *1* to the left part of the answer and keep the *43* as the right part of the answer.
- That is, perform **76 + 1 = 77**—this is the updated left part of the answer. Link *77* to *multiplex*. Then link *43* to *77*.
- Therefore, the answer is **77 & 43 = 7,743.**

EXAMPLE 5: EXTENDING THE TECHNIQUE TO LARGER NUMBERS

Multiply 912 by 903:

$$912$$
$$x \quad 903$$

Both numbers are near and above the same 100. In this case, the nearest 100 is 900. The application of the technique requires only one additional step.

(Note again that both numbers must be near and above/below the <u>same</u> 100. So if, instead, we wanted to multiply 812 x 903, the trick would not work in its current form, since one number is over 800 whilst the other is over 900.)

- The amounts by which the numbers are over the nearest 100 are 12 and 3.
- Perform either **912 + 3 = 915** or **903 + 12 = 915**.
- **Additional Step**: Since the nearest 100 that the two numbers are over is 900, we need to multiply the result by 9. So calculate **915 x 9 = 8,235**. (The general rule is to multiply by the hundreds digit. That is, for numbers near 300, we would multiply by 3; for number near 500, we would multiply by 5; and, in general, for numbers near $q \cdot 100$, we would multiply by q.)
- This is the left part of the answer, so link *8,235* to *multiplex*. You could employ, say, a **VWYZ** convention, or you could simply link *82* to *multiplex* and then link *35* to *82*. [The author assumes, with much hope, that through diligent practice, by the time you read this section, the memory techniques from Part 2 will have been mastered.]
- Now, multiply together the amount by which each number is over the nearest 100—i.e., **3 x 12 = 36**. This is the right part of the answer. Since it is only two digits in length, no further calculation is required. Link *36* to *8,235*.
- Therefore, the answer is **8,235 & 36 = 823,536**.

EXAMPLE 6

Multiply 289 by 288:

$$
\begin{array}{r}
289 \\
\times \ \underline{288}
\end{array}
$$

- Both numbers are near and below the same 100. In this case, the nearest 100 is 300.

- The amounts by which the numbers are below the nearest 100 are 11 and 12.
- Perform either **288 − 11 = 277** or **289 − 12 = 277**.
- Since the nearest 100 that the two numbers are below is 300, we need to multiply the result by 3. So calculate **277 x 3 = 831**. This is the left part of the answer, so link *831* to *multiplex*.
- Now, multiply together the amount by which each number is below the nearest 100—i.e., **11 x 12 = 132**. This is the right part of the answer. However, since it is three digits in length, add the *1* to the left part of the answer and keep the *32* as the right part of the answer.
- That is, perform **831 + 1 = 832**—this is the updated left part of the answer. Link *832* to *multiplex*. Then link *32* to *832*.
- Therefore, the answer is **832 & 32 = 83,232**.

EXAMPLE 7: ONE BELOW AND ONE ABOVE 100

Multiply 104 by 91:

$$
\begin{array}{r}
104 \\
\times \quad 91 \\
\hline
\end{array}
$$

- Since both numbers are near the same 100, we can use the technique.
- The amounts by which the numbers are away from the nearest 100 are 4 and 9.
- Perform either **104 − 9 = 95** or **91 + 4 = 95**.
- Then multiply the result by 100: **95 x 100 = 9,500**.
- Link *9,500* to *multiplex*.

- Now, multiply together the amount by which each number is away from the nearest 100—i.e., **4 x 9 = 36**.
- Take the temporary answer, 9500, and from it subtract the above result. That is, perform **9,500 – 36 = 9,464**. Then link *9,464* to *multiplex*.
- Therefore, the answer is 9,464.

EXAMPLE 8

Multiply 814 by 798:

$$\begin{array}{r} 814 \\ \times\ \ 798 \\ \hline \end{array}$$

- Since both numbers are near the same 100 (in this case, 800), we can use the technique.
- The amounts by which the numbers are away from the nearest 100 are 14 and 2.
- Perform either **814 – 2 = 812** or **798 + 14 = 812**.
- Since the 100 that the two numbers are near is 800, we need to multiply the result by 8. So calculate **812 x 8 = 6,496**.
- Then multiply the result by 100: **6,496 x 100 = 649,600**.
- Link *649,600* to *multiplex*.
- Now, multiply together the amount by which each number is away from the nearest 100—i.e., **14 x 2 = 28**.
- Take the temporary answer, 649,600, and from it subtract the above result. That is, perform **649,600 – 28 = 649,572**. Then link *649,572* to *multiplex*.
- Therefore, the answer is 649,572.

EXAMPLE 9: THOUSANDS AND UPWARDS

Multiply 1,004 by 1,008:

$$
\begin{array}{r}
1,004 \\
\times \ \ 1,008 \\
\hline
\end{array}
$$

The technique here is the same, the only difference is that we now work to the nearest thousand rather than the nearest hundred. And, for that reason, the right part of the answer should be three digits in length—rather than two digits, as is the case for hundreds.

- The amounts by which the numbers are above the nearest 1,000 are 4 and 8.
- Perform either **1,004 + 8 = 1,012** or **1,008 + 4 = 1,012**.
- This is the left part of the answer, so link *1,012* to *multiplex*.
- Now, multiply together the amount by which each number is above the nearest 1,000—i.e., **4 x 8 = 32**. Since we are working with thousands, and since this result is only two digits in length, we need to attach a zero to its left. That is, **0 & 32 = 032**. This is the right part of the answer. Link *032* to *1,012*.
- Therefore, the answer is **1,012 & 032 = 1,012,032.**

EXAMPLE 10

Multiply 2,015 by 1,988:

$$
\begin{array}{r}
2,015 \\
\times \ \ 1,988 \\
\hline
\end{array}
$$

- Since both numbers are near the same 1,000 (in this case, 2,000), we can use the technique.
- The amounts by which the numbers are away from the nearest 1,000 are 15 and 12.
- Perform either **2,015 − 12 = 2,003** or **1,988 + 15 = 2,003**.
- Since the 1,000 that the two numbers are near is 2,000, we need to multiply the result by 2 (in general, for numbers near $q \cdot 1,000$, we would multiply by q). So calculate **2,003 x 2 = 4,006**.
- Then multiply the result by 1,000: **4,006 x 1,000 = 4,006,000**.
- Link *4,006,000* to *multiplex*.
- Now, multiply together the amount by which each number is away from the nearest 1,000—i.e., **15 x 12 = 180**.
- Take the temporary answer, 4,006,000, and from it subtract the above result. That is, perform **4,006,000 − 180 = 4,005,820**. Then link *4,005,820* to *multiplex*.
- Therefore, the answer is 4,005,820.

The same technique can be extended, along similar arguments, to millions, billions, and so forth.

CONTRAINDICATIONS

The tricks presented above speed up the calculation when the numbers are near the same 100 (or the same 1,000, or the same 1,000,000, etc.). When the numbers involved are too far from such mark, the tricks can still be used, but they do not offer a speedy solution. For such cases, it is better to use the Principal Multiplication Technique. Here are some examples:

- **219 x 912**: the hundreds that the numbers are above differ.
- **254 x 262**: both numbers are near the middle of the hundred, so the trick does not offer a significant simplification.
- **1,456 x 1,589**: using the thousands variation would not be advisable here, as it would amount to calculating 456 x 589. Using the nearest 100 would not be advisable either, as it would require multiplying a 4-digit number by 15; then multiplying 44 by 89, and subtracting this result from the previous.

The Principal Multiplication Technique is more efficient in such cases.

PRINCIPAL MULTIPLICATION TECHNIQUE

The Principal Multiplication Technique should be applied to all problems that cannot be easily solved with the tricks presented in the previous section. The tricks are essentially shortcuts that make the problem easier to solve, which is why they should always be deployed where appropriate. For everything else, the Principal Multiplication Technique is the approach to take.

The Principal Multiplication Technique is still a very rapid way to mentally perform the calculation, but its real advantage is its versatility. It is simple and can be applied to any multiplication problem, irrespective of the magnitudes of the numbers involved.

As with most of the techniques presented in this Part of the book, you can use the Principal Multiplication Technique to calculate in your mind more than what is feasible on a standard calculator or Microsoft Excel.

PROCEDURE

1. **If the numbers are not of the same magnitude**, add zeros to the left side of the shorter number until the two numbers are of the same length.
2. **Begin multiplying the numbers across the *multiplication arches* in the following order:**
   a. Travel from right to left.
   b. With each step in the calculation, extend the existing arches by one digit, and add an inner arch. The sequence is as follows:

Step 1	abc x def
Step 2	abc x def
Step 3	abc x def

c. In each step, for each arch, multiply together the two digits at its ends. For example, in Step 1, multiply c by f; in Step 2, multiply b by f, then multiply c by e; and in Step 3, multiply a by f, b by e, and c by d.

d. In each step, sum the results across the arches. It is recommended that you keep a running total as you multiply each arch, rather than multiply all the arches first and then sum them together. For in the former there is no need to memorise the results of the intra-arch multiplication; you only need to keep the running total.

e. In each step, the rightmost digit of the sum total from Clause (2.d.) is a digit of the answer. The rest of the digits from the sum total are carried over to the next step (where the running total commences with the amount carried over).

f. Memorise each such digit of the answer using the Loci System. In each step, peg the image for the digit from Clause (2.e.) to an object in the locus.

3. **Once the arches encompass the outermost digits** (Step 3 in the table above), with each step, remove the outermost arch and extend the remaining arches by one digit:

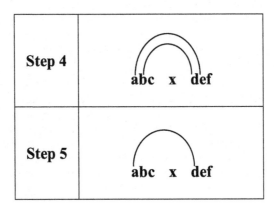

Step 4	abc x def
Step 5	abc x def

4. **Once you have multiplied the numbers connected to the last remaining arch** (Step 5), the computation is complete.
5. **You can then recover the answer by mentally travelling through your locus** and recalling the numbers that you have pegged to the objects along the way. This provides the answer from right to left.

For added clarity, let us isolate the mechanics of the arches:

- The arches are anchored at the right operand. That is, the right side of the arch remains fixed; the left side, however, shifts leftwards with each step.
- With each step, existing arches are extended (at the left operand) by one digit. For example, the arch connecting f and c in Step 1, is extended to connect f and b in Step 2.
- With each step, after extending the existing arches, one inner arch is added.

- Once all the digits are connected with arches, subsequent steps involve removing the outermost arch and extending the remaining arches. For example, the arch connecting *f* and *a* in Step 3, is removed in Step 4, and the remaining arches are extended.
- **Note that the arches are a mental instrument: you should not physically draw them when solving.**

In order to better illustrate the procedure, let us apply the technique to specific examples. In the workings that follow, let us use an example journey (across a locus) that has, in order of appearance, the following monuments along the way:

A *boat,* a *pier,* a *gate,* a *car park,* an *ice-cream van,* a *golf course,* a *flower garden,* a *statue,* a *fountain.*

(This is just to illustrate the technique; you are, as mentioned previously, advised to use your own loci.)

As before, if the problem is delivered verbally, memorise the numbers involved using either the Link System or the Loci System, and then solve. If, on the other hand, the problem is delivered in writing, there is no need to memorise the numbers in the problem: you can immediately commence the calculation.

EXAMPLE 1

Multiply 12 by 34:

Step 1	12 x 34
Step 2	12 x 34
Step 3	12 x 34

- **Step 1**: Mentally form the first arch—connecting *2* and *4*.
- Multiply together the digit at each end of this arch: **2 x 4 = 8**. This is the first digit of the answer (**from right to left**).
- Peg the unique identifier for this number, *foe*, to the first object in the locus, *boat*.
- **Step 2:** Extend the existing arch, so it now connects *1* and *4*; and add an inner arch to connect *2* and *3*.
- For each arch, multiply together the digits at its ends, and, as you do so, keep a running total of the sum. So perform **1 x 4 = 4**, keeping the result as the running total. Then perform **2 x 3 = 6**, and add it to the running total: **4 + 6 = 10**.
- Take the rightmost digit of this result, the *0*, and peg it to the next object in the locus, *pier*.

- Then take the remainder, the *1*, and carry it over to the next step.
- **Step 3:** Since all the digits of the problem are encompassed within the arches in Step 2, begin Step 3 by removing the outermost arch. Then extend the remaining arch—so that it now connects *1* and 3.
- Begin with the number that you carried over from the previous step, the *1*. **This is your start running-total**.
- Now, multiply together the digits at the ends of the arch; that is, perform **1 x 3 = 3**. And add this result to the running total: **1 + 3 = 4**.
- Since it is the last remaining arch, the above result is the final digit of the answer. Therefore, peg *4* to the third object in the locus, *gate*.
- To recall the answer, simply journey through the locus—in the same order in which it was specified (constancy in the order is critical)—and recall the numbers pegged along the way. Note, again, that the locus provides the answer from **right to left**.
- Therefore, the answer is 408.

EXAMPLE 2

Multiply 345 by 857:

Step 1	
Step 2	
Step 3	
Step 4	
Step 5	

- **Step 1**: Mentally form the first arch—connecting 5 and 7.
- Multiply together the digit at the each end of this arch: **5 x 7 = 35**. The rightmost digit, 5, is the first digit of the answer **(from right to left)**.
- So peg 5 to *boat*, and carry over the 3 to the next step.
- **Step 2:** Extend the existing arch and add an inner arch.

- Start with the amount carried over from the previous step and to it add the results of the intra-arch multiplication. That is, perform **3 + 4 x 7 = 31**. Then, with the updated running total, proceed to the inner arch: **31 + 5 x 5 = 56**. In short-form notation, the step can be written as follows: **3 + 4 x 7 + 5 x 5 = 56**.
- Peg *6* to *pier*, and carry the *5*.
- **Step 3:** Extend the existing arches and add an inner arch.
- Start with the amount carried over from the previous step, the *5*, and to it add the results of the intra-arch multiplication. That is, perform **5 + 3 x 7 + 4 x 5 + 5 x 8 = 86**.
- Peg *6* to *gate*, and carry the *8*.
- **Step 4:** Since all the digits of the problem are encompassed within the arches in Step 3, begin Step 4 by removing the outermost arch. Then extend the remaining arches.
- Start with the amount carried over from the previous step, the *8*, and to it add the results of the intra-arch multiplication. That is, perform **8 + 3 x 5 + 4 x 8 = 55**.
- Peg *5* to *car park*, and carry the other *5*.
- **Step 5:** Remove the outermost arch and extend the remaining arch.
- Start with the amount carried over from the previous step, the *5*, and to it add the results of the intra-arch multiplication. That is, perform **5 + 3 x 8 = 29**.
- Since it is the last remaining arch, the above result is the final portion of the answer. Therefore, peg *29* to *ice-cream van*.
- Notice that the entire result, *29*, was pegged to the object in the locus. As there are no further steps in the calculation, there is no place but the answer to which the *2* can be carried.
- Therefore, the answer is 295,665.

EXAMPLE 3: NUMBERS OF DIFFERENT MAGNITUDE

Multiply 897 by 23.

When the numbers to be multiplied are of different magnitude, an additional step is required. You should (mentally) add zeros to the left side of the smaller number until it is of equal length to the other. Thus, the problem becomes:

897 x 023

Proceed as before:

- **Step 1**:
  - $7 \times 3 = 21$.
  - Peg *1* to *boat*, and carry the *2*.
- **Step 2**:
  - $2 + 9 \times 3 + 7 \times 2 = 43$.
  - Peg *3* to *pier*, and carry the *4*.
- **Step 3**:
  - $4 + 8 \times 3 + 9 \times 2 + 7 \times 0 = 46$.
  - Peg *6* to *gate*, and carry the *4*.
- **Step 4**:
  - $4 + 8 \times 2 + 9 \times 0 = 20$.
  - Peg *0* to *car park*, and carry the *2*.
- **Step 5**:
  - $2 + 8 \times 0 = 2$.
  - Peg *2* to *ice-cream van*.
- Therefore, the answer is 20,631.

Note that this approach extends to numbers of any magnitude. For example, to solve **9,837,672,123 x 5,546**, it should be tackled as **9,837,672,123 x 0,000,005,546**.

EXAMPLE 4: LARGER NUMBERS

Multiply 67,583 by 88,504:

$$67,583 \times 88,504$$

The procedure remains the same, the only difference is that there are now more arches—and thus more steps.

- **Step 1**:
  - ○ 3 x 4 = 12.
  - ○ Peg *2* to *boat*, and carry the *1*.
- **Step 2**:
  - ○ 1 + 8 x 4 + 3 x 0 = 33.
  - ○ Peg *3* to *pier*, and carry the other *3*.
- **Step 3**:
  - ○ 3 + 5 x 4 + 8 x 0 + 3 x 5 = 38.
  - ○ Peg *8* to *gate*, and carry the *3*.
- **Step 4**:
  - ○ 3 + 7 x 4 + 5 x 0+ 8 x 5 + 3 x 8 = 95.
  - ○ Peg *5* to *car park*, and carry the *9*.
- **Step 5**:
  - ○ 9 + 6 x 4 + 7 x 0 + 5 x 5 + 8 x 8 + 3 x 8 = 146.
  - ○ Peg *6* to *ice-cream van*, and carry *14*.
- **Step 6**:
  - ○ 14 + 6 x 0 + 7 x 5 + 5 x 8 + 8 x 8 = 153.
  - ○ Peg *3* to *golf course*, and carry *15*.
- **Step 7**:
  - ○ 15 + 6 x 5 + 7 x 8 + 5 x 8 = 141.
  - ○ Peg *1* to *flower garden*, and carry *14*.
- **Step 8**:
  - ○ 14 + 6 x 8 + 7 x 8 = 118.
  - ○ Peg *8* to *statue*, and carry *11*.
- **Step 9**:
  - ○ 11 + 6 x 8 = 59.

      ○ Peg *59* to *fountain*.
- Therefore, the answer is 5,981,365,832.

There are no limits. One could use this technique to multiply together two 200-digit numbers, if one feels the urge to do so.

SQUARING

Squaring is simply an instance of multiplication in which the two numbers involved are the same. Therefore, the approach to squaring is similar to the one described for multiplication—with one small exception. Numbers that end with *5* should be squared using a *squaring trick*; everything else should be calculated exactly the same as for general multiplication problems.

Hence, the overall strategy is as follows:

1. **If the number to be squared ends with 5**, use the squaring trick.
2. **If the number to be squared does not end with 5, is it near a 100?** If so, use the multiplication tricks.
3. **If it neither ends with 5 nor is it near a 100**, use the Principal Multiplication Technique.

SQUARING TRICK

When squaring numbers whose rightmost digit is *5*, there is a simple trick that simplifies the calculation. The procedure for this trick is as follows:

1. **Split the number to be squared into two portions**. The rightmost *5* forms the **right portion**, and everything else is the **left portion**.

2. **Take the number that represents the left portion,**
   a. And to it add 1.
   b. Then multiply the number that represents the left portion by the result from Clause (2.a.). This provides the left part of the answer.
3. **The right part of the answer is always 25.**

EXAMPLE 1

Square the number 25:

$$25^2$$

- Begin by splitting the number into two portions: the *5* on the right and everything else on the left. That is, perform **25 = 2 & 5.**
- Take the number that represents the left portion, *2*, and to it add 1: **2 + 1 = 3.**
- Then multiply this result by the number that represents the left portion, *2*; that is, perform **3 x 2 = 6.** This gives the left part of the answer.
- The right part of the answer is always 25.
- Connect together the two parts of the answer: **6 & 25 = 625.**
- Therefore, the answer is 625.

EXAMPLE 2

Square the number 85:

$$85^2$$

- Begin by splitting the number into two portions: the *5* on the right and everything else on the left. That is, perform **85 = 8 & 5.**
- Take the number that represents the left portion, *8*, and to it add 1: **8 + 1 = 9.**
- Then multiply this result by the number that represents the left portion, *8*; that is, perform **9 x 8 = 72.** This gives the left part of the answer.
- The right part of the answer is always 25.
- Connect together the two parts of the answer: **72 & 25 = 7,225.**
- Therefore, the answer is 7,225.

EXAMPLE 3

Square the number 115:

$$115^2$$

- Begin by splitting the number into two portions: the *5* on the right and everything else on the left. That is, perform **115 = 11 & 5.**
- Take the number that represents the left portion, *11*, and to it add 1: **11 + 1 = 12.**
- Then multiply this result by the number that represents the left portion, *11*; that is, perform **12 x 11 = 132.** This gives the left part of the answer.
- The right part of the answer is always 25.
- Connect together the two parts of the answer: **132 & 25 = 13,225.**
- Therefore, the answer is 13,225.

EXAMPLE 4

Square the number 985:

$$985^2$$

- We begin by splitting the number into two portions: the *5* on the right and everything else on the left. That is, perform **985 = 98 & 5**.
- Take the number that represents the left portion, *98*, and to it add 1: **98 + 1 = 99**.
- Then multiply this result by the number that represents the left portion, *98*. Since both numbers are near 100, this calculation can be easily performed with the multiplication tricks. So, calculate **99 x 98 = 9,702**. This gives the left part of the answer.
- The right part of the answer is always 25.
- Connect together the two parts of the answer: **9,702 & 25 = 970,225**.
- Therefore, the answer is 970,225.

EXAMPLE 5

Square the number 98:

$$98^2$$

- This number does not end with 5, but it is near 100, so we can use the multiplication tricks.
- The amount by which the number is below 100 is 2.
- Perform **98 – 2 = 96**. This is the left part of the answer. Link *96* to *multiplex*.
- Now, square the amount by which the number is below 100—i.e., $2^2 = 4$. Since it is only one digit in length, add

0 to its left. That is, perform **0 & 4 = 04**. This is the right part of the answer.

- Link *04* to *96*.
- Therefore, the answer is **96 & 04 = 9,604**.

EXAMPLE 6

Square the number 362:

$$362^2$$

The number neither ends with *5* nor is it near a 100, so use the Principal Multiplication Technique.

$$362 \times 362$$

- **Step 1**:
  - ○ **2 x 2 = 4**.
  - ○ Peg *4* to *boat*.
- **Step 2**:
  - ○ **6 x 2 + 2 x 6 = 24**.
  - ○ Peg *4* to *pier*, and carry the *2*.
- **Step 3**:
  - ○ **2 + 3 x 2 + 6 x 6 + 2 x 3 = 50**.
  - ○ Peg *0* to *gate*, and carry the *5*.
- **Step 4**:
  - ○ **5 + 3 x 6 + 6 x 3 = 41**.
  - ○ Peg *1* to *car park*, and carry the *4*.
- **Step 5**:
  - ○ **4 + 3 x 3 = 13**.
  - ○ Peg *13* to *ice-cream van*.
- Therefore, the answer is 131,044.

SUBTRACTION

Similar to the procedure for addition, the strategy for subtraction does not involve any tricks. A single versatile approach is applied to all problems.

PROCEDURE

1. **Mentally right-align the two numbers.** That is, ensure that the digits belonging to the *ones column* are vertically aligned with each other; the digits belonging to the *tens column* are vertically aligned with each other; and so forth.
2. **Is the top number (the minuend) larger than the number (to be subtracted) below it (the subtrahend)?** If not, (mentally) switch their positions and add a minus sign in front of the answer.
3. **Solve from right to left.** Starting from the *ones column*, subtract the bottom digit from the one directly above it.
   a. If the top digit is smaller than the one below it, add 10 to the top digit. Then, from this sum subtract the digit below and carry a **minus 1**.
   b. If the top digit is larger than the one below, simply subtract the digit below (nothing to carry).
   c. The result of each such step is a digit of the answer **(from right to left)**.
4. **Link the digit of the result from Clause (3.c.) to** *submarine*. The word *subtraction* can be shortened to "sub", and *sub* can mean submarine. If this association seems whimsical to you, think of a different one in order to generate a unique identifier for *subtraction*.
5. **Step one column to the left, and repeat the procedure.**

   a. Any amount carried over—i.e., the minus 1, if Clause (3.a.) was applicable—should be added to the digit at the top before solving. Then proceed to solving as in Step 3 above.

   b. If nothing was carried, simply proceed to solving as in Step 3 above.

   c. With each step leftwards, link the new digit of the answer to the previous one.

As before, if the problem is delivered verbally, memorise the numbers involved using either the Link System or the Loci System, and then solve. If, on the other hand, the problem is delivered in writing, there is no need to memorise the numbers in the problem: you can immediately commence the calculation.

EXAMPLE 1

Subtract 325 from 987:

$$
\begin{array}{r}
987 \\
-\ 325 \\
\hline
\end{array}
$$

- Begin at the rightmost column. Subtract the bottom digit from the one above it; that is, perform **7 – 5 = 2**. This is the rightmost digit of the answer.
- Link *2* to *submarine*.
- Step leftwards to the next column. Subtract the bottom digit from the one above it; that is, perform **8 – 2 = 6**. This is the next digit of the answer (from right to left).
- Link *6* to *2*.
- Proceed leftwards to the final column. Subtract the bottom digit from the one above it; that is, perform **9 – 3 = 6**. This is the final digit of the answer.

- Link *6* to *6*. (Perhaps visualise a shoe tying the laces of another shoe.)
- To recall the answer, think of *submarine*, and the rest of the objects—and thus the digits of the answer from right to left—will flow into conscious awareness.
- Therefore, the answer is 662.

Note that for subtraction problems that involve large numbers, it is advisable to use the Loci System, which obviates the issue of repeated digits. For example, say the answer to a subtraction problem was the following number: 54,555,535,535,553. It is easy to see that some confusion may occur with the links that involve *5*, due to it featuring repeatedly in the answer. With the Loci System, no such confusion can occur.

An alternative solution is to solve—and thus memorise—in digit pairs or triplets. The larger "chunks" reduce the possibility for confusion when recalling the answer. This approach will be covered later in this section.

EXAMPLE 2

Subtract 3,628 from 9,571:

$$
\begin{array}{r}
9,571 \\
-\ \ 3,628 \\
\hline
\end{array}
$$

- Begin at the rightmost column. Subtract the bottom digit from the one above it; but since the top digit is smaller, add 10 to the top digit. That is, perform **1 + 10 = 11.**
- Then perform the subtraction with the updated top number: **11 − 8 = 3.** This is the rightmost digit of the answer.

- Link *3* to *submarine*, and carry *minus 1*.
- Next column: add *minus 1* to the top digit; i.e., perform **7 − 1 = 6**. Then subtract the bottom digit from this updated top digit; i.e., perform **6 − 2 = 4**. This is the next digit of the answer.
- Link *4* to *3*. (Nothing to carry in this step.)
- Step leftwards to the next column. Subtract the bottom digit from the one above it; but since the top digit is smaller, add 10 to the top digit. That is, perform **5 + 10 = 15**.
- Then perform the subtraction with the updated top number: **15 − 6 = 9**. This is the next digit of the answer.
- Link *9* to *4*, and carry a *minus 1* to the next step.
- Step leftwards to the final column, and add the carried *minus 1* to the top digit; i.e., perform **9 − 1 = 8**. Then subtract the bottom digit from this updated top digit; i.e., perform **8 − 3 = 5**. This is the final digit of the answer.
- Link *5* to *9*.
- To recall the answer, think of *submarine*, and the rest of the objects—and thus the digits of the answer from right to left—will flow into conscious awareness.
- Therefore, the answer is 5,943.

EXAMPLE 3: SOLVING IN PAIRS

After some practice, you may suspect that solving two digits at a time is actually a superior approach. That is indeed the case, for it is more efficient to memorise two digits at a time, and the corresponding increase in calculation complexity is marginal.

Such approach requires one to memorise less objects altogether, and the flow of calculations is interrupted less frequently. The procedure is overall the same; the only difference is that solving—and thus memorising—is performed two digits at a time instead of one.

Subtract 354,978 from 665,802:

$$
\begin{array}{r}
665,802 \\
- \ 354,978 \\
\hline
\end{array}
$$

- Begin with the rightmost two columns. Subtract the bottom 2-digit number from the 2-digit number above it. But since the top 2-digit number is smaller, **add 100** to the top number (rather than adding 10, as we are solving two digits at a time). That is, perform **02 + 100 = 102**.
- Then perform the subtraction with the updated top number: **102 − 78 = 24**. These are the rightmost two digits of the answer.
- Link *24* to *submarine*, and carry *minus 1*.
- Step leftwards to the next two columns, and add the carried *minus 1* to the top 2-digit number; i.e., perform **58 − 1 = 57**. Then subtract the bottom 2-digit number from this updated top number; i.e., perform **57 − 49 = 08**. These are the next two digits of the answer.
- Link *08* to *24*. (Nothing to carry in this step.)
- **It is important to note that this portion of the solution is *08* rather than *8*.** This is a consequence of solving two digits at a time.
- Step leftwards to the final two columns. Subtract the bottom 2-digit number from the 2-digit number above it. That is, perform **66 − 35 = 31**. This is the final portion of the answer.
- Link *31* to *08*.
- To recall the answer, think of *submarine*, and the rest of the objects—and thus the digits of the answer from right to left—will flow into conscious awareness.

- Therefore, the answer is 310,824.

EXAMPLE 4: NEGATIVE ANSWERS

When the number at the top (the minuend) is smaller than the one at the bottom (the subtrahend), the answer will be negative. It is therefore important to check, before solving, whether the number at the top is indeed larger. If it is not larger, (mentally) switch the positions of the two numbers, and add a minus sign in front of the answer. Below is an example.

Subtract 415,691 from 414,729:

$$\begin{array}{r} 414,729 \\ - \ \ 415,691 \\ \hline \end{array}$$

The top number is clearly smaller than the one below, so switch the numbers and remember to add a minus sign in front of the answer:

$$\begin{array}{r} 415,691 \\ - \ \ 414,729 \\ \hline \end{array}$$

- Begin with the rightmost two columns. Perform **91 – 29 = 62**.
- Link *62* to *submarine*.
- Then, step two columns leftwards and perform **56 – 47 = 09**.
- Link *09* to *62*.
- Finally, for the last two columns, calculate **41 – 41 = 0**.
- Remember to add a minus sign in front of the answer.
- Therefore, the answer is -962.

DIVISION

Division involves a single technique that should be applied to all problems.

To memorise the answer to a division problem, we utilise the Loci System.

PROCEDURE

1. **Is the number being divided (the dividend) greater than the number dividing it (the divisor)?**
   a. If so, proceed to the rest of the steps.
   b. If not, repeatedly multiply the dividend by 10 until it is larger than the divisor. Each time you multiply by 10, shift the beginning of the answer by one decimal place.
2. **Search the dividend from left to right until you find a leftmost portion that is greater than the divisor.** Then on this portion perform integer division[19] by the divisor. The result is the first digit of the answer (**from left to right**).
3. **Peg the result from Step 2 to the first item in your locus.**
4. **Multiply the result obtained in Step 2 by the divisor.** Then subtract this product from the leftmost portion of the dividend that was used in Step 2.
5. **If after subtracting there is a remainder:**
   a. If there are no further (unused) digits in the dividend, go to Step 7.

---

[19] *Integer division* of a dividend x by a divisor y is a division in which the remainder is discarded. It involves finding the largest integer that, when multiplied by y, yields a product that is smaller than or equal to x.

b. Otherwise, append the next (unused) digit in dividend to the right side of the remainder. Let us name such appended remainder as the *intra-dividend*.

c. If the intra-dividend is smaller than the divisor, go to Step 6.

d. Otherwise, on the intra-dividend perform integer division by the divisor. The result is the next digit of the answer.

e. Peg the result from Clause (5.d.) to the next item in the locus.

f. Multiply the result obtained in Clause (5.d.) by the divisor. Then subtract this product from the intra-dividend that was used in Clause (5.d).

g. **Repeat Step 5** until there is no remainder, or until there are no more dividend digits to append—in which case, go to Step 7.

6. **If, after appending another digit in Clause (5.b.), the intra-dividend is smaller than the divisor**, simply peg *0* to the next item in the locus, and repeat Step 5. (Repeat this loop until the intra-dividend is larger than the divisor.)

7. **If there are no further (unused) dividend digits to append**, simply append a *0* to the right side of the remainder (or to the intra-dividend, where applicable)— this yields the intra-dividend (or the updated intra-dividend, where applicable). In addition, peg *Johnny Depp*[20] to the next item in the locus. Then,

a. If the intra-dividend is larger than the divisor, on the intra-dividend perform integer division by the divisor. Then peg the result to the next item in the locus.

---

[20] *Johnny Depp* is the unique identifier for *decimal point*. For decimal place is commonly abbreviated as d.p.—hence Depp.

b. If the intra-dividend is smaller than the divisor, append another *0* to the right side of the intra-dividend, and peg *0* to the next item in the locus. Repeat until the updated intra-dividend is larger than the divisor. Once it is larger, on the intra-dividend perform integer division by the divisor, and peg the result to the next item in the locus.

c. Multiply the result—from either Clause (7.a.) or Clause (7.b.), whichever applies—by the divisor. Then subtract this product from the intra-dividend.

d. If in Clause (7.c.) there is a remainder, to it append a *0*.

e. **Repeat Clauses (7.a.) to (7.d.)** until either no remainder is left or the answer has been calculated to the desired number of decimal places.

The procedure appears to be long and complicated but, in fact, it is much easier to perform than its written description allows to portray. After only a little practice, the procedure will become quite natural to execute. The examples below will better illustrate this.

For division problems that involve large numbers, the intra-dividend may be quite long. It may, therefore, prove useful to temporarily anchor the unique identifier for the intra-dividend. One approach is to peg the intra-dividend to *a fakir's rope*[21]. This then allows one to remember the intra-dividend for subsequent steps in which it is used.

For example, in Clause (5.f.) we multiply the result from the integer division by the divisor. If the intra-dividend is long, it

---

[21] *A fakir's rope* refers to the Indian rope trick, in which a fakir "magically" raises a rope skywards from a basket on the ground. The rope is usually depicted as snaking upwards to the tune of a flute, sometimes with a young assistant climbing to its peak.

may be difficult to recall it after having performed a multiplication that did not involve it. But recall it we must, for the product of the multiplication is subtracted from it shortly afterwards.

Pegging the intra-dividend to *a fakir's rope* thus avoids confusion during the calculation procedure; it is, however, only necessary when the intra-dividend is large.

Lastly, as before, note that if the problem is delivered verbally, memorise the numbers involved using either the Link System or the Loci System, and then solve. If, on the other hand, the problem is delivered in writing, there is no need to memorise the numbers in the problem: you can immediately commence the calculation.

EXAMPLE 1

Divide 789 by 12:

$$789 \div 12$$

- Firstly, note that the dividend is larger than the divisor. So there is no need to begin the answer beyond the decimal point.
- Search the dividend to identify the leftmost portion that is greater than the divisor. Since the dividend's first digit, *7*, is smaller than the divisor, *12*, proceed further. The first two digits, *78*, however, are sufficiently large. Therefore, begin the calculation with this portion of the dividend.
- On this first portion, *78*, perform integer division by the divisor, *12*. That is, perform[22] **78 ÷ 12 = 6 + x**. Given that

---

[22] More formally, the calculation should be written as either **78 \ 12 = 6** or **⌊78 / 12⌋ = 6**, where " **** " is the integer division operator. However, to make

you are performing integer division, discard the remainder—i.e., discard **x = 6/12 = 0.5**.

- Peg *6* to the first item in your locus.
- Multiply the result from the integer division by the divisor; that is, perform **6 x 12 = 72**. Then subtract this product from the leftmost portion of the dividend that was used to derive this part of the answer (i.e., subtract from 78)—hence, perform **78 − 72 = 6**. This is the remainder.
- Append the next (unused) digit of the dividend to the right side of the remainder. That is, append *9* to the right side of *6*: **6 & 9 = 69**. This is the intra-dividend.
- On the intra-dividend perform integer division by the divisor. That is, perform **69 ÷ 12 = 5 + y**. Given that you are performing integer division, discard the *y*. The *5* is the next digit of the answer.
- Peg *5* to the next item in the locus.
- Multiply the result from the integer division by the divisor; that is, perform **5 x 12 = 60**. Then subtract this product from the intra-dividend—i.e., perform **69 − 60 = 9**. This is the new remainder.
- Since there are no more (unused) digits in the dividend, append a *0* to the right side of the remainder. That is, append *0* to the right side of *9*: **9 & 0 = 90**. This is the new intra-dividend. Then peg *Johnny Depp* to the next item in the locus, to indicate where in the answer the decimal point is placed.
- On the intra-dividend perform integer division by the divisor. That is, perform **90 ÷ 12 = 7 + z**. Given that you are performing integer division, discard the *z*. The *7* is the next digit of the answer.
- Peg *7* to the next item in the locus.

---

this text approachable to a common level of mathematical knowledge, we employ the more familiar notation.

- Multiply the result from the integer division by the divisor; that is, perform **7 x 12 = 84**. Then subtract this product from the intra-dividend—i.e., perform **90 – 84 = 6**. This is the new remainder.
- Since there are no more (unused) digits in the dividend, and since you already added a decimal point, proceed by appending a *0* to the right side of the remainder. That is, append *0* to the right side of *6*: **6 & 0 = 60**. This is the new intra-dividend.
- On the intra-dividend perform integer division by the divisor. That is, perform **60 ÷ 12 = 5**. As there is no remainder, the *5* is the final digit of the answer.
- Peg *5* to the next item in the locus.
- To recall the answer, simply journey through the locus and recall the numbers pegged along the way. Note again that, for division, the locus provides the answer from **left to right**.
- Therefore, the answer is 65.75.

EXAMPLE 2

Divide 98,256 by 564:

$$98,256 \div 564$$

- It is clear that *982* is the first leftmost portion of the dividend that is greater than the divisor. Thus perform **982 ÷ 564 = 1 + x**.
- Peg *1* to the first item in the locus.
- **Find the remainder.** First perform **1 x 564 = 564**, and then subtract this product from 982—i.e., **982 – 564 = 418**.

- **Find the intra-dividend**. Append the next (unused) dividend digit to the remainder: **418 & 5 = 4,185**. You can then peg the unique identifier for this number (perhaps *Rat-Ville*) to *a fakir's rope*, so that it is easy to recall it in subsequent steps.
- Perform **4,185 ÷ 564 = 7 + y**. Peg *7* to the next item in the locus.
- **Find the remainder**. First perform **7 x 564 = 3,948**, and then subtract this product from 4,185—i.e., **4,185 – 3,948 = 237**.
- **Find the intra-dividend**. Append the next (unused) dividend digit to the remainder: **237 & 6 = 2,376**. You can peg the unique identifier for this number to *a fakir's rope*, so that it is easy to recall it in subsequent steps.
- Perform **2,376 ÷ 564 = 4 + z**. Peg *4* to the next item in the locus.
- **Find the remainder**. First perform **4 x 564 = 2,256**, and then subtract this product from 2,376—i.e., **2,376 – 2,256 = 120**.
- **Find the intra-dividend**. Since there are no more (unused) digits in the dividend, to the remainder append a *0*. That is, **120 & 0 = 1,200**. Peg *1200* to *a fakir's rope*, and then peg *Johnny Depp* to the next item in the locus.
- Perform **1200 ÷ 564 = 2 + u**. Peg *2* to the next item in the locus.
- **Find the remainder**. First perform **2 x 564 = 1128**, and then subtract this product from 1200—i.e., **1200 – 1128 = 72**.
- **Find the intra-dividend**. Since there are no more (unused) digits in the dividend, and since you already added a decimal point, proceed by appending a *0* to the right side of the remainder. That is, perform **72 & 0 = 720**. (As before, *720* can be pegged to *a fakir's rope*.)

- Perform $720 \div 564 = 1 + v$. Peg *1* to the next item in the locus.
- You can loop through the procedure until the answer is calculated to the desired number of decimal places. If you stop now and journey through the locus, the answer from left to right would be correct to two decimal places.
- Therefore, the answer, correct to two decimal places, is 174.21.

EXAMPLE 3

In this example we demonstrate the procedure when the dividend is smaller than the divisor.

Divide 9 by 73:

$$9 \div 73$$

- As the divisor is larger than the dividend, repeatedly multiply the dividend by 10 until it is larger than the divisor. Each time you multiply by 10, shift the beginning of the answer by one decimal place. In this example, a single multiplication by 10 is sufficient. Thus perform **9 x 10 = 90**, and peg *Johnny Depp* to the first item in the locus (to remember that the answer begins with a decimal point).
- Perform the rest of the procedure on the adjusted dividend, *90*. So, **90 $\div$ 73 = 1 + x**. Peg *1* to the next item in the locus.
- **Find the remainder**. First perform **1 x 73 = 73**, and then subtract this product from 90—i.e., **90 – 73 = 17**.
- **Find the intra-dividend**. Since there are no more (unused) digits in the dividend, and since you already added a decimal point, proceed by appending a *0* to the

right side of the remainder. That is, perform **17 & 0 = 170**.

- Perform **170 ÷ 73 = 2 + y**. Peg *2* to the next item in the locus.
- **Find the remainder**. First perform **2 x 73 = 146**, and then subtract this product from 170—i.e., **170 – 146 = 24**.
- **Find the intra-dividend**. Since there are no more (unused) digits in the dividend, and since you already added a decimal point, proceed by appending a *0* to the right side of the remainder. That is, perform **24 & 0 = 240**.
- Perform **240 ÷ 73 = 3 + z**. Peg *3* to the next item in the locus.
- You can loop through the procedure until the answer is calculated to the desired number of decimal places. If you stop now and journey through the locus, the answer from left to right would be correct to three decimal places.
- Therefore, the answer, correct to three decimal places, is 0.123.

CUBE ROOT

The technique presented here for the extraction of the cube root is only applicable to integer roots. That is, it will only give a precise answer when the root is an integer. However, a simple modification of the technique provides an approximation when the root is not an integer.

Therefore, if you are informed (or are aware) that the root is an integer, use the main procedure. Otherwise, use the approximation.

Preparatory step: Memorise the table of cubes. The cubes for the numbers 0 to 9 are provided below for ease of reference. With these you will be able to extract the cube root of any number between 0 to 1,000,000.

PROCEDURE

1. **Split the number whose cube root you wish to extract into two portions.** The **right portion** consists of the three rightmost digits, whilst the **left portion** consists of the rest.
2. **In the table of cubes, find the number whose cube ends with the same digit as the right portion derived in Step 1.** This gives you the right part of the answer.
3. **Now look at the left portion. In the table of cubes, find the closest cube that is smaller than the left portion.** The number whose cube it is forms the left part of the answer.

APPROXIMATION PROCEDURE

When you are not specifically informed (or aware) that the root is an integer, the approximation procedure below should be deployed instead.

1. **Split the number whose cube root you wish to extract into two portions.** The **right portion** consists of the three rightmost digits, whilst the **left portion** consists of the rest.
2. **Focus on the left portion. In the table of cubes, find the closest cube that is smaller than the left portion.** The number whose cube it is forms the left part of the answer.

3. **From the left portion of the problem, subtract the cube found in Step 2.** Call the result the *dividend*.

4. **Find the next cube that is above the cube from Step 2.** You are essentially trying to identify between which two cubes the left portion resides. The lower boundary, which is the cube found in Step 2, is called the *lower cube*, and the upper boundary, found here, is called the *upper cube*.

5. **Subtract the lower cube from the upper cube.** Call the result the *divisor*.

6. **Divide the dividend by the divisor** (to two decimal places). Then multiply the result by 10. This is the right part of the answer.

TABLE OF CUBES

Base	Cube
0	0
1	1
2	8
3	27
4	64
5	125
6	216
7	343
8	512
9	729

EXAMPLE 1

Extract the cube root of 17,576; the root is an integer:

$$\sqrt[3]{17,576}$$

- Begin by splitting the number into two portions: **17,576 = 17 & 576**.
- The right portion consists of *576*, which ends with a *6*. Consult the table of cubes[23] and find the cube that ends with a *6*. The table suggests that the cube of 6 (which is *216*) ends with a *6*. Therefore, the right part of the answer is *6*.
- The left portion of the problem consists of *17*. Consult the table of cubes again and find the closest cube that is smaller than 17. The table suggests that 8 is the closest cube that is smaller than 17. And 8 is the cube of 2. Thus the left part of the answer is *2*.

---

[23] It is important to commit the table of cubes to memory, so that it is not physically required when performing calculations

- Therefore the answer is **2 & 6 = 26**.

EXAMPLE 2

Extract the cube root of 912,673; the root is an integer:

$$\sqrt[3]{912,673}$$

- Begin by splitting the number into two portions: **912,673 = 912 & 673**.
- The right portion consists of *673*, which ends with a *3*. Consult the table of cubes and find the cube that ends with a *3*. The table suggests that the cube of 7 (which is 343) ends with a *3*. Therefore, the right part of the answer is *7*.
- Consult the table of cubes again and find the closest cube that is smaller than 912. The table suggests that 729 is the closest cube that is smaller than 912. And 729 is the cube of 9. Thus the left part of the answer is *9*.
- Therefore, the answer is **9 & 7 = 97**.

EXAMPLE 3: APPROXIMATION

Extract the cube root of 854,365:

$$\sqrt[3]{854,365}$$

- Begin by splitting the number into two portions: **854,365 = 854 & 365**.
- Consult the table of cubes and find the closest cube that is smaller than 854. The table suggests that 729 is the closest cube that is smaller than 854. And 729 is the cube of 9. Thus the left part of the answer is *9*.
- From the left portion of the problem, *854*, subtract the cube found in the previous step, *729*. That is, perform **854 – 729 = 125**.
- Find the next cube that is above the cube from the previous step. Since 729 is the cube of 9, the next cube is the one belonging to 10, which is 1,000.
- Subtract the lower cube from the upper cube. That is, perform **1,000 – 729 = 271**.
- Divide 125 by 271 (to two decimal places). That is, perform **125 ÷ 271 = 0.46**. Then multiply by 10: **0.46 x 10 = 4.6**. This is the right part of the approximate answer.
- Therefore, the <u>approximate</u> answer is **9 & 4.6 = 94.6** [for comparison, the precise answer to four decimal places is 94.8887].

It is important to reiterate that this technique only offers an approximation.

HIGHER ORDER ROOTS

The technique introduced for the extraction of cube roots can be extended to odd higher-order roots. The main procedure and the approximation remain the same; the only differences are in the lookup table and in where the radicand should be split.

As with cube roots, the technique is only precise when the root is an integer. Therefore, as before, if you are informed (or are aware) that the root is an integer, use the main procedure. Otherwise, use the approximation.

Preparatory step: Memorise the table of higher powers. The odd powers for the numbers 0 to 9 are provided below for ease of reference.

PROCEDURE

1. **Split the number whose nth root you wish to extract into two portions**. The **right portion** consists of the n rightmost digits, whilst the **left portion** consists of the rest. The number of digits, n, is equal to the degree of the root you are attempting to extract. That is, for cube root, $n = 3$; for penteract root, $n = 5$, for hepteract root, $n = 7$, etc.

2. **In the table of higher powers, find the number whose power ends with the same digit as the right portion derived in Step 1**. This gives you the right part of the answer.

3. **Now look at the left portion. In the table of higher powers, find the closest power that is smaller than the left portion**. The number whose power it is forms the left part of the answer.

APPROXIMATION PROCEDURE

When you are not specifically informed (or aware) that the root is an integer, the approximation procedure below should be deployed instead.

1. **Split the number whose *n*th root you wish to extract into two portions.** The **right portion** consists of the *n* rightmost digits, whilst the **left portion** consists of the rest. The number of digits, *n*, is equal to the degree of the root you are attempting to extract. That is, for cube root, *n* = 3; for penteract root, *n* = 5, for hepteract root, *n* = 7, etc.

2. **Focus on the left portion. In the table of higher powers, find the closest power that is smaller than the left portion.** The number whose power it is forms the left part of the answer.

3. **From the left portion of the problem, subtract the power found in Step 2.** Call the result the *dividend*.

4. **Find the next power that is above the power from Step 2.** You are essentially trying to identify between which two powers the left portion resides. The lower boundary, which is the power found in Step 2, is called the *lower power*, and the upper boundary, found here, is called the *upper power*.

5. **Subtract the lower power from the upper power.** Call the result the *divisor*.

6. **Divide the dividend by the divisor (to two decimal places). Then multiply the result by 10.** This is the right part of the answer.

TABLE OF HIGHER POWERS

Base	Penteract (to the power of 5)	Hepteract (to the power of 7)	Enneract (to the power of 9)
0	0	0	0
1	1	1	1
2	32	128	512
3	243	2,187	19,683
4	1,024	16,384	262,144
5	3,125	78,125	1,953,125
6	7,776	279,936	10,077,696
7	16,807	823,543	40,353,607
8	32,768	2,097,152	134,217,728
9	59,049	4,782,969	387,420,489

EXAMPLE 1

Extract the fifth root of 229,345,007; the root is an integer:

$$\sqrt[5]{229,345,007}$$

- Since it is an extraction of the fifth root, split the number at the rightmost five digits: **229,345,007 = 2,293 & 45,007.**
- The right portion consists of *45,007*, which ends with a *7*. Consult the table of higher powers[24] and find the penteract that ends with a *7*. The table suggests that the penteract of 7 (which is 16,807) ends with a *7*. Therefore, the right part of the answer is *7*.
- The left portion of the problem consists of *2,293*. Consult the table of higher powers again and find the closest penteract that is smaller than 2,293. The table suggests

---

[24] As was the case for the table of cubes, it is important to commit the table of higher powers to memory, so that it is not physically required when performing calculations

that 1,024 is the closest penteract that is smaller than 2,293. And 1024 is the penteract of 4. Thus the left part of the answer is *4*.
- Therefore the answer is **4 & 7 = 47**.

EXAMPLE 2

Extract the seventh root of 17,565,568,854,912; the root is an integer:

$$\sqrt[7]{17,565,568,854,912}$$

- Since it is an extraction of the seventh root, split the number at the rightmost seven digits: **17,565,568,854,912 = 1,756,556 & 8,854,912.**
- The right portion consists of *8,854,912*, which ends with a *2*. Consult the table of higher powers and find the hepteract that ends with a *2*. The table suggests that the hepteract of 8 (which is 2,097,152) ends with a *2*. Therefore, the right part of the answer is *8*.
- The left portion of the problem consists of *1,756,556*. Consult the table of higher powers again and find the closest hepteract that is smaller than 1,756,556. The table suggests that 823,543 is the closest hepteract that is smaller than 1,756,556. And 823,543 is the hepteract of 7. Thus the left part of the answer is *7*.
- Therefore the answer is **7 & 8 = 78**.

EXAMPLE 3: APPROXIMATION

Extract the ninth root of 208,728,001,158,759:

$$\sqrt[9]{208,728,001,158,759}$$

- Since it is an extraction of the ninth root, split the number at the rightmost nine digits: **208,728,001,158,759 = 208,728 & 001,158,759.**
- Consult the table of higher powers and find the closest enneract that is smaller than 208,728. The table suggests that 19,683 is the closest enneract that is smaller than 208,728. And 19,683 is the enneract of 3. Thus the left part of the answer is *3*.
- From the left portion of the problem, *208,728*, subtract the enneract found in the previous step, 19,683. That is, perform **208,728 − 19,683 = 189,045.**
- Find the next enneract that is above the enneract from the previous step. Since 19,683 is the enneract of 3, the next enneract is the one belonging to 4, which is 262,144.
- Subtract the lower enneract from the upper enneract. That is, perform **262,144 − 19,683 = 242,461.**
- Divide 189,045 by 242,461 (to two decimal places). That is, perform **189,045 ÷ 242,461 ≈ 189 ÷ 242 = 0.78.** Then multiply by 10: **0.78 x 10 = 7.8.** This is the right part of the approximate answer.
- Therefore, the <u>approximate</u> answer is **3 & 7.8 = 37.8** [for comparison, the precise answer to six decimal places is 38.999993].

It is important to reiterate that this technique only offers an approximation.

SQUARE ROOT

Similar to the techniques for cube roots and odd higher-order roots, the main technique presented here is only applicable to integer roots. For all other problems, the approximation procedure should be used instead.

There are, however, some subtle differences. The main difference is that the technique for square roots requires an extra step. This is a consequence of some squares having the same rightmost digit.

The other difference between the techniques is in the type of approximation. The square root approximation follows a different route to the one previously covered. Such approximation is practical for the square root operation given the low degree of the root.[25]

PROCEDURE

1. **Split the number whose square root you wish to extract into two portions**. The **right portion** consists of the two rightmost digits, whilst the **left portion** consists of the rest.
2. **Look at the left portion. Find the closest square that is smaller than the left portion**. The number whose square it is forms the left part of the answer.
3. **Next, find the number whose square ends with the same digit as the right portion derived in Step 1**. For right portions that end with 5 or 0, this mapping is unique, but, for the rest, there are two possibilities. Therefore, if the rightmost digit of the right portion is 5,

---

[25] For the interested reader, the approximation applied here to square roots is based on the nth-root algorithm, which is a special case of Newton's method (also commonly known as the Newton-Raphson method). The general formula is $x_{k+1} = \frac{1}{n}\left((n-1)x_k + \frac{A}{x_k^{n-1}} \right)$, where k enumerates the sequence of iterations, n is the degree of the root, and A is the radicand.

then the right part of the answer is *5*; if the rightmost digit is *0*, then the right part of the answer is *0*. For all other digits, take the <u>left part</u> of the answer and add it to its square. Then,

a. If the result is greater than the left portion of the problem, then, of the digits whose square ends with the same digit as the right portion of the problem, choose the <u>lower digit</u>.

b. If, on the other hand, the result is lower than the left portion of the problem, then, of the digits whose square ends with the same digit as the right portion of the problem, choose the <u>higher digit</u>.

APPROXIMATION PROCEDURE
When you are not specifically informed (or aware) that the root is an integer, the approximation procedure below should be deployed instead.

1. **Split the number whose square root you wish to extract into two portions.** The **right portion** consists of the two rightmost digits, whilst the **left portion** consists of the rest.

2. **Look at the left portion. Find the closest square that is smaller than the left portion.** The number whose square it is forms the left part of the answer.

3. **Evaluate the distance between the square of the left part of the answer and the left portion of the problem.** If the left portion of the problem resides roughly[26] halfway between the square of the left part of the answer

---

[26] The reader may note that in Step 3, something akin to guessing appears to be taking place. That is correct. However, doing so is mathematically justifiable, for the next step iterates from this guess towards the correct answer. And the iterative procedure converges very fast—thus making the reasoned guess an efficient way of rapidly arriving at the answer. Try it and see for yourself.

(*lower square*) and the next square above it (*upper square*), then set the right part of the answer to *5*. If it is closer to the lower square, set *3* as the right part of the answer; if closer to the upper square, set *7* as the right part of the answer.

4. **Apply a single iteration of the *n*th-root algorithm.**

   a. Take the answer provided by Steps 1 to 3. Call it the *estimate.*

   b. Divide the number whose square root you wish to extract by the estimate.

   c. To the result from Clause (4.b.) add the estimate. And then divide by 2. This is your approximation.

EXAMPLE 1

Extract the square root of 6,084; the root is an integer:

$$\sqrt{6,084}$$

- Split the number at the rightmost two digits: **6,084 = 60 & 84.**
- The left portion of the problem consists of *60*. Find the closest square that is smaller than 60. This is 49, which is the square of 7. Thus the left part of the answer is *7*.
- Take the left part of the answer and add it to its square. That is, perform **7 x 7 + 7 = 56.** Then evaluate whether the result is below the left portion of the problem.
- As you evaluate that **56 < 60**, and as the right portion of the problem ends with *4*, find the <u>higher</u> digit whose square ends with *4*. Since the two digits whose square ends with *4* are *2* and *8*, set *8* (the higher of the two) as the right part of the answer.
- Therefore the answer is **7 & 8 = 78.**

EXAMPLE 2

Extract the square root of 8,649; the root is an integer:

$$\sqrt{8,649}$$

- Split the number at the rightmost two digits: **8,649 = 86 & 49**.
- The left portion of the problem consists of *86*. Find the closest square that is smaller than 86. This is 81, which is the square of 9. Thus the left part of the answer is *9*.
- Take the left part of the answer and add it to its square. That is, perform **9 x 9 + 9 = 90**. Then evaluate whether the result is below the left portion of the problem.
- As you evaluate that **90 > 86**, and as the right portion of the problem ends with *9*, find the <u>lower</u> digit whose square ends with *9*. Since the two digits whose square ends with *9* are *3* and *7*, set *3* (the lower of the two) as the right part of the answer.
- Therefore the answer is **9 & 3 = 93**.

EXAMPLE 3: APPROXIMATION

Extract the square root of 18,321:

$$\sqrt{18,321}$$

- Split the number at the rightmost two digits: **18,321 = 183 & 21**.
- The left portion of the problem consists of *183*. Find the closest square that is smaller than 183. This is 169, which is the square of 13. Thus the left part of the answer is *13*.
- Evaluate where in between the lower square and the upper square the left portion of the problem resides. That

is, roughly estimate to which of 169 (square of 13) and 196 (square of 14) the left portion (183) is closer.

- Given that 183 is 14 away from 169, and 13 away from 196, it is reasonable to guess that the answer is roughly in between the two roots. Therefore, set the right part of the estimate to 5. Together with the left part of the answer, the estimate is **13 & 5 = 135**.

- Divide the number whose square root you wish to extract by the estimate. That is, perform **18,321 ÷ 135 = 135.71**.

- To the result add the estimate, then divide by 2. That is, perform **(135.71 + 135) ÷ 2 = 135.355**.

- Therefore, the <u>approximate</u> answer is 135.355 [for comparison, the precise answer to six decimal places is 135.355089].

It is important to reiterate that this technique only offers an approximation.

HIGHER PRECISION

The root extractions in the previous sections involved, at least when the root was not an integer, some approximations. An alternative strategy could be to use a long-division-type procedure to arrive at the precise answer; but—especially for higher-order roots—that procedure can be cumbersome and inefficient.

Another route is to employ an iterative procedure to arrive at a better approximation. Such an approach was used to arrive at an approximation for the square root. Given the simplicity of the iterative formula when the degree of the root is two, it is practical to apply it as the first line of attack. For higher-order roots, however, using it straightaway is inefficient: only when the required precision is high should it be deployed.

Therefore, for high-precision approximations, the general strategy is as follows:

1. Compute a reasonable estimate.
2. Perform one iteration to improve the approximation.

PROCEDURE

1. **Following the previously presented techniques, compute an approximation of the root**. For even higher-order roots, perform the same approximation as for odd higher-order roots.
2. **Apply a single iteration of the nth-root algorithm.** (Where n is the degree of the root.)
   a. Take the answer provided by Step 1. Call it the *estimate.*
   b. Raise the estimate to the power of $(n - 1)$.
   c. Divide the number whose root you wish to extract by the result from Clause (2.b.). (If the result of this step is long, you can peg it to *a fakir's rope,* to remember it for subsequent steps.)
   d. Multiply the estimate by $(n - 1)$.
   e. To the result of Clause (2.c.) add the result of Clause (2.d.).
   f. Divide the result from Clause (2.e.) by n. This is your improved approximation.

Note that every calculation in Step 2 should be correct to at least the number of decimal places you are aiming for in the answer. But, to be clear, the answer may not always be correct to the same number of decimal places. That is, it is a necessary condition, not a sufficient one.

EXAMPLE

Take Example 3 from the Cube Root section:

$$\sqrt[3]{854,365}$$

In that example, we already derived an estimate of 94.6. We can now improve this estimate using the procedure described above.

1. Raise the estimate to the power of $(n - 1) = (3 - 1) = 2$. That is perform **94.6 x 94.6 = 8,949.16**.
2. Divide the number whose root you wish to extract by 8,949.16. That is perform **854,365 ÷ 8,949.16 = 95.47**.
3. Multiply the estimate by $(n - 1)$; i.e., perform **94.6 x 2 = 189.2**. Then add this to the previous result; that is, perform **95.47 + 189.2 = 284.67**.
4. Divide the sum from the previous step by n: **284.67 ÷ 3 = 94.89**. This is your improved approximation. The precise answer to two decimal places is 94.89; thus, in this instance, the approximation is precise to two decimal places.

Applying the same procedure to Example 3 from the Higher Order Roots section, $\sqrt[9]{208,728,001,158,759}$, yields 39.16, which is precise to two significant figures.

DECIMALS

All the mental arithmetic techniques presented in the previous sections can be applied to non-integers. To do so, however, requires some modification to the problem.

For multiplication, the easiest approach is to multiply the non-integers by 10 until each becomes an integer. This modification is then reversed in the answer. For example, multiplying **1.2 x 1.4** is the same as multiplying **14 x 12** and then dividing the answer by 100.

For addition and subtraction, no modification is necessary. The only aspect that requires attention is the right-alignment of the numbers. If one number is an integer and the other is not, the integer should be specified to the same number of decimal places—so that the numbers can be right-aligned. For example, **568.65 + 389** should be mentally viewed as **568.65 + 389.00**.

For division, the approach is the same as for multiplication, but care needs to be taken when reversing the operation in the answer. For example **124 ÷ 7.2** is the same as **124 ÷ 72** followed by a multiplication of the answer by 10. On the other hand, say we had **12.4 ÷ 7.2**. It would then be the same as performing **124 ÷ 72,** and there would be no need to reverse anything, since the two multiplications by 10 cancel each other out.

For root extraction, it is necessary to multiply the radicand by a number that has an integer root. For instance, if it is a square root problem, we can multiply the radicand by 100 and then divide the answer by 10. If it is a cube root problem, we can multiply the radicand by a 1,000 and then divide the answer by 10. For example, the cube root of 474.552 is the same as the cube root of 474,552 divided by 10.

The key point is: **any simplification that is introduced needs to be reversed in accordance with the arithmetic operation being performed.**

TRAINING PLAN

T he training plan, quite simply, involves practising the techniques presented herein on a regular basis and incorporating them, as much as possible, into daily life.

At the beginning, it is recommended to practise the techniques on problems that are written down, preferably in the format utilised for the examples presented along with the techniques. To be clear: only write down the problem; solving should still be performed mentally.

It is recommended to begin with small numbers: for example, by adding three 3-digit numbers together. Once you can perform such calculations comfortably, you can increase the complexity by, for example, adding more numbers together, and by increasing the magnitude of the numbers involved. This is the approach taken in the Training Schedule below.

TRAINING SCHEDULE

You can use Microsoft Excel's RANDBETWEEN function to generate random numbers of the length you wish to solve. Produce one problem for each arithmetic operation; i.e., one for addition, one for multiplication, one for subtraction, one for squaring, one for division, one for square root, one for cube root, and one for higher-order roots.

Spend **ten minutes** each day solving the problems using the techniques presented in this Part of the book.

The training is split into several levels of difficulty. Once you are comfortable with the degree of difficulty of a given level, progress to the next.

At the beginning, depending on your initial level of proficiency, it may not be possible to complete all the exercises of a given level within ten minutes. That is absolutely fine. Simply perform half of the exercises on Day 1 and the other half on Day 2. Then repeat the cycle—spending a maximum of ten minutes per day. The same split-training approach can be employed when you start including larger numbers in the problems.

LEVEL 1: RECOMMENDED STARTING POINT

1. **Addition**: Add three 3-digit numbers together.
2. **Multiplication**: Multiply together two 3-digit numbers.
3. **Squaring**: Square a 3-digit number.
4. **Subtraction**: Subtract one 3-digit number from another.
5. **Division**: Divide a 3-digit number by a 2-digit number.
6. **Square root**: Extract the integer square root of a 4-digit number.[27]
7. **Cube root**: Extract the integer cube root of a 6-digit number.
8. **Square root approximation**: Approximate the square root of a 4-digit number.
9. **Higher-order root approximation**: In your spreadsheet, generate a random non-integer between 0 and 100. Raise the non-integer to a randomly generated power (the

---

[27] The problem can be produced in your spreadsheet by first generating a random integer between 0 and 100. And then, in another cell, squaring that random integer. The result of the cell should be the only visible quantity.

power should be an integer between 3 and 9). Then mentally perform a root extraction on the result.

LEVEL 2

Once the exercises in Level 1 are considered as easy, proceed to:

1. **Addition**: Add five 5-digit numbers together.
2. **Multiplication**: Multiply together two 5-digit numbers.
3. **Squaring**: Square a 5-digit number.
4. **Subtraction**: Subtract one 5-digit number from another.
5. **Division**: Divide a 5-digit number by a 3-digit number.
6. **Square root**: Extract the integer square root of a 5-digit number.
7. **Cube root**: Extract the integer cube root of a 6-digit number.
8. **Square root approximation:** Approximate the square root of a 4-digit number.
9. **Higher-order root approximation**: In your spreadsheet, generate a random non-integer between 0 and 100. Raise the non-integer to a randomly generated power (the power should be an integer between 3 and 9). Then mentally perform a root extraction on the result.

LEVEL 3

Once the exercises in Level 2 are considered as easy, proceed to:

1. **Addition**: Add nine 9-digit numbers together.

2. **Multiplication**: Multiply together two 9-digit numbers. Note that you will need to use a scientific calculator[28] to evaluate the answer (as Excel will round to 15 significant figures).

3. **Squaring**: Square a 9-digit number.

4. **Subtraction**: Subtract one 9-digit number from another.

5. **Division**: Divide a 9-digit number by a 4-digit number.

6. **Square root**: Extract the integer square root of a 5-digit number.

7. **Cube root**: Extract the integer cube root of a 6-digit number.

8. **Square root approximation:** Approximate the square root of a 5-digit number.

9. **Higher-order root approximation**: In your spreadsheet, generate a random non-integer between 0 and 100. Raise the non-integer to a randomly generated power (the power should be an integer between 3 and 9). Then mentally perform a root extraction on the result.

LEVEL 4

Once the exercises in Level 3 are considered as easy, introduce non-integers to the problems. That is, generate non-integer random numbers (in Excel, for example, you could use the RAND function[29]) and perform the same exercises.

---

[28] Across the Internet there are many free calculators that are able to accurately perform arithmetic operations on large numbers. For example, at the time of writing, web2.0calc.com appears at the top of the Google Search results.

[29] For example, through formulas in a spreadsheet, first use the RAND function to generate a random number between 0 and 1. Then multiply by 10,000,000 and round to two decimal places. This yields a 9-digit non-integer.

Split the training into a 2-day cycle: one day for solving integer problems, and the other day for non-integer problems:

1. **Day 1**: perform the exercises from Level 3.
2. **Day 2**: perform the exercises from Level 3 using non-integer problem numbers that are rounded to two decimal places.

LEVEL 5

Once the exercises in Level 4 are considered as easy, instead of training with visually presented problems, either memorise the problems or have them called out to you (using a voice recorder, for example). Then perform the calculations in your mind without referring to the written version of the problems.

The training should be split into a 3-day cycle as follows:

1. **Day 1**: perform the exercises from Level 3.
2. **Day 2**: perform the exercises from Level 3 using non-integer problem numbers that are rounded to two decimal places.
3. **Day 3**: perform the exercises from Level 1, but do not refer to the written version of the problems. (As you improve, you can perform this portion of the 3-day cycle on the exercises from Level 2, and, once mastered, Level 3.)

MEASURE YOUR PROGRESS

You can measure your progress by tabulating how long it takes you to perform each arithmetic operation. Keep the magnitude of the numbers in the problem constant, in order to make the measurement consistent.

For example, once a week, time how long it takes you to multiply together two 3-digit numbers. Tabulate the result and track your progress.

INCORPORATION INTO DAILY LIFE

1. **Shopping.** Get used to adding the cost of your groceries as you shop. Verify your answer when you arrive at the checkout.
2. **Restaurants.** Get used to adding your dinning bill and calculating the service charge. Verify your answer when the bill arrives.
3. **In general, perform all arithmetic calculations in your mind as you encounter such problems in daily life** (e.g., discount price, return on investment, cooking measurements, dividend yield, compound interest, price per square foot, tax calculations, etc.). Until you gain confidence in your abilities, you can always resort to checking your answers. The main point is to develop the habit of first solving in the mind, instead of immediately reaching out for a calculator.

SUMMARY AND REVISION MAP

KEY POINTS

- Practising mental arithmetic exercises the brain and can improve the skill with time. In addition, regular practice can also improve other mathematical abilities and general problem-solving skills.
- Mental arithmetic involves several mental faculties, including concentration, visualisation, memory, problem-solving and logic. It is thus an excellent all-round brain exercise.
- In the Rapid Math System, for addition, subtraction and division, a single procedure for each is deployed to all problems.
- For multiplication, the Rapid Math System relies on tricks to facilitate the calculation for numbers near 100. For everything else, a general method is employed.
- For squaring, the Rapid Math System deploys a trick for numbers that end with 5. To everything else, the multiplication procedures are applied.
- The root extraction procedures rely on memorising the values of key powers in order to speed up the calculation for integer root problems.
- Root approximations can be improved using a single iteration of the nth-root algorithm.
- To master the techniques, introduce a daily practice and apply in daily life.

REVISION MAP

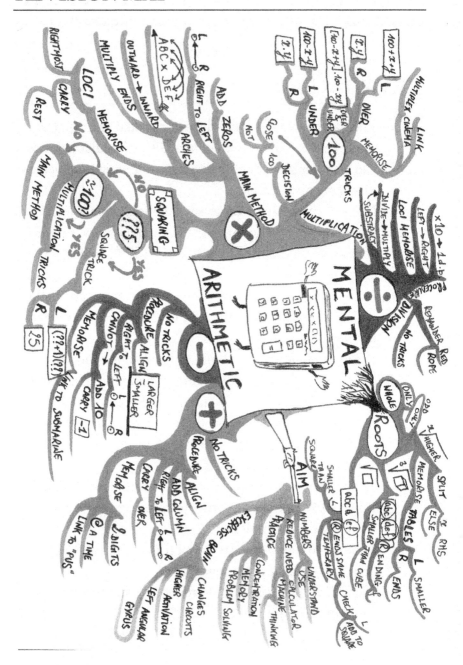

AFTERWORD

The systems presented in the book work, but they work best for those who persevere with the training.

In the first outline for *The Manual*, a full Part was set aside to cover the topic of Discipline and Perseverance. However, after several iterations, I felt that going into great detail about this topic may risk missing the point, for it is essentially a character trait. And it is a trait that evolves only after certain life decisions have been made. Any views and facts provided prior to that are just "interesting", but ultimately have little impact. Moreover, the likelihood of one patiently reading through long passages to be thus stimulated is low before such character trait has taken hold.

The route to self-discipline usually involves a person evaluating (sometimes subconsciously) the degree and ratio of present pleasure/pain versus future pleasure/pain, and of goals versus present desires. Pondering who he is now versus who he would like to be in the future, and which path to get there is the optimal one. All of these considerations are specific to the individual and are often quite personal.

Attempting to cover the spirit of each case and variation in a single text is not feasible. Nor is it necessary, for there is a basic common theme: At the root of the trait lie specific proclivities and lifetime goals. These provide the energy required to impose the rules and persevere through setbacks. Ultimately, discipline and perseverance are merely a product of your **desire** and **belief** in your ability to succeed.

For the abovementioned reasons, the approach taken here is to provide three quotes that embody the essence of the topic. These are pithy sayings that require little effort to read, but the ideas contained within their lines can change a life. Consider them as food for thought:

Discipline is the refining fire by which talent becomes ability.

—Roy L. Smith

It was character that got us out of bed, commitment that moved us into action, and discipline that enabled us to follow through.

—Zig Ziglar

Success is not final, failure is not fatal: it is the courage to continue that counts.

—Winston Churchill

CONTACT INFORMATION

For comments and enquiries about the book, as well as private seminars/personal tuition provided by the author, please contact:

TheUSMmanual@gmail.com

You can also visit our website at:

www.UltimateStudyMethod.com

REFERENCES AND EXTRA READING

References of particular significance are starred. Such allocation is reserved for resources that, to the author's belief, provide an authoritative, comprehensive, yet practical coverage of a topic.

CONCENTRATION

BOOKS

Anderson , John R. 2009. *Cognitive Psychology and its Implications.* Worth Publishers.

Bodian, Stephan. 2012. *Meditation for Dummies.* John Wiley & Sons.

Kaplan, Aryeh. 1995. *Jewish Meditation: A Practical Guide.* Schocken. ★

Liang, Shou-Yu, and Wen-Ching Wu. 1997. *Qigong Empowerment: A Guide to Medical, Taoist, Buddhist, and Wushu Energy Cultivation.* Way of the Dragon Pub.

Ostrander, Sheila. 1979. *Superlearning.* Delta/Confucian Press.

Ostrander, Sheila, and Lynn Schroeder. 2012. *Super-Learning 2000: New Triple Fast Ways You Can Learn, Earn, and Succeed in the 21st Century.* Random House Publishing Group.

Rose, Colin. 1985. *Accelerated Learning*. Accelerated Learning Systems.

Sadhu, Mouni. 1980. *Concentration: A Guide to Mental Mastery*. Wilshire Book Company. ★

Saraswati, Satyananda. 2002. *Kundalini Tantra*. Yoga Publications Trust. ★

Silva, José, and Philip Miele. 1991. *The Silva Mind Control Method*. Simon and Schuster. ★

Winner, Jay. 2008. *Take Stress Out of Your Life: A Medical Doctor's Proven Program to Minimize Stress and Maximize Health*. De Capo Press.

Yang, Jwing-Ming. 1997. *The Root of Chinese Qigong*. YMAA Publication Center. ★

SCIENTIFIC JOURNALS

Cahn, Rael B., and John Polich. 2006. "Meditation states and traits: EEG, ERP, and neuroimaging studies." *Psychological Bulletin* (American Psychological Association) 132 (2): 180-211.

Dukas, Reuven. 2002. "Behavioural and ecological consequences of limited attention." *Philosophical Transactions of the Royal Society B: Biological Sciences* (The Royal Society) 357 (1427): 1539-1547.

Hasenkamp, Wendy, Christine D. Wilson-Mendenhall, Erica Duncan, and Lawrence W. Barsalou. 2012. "Mind wandering and attention during focused meditation: A fine-grained temporal analysis of fluctuating cognitive states." *NeuroImage* (Academic Press) 59 (1): 750-760.

Lutz, Antoine, Heleen A. Slagter, Nancy B. Rawlings, Andrew D. Francis, Lawrence L. Greischar, and Richard J. Davidson. 2009. "Mental training enhances attentional stability: Neural and behavioural evidence." *Journal of Neuroscience* (Society for Neuroscience) 29 (42): 13418-13427.

MacLean, Katherine A., Emilio Ferrer, Stephen R. Aichele, David A. Bridwell, Anthony P. Zanesco, Tonya L. Jacobs, Brandon G. King, et al. 2010. "Intensive meditation training improves perceptual discrimination and sustained attention." *Psychological Science* (Sage Publications) 21 (6): 829-839.

Newberg, Andrew B., and J. Iversen. 2003. "The neural basis of the complex mental task of meditation: neurotransmitter and neurochemical considerations." *Medical Hypotheses* (Elsevier Science Ltd.) 51 (2): 282-291.

Richard, Matthieu, Antoine Lutz, and Richard J. Davidson. 2014. "Mind of the meditator." *Scientific American* (Nature Publishing Group) 311 (5): 38-45.

Rossano, Matt J. 2007. "Did meditating make us human?" *The Cambridge Archaeological Journal* (The McDonald Institute for Archaeological Research) 17 (01): 47-58.

Strayer, David L., Frank A. Drews, and William A. Johnston. 2003. "Cell phone-induced failures of visual attention during simulated driving." *Journal of Experimental Psychology: Applied* (American Psychological Association) 9 (1): 23-32.

MEMORY

BOOKS

Brown, Derren. 2009. *Tricks of the Mind.* Random House.

Buzan, Tony. 1991. *Use Your Perfect Memory: Dramatic New Techniques for Improving Your Memory.* Plume.

Campayo, Ramon. 2010. *Maximize Your Memory.* Career Press.

Lorayne, Harry. 1996. *Harry Lorayne's Page-a-minute Memory Book.* Ballantine Books.

—. 1995. *How to Develop a Super Power Memory.* Frederick Fell .

—. 1990. *Super Memory - Super Student: How to Raise Your Grades in 30 Days.* Little, Brown and Company. ★

Lorayne, Harry, and Jerry Lucas. 1974. *The Memory Book.* Stein and Day.

Neath, Ian, and Aimée M. Surprenant. 2003. *Human Memory: An Introduction to Research, Data, and Theory.* Thomson/Wadsworth.

Trudeau, Kevin. 1995. *Kevin Trudeau's Mega Memory: How To Release Your Superpower Memory In 30 Minutes Or Less A Day.* HarperCollins. ★

SCIENTIFIC JOURNALS

Anderson, Michael C., and James H. Neely. 1996. "Interference and inhibition in memory retrieval." *Memory* (Academic Press) 237-317.

Baddeley, Alan D. 1966. "The influence of acoustic and semantic similarity on long-term memory for word sequences." *Quarterly Journal of Experimental Psychology* (Taylor & Francis Group) 18 (4): 302-309.

Ebbinghaus, Hermann. (1885) 2013. "Memory: A contribution to experimental psychology." *Annals of Neurosciences* 20 (4): 155-156.

Miller, George A. 1956. "The magical number seven, plus or minus two: some limits on our capacity for processing information." *Psychological Review* 63 (2): 81-97.

Small, Gary W., Daniel H.S. Silverman, Prabha Siddarth, Linda M. Ercoli, Karen J. Miller, Helen Lavretsky, Benjamin C. Wright, Susan Y. Bookheimer, Jorge R. Barrio, and Michael E. Phelps. 2006. "Effects of a 14-day healthy longevity lifestyle program on cognition and brain function." *The American Journal of Geriatric Psychiatry* (Elsevier) 14 (6): 538-545.

SPEED READING

BOOKS

Beale, Abby, and Pam Mullan. 2008. *The Complete Idiot's Guide to Speed Reading*. Penguin.

Berg, Howard Stephen. 1992. *Super Reading Secrets*. Grand Central Publishing.

Buzan, Tony. 2006. *The Speed Reading Book: The Revolutionary Approach to Increasing Reading Speed, Comprehension and General Knowledge*. BBC Active.

Cutler, Wade E. 2003. *Triple Your Reading Speed: 4th Edition*. Simon and Schuster.

Dudley, Geoffrey A. 1995. *Rapid Reading: The High Speed Way to Increase Your Learning Power*. Thorsons.

Frank, Stanley D. 1994. *The Evelyn Wood Seven-Day Speed Reading and Learning Program*. Times Books.

Gray, William S. 1941. *Reading: A Research Retrospective, 1881-1941*. Edited by John T. Guthrie. International Reading Association.

Kump, Peter. 1998. *Breakthrough Rapid Reading*. Penguin. ★

Richaudeau, François. 2004. *Méthode de lecture rapide Richaudeau*. Retz.

Scheele, Paul R. 1999. *The PhotoReading Whole Mind System*. Learning Strategies Corporation. ★

SCIENTIFIC JOURNALS

Brown, B., D. Inouye, K. Barrus, and D. Hansen. 1981. "An analysis of the rapid reading controversy." *The Social Psychology of Reading*.

Brozo, William G., and Jerry L. Johns. 1986. "A content and critical analysis of 40 speed reading books." *Journal of Reading* (International Reading Association) 30 (3): 242-247.

Cranney, A. Garr, Bruce L. Brown, Dorothy M. Hansen, and Dillon K. Inouye. 1982. "Rate and reading dynamics reconsidered." *Journal of Reading* (Wiley) 25 (6): 526-533 .

Fujimaki, Norio, Tomoe Hayakawa, Shinji Munetsuna, and Toyofumi Sasaki. 2004. "Neural activation dependent on reading speed during covert reading of novel." *NeuroReport* 15 (2): 239-243.

Macalister, John. 2010. "Speed reading courses and their effect on reading authentic texts: A preliminary investigation." *Reading in a Foreign Language* 22 (1): 104-116.

McNamara, Danielle S. 2000. *Preliminary analysis of Photoreading.* NASA Technical Report, Moffett Field, CA : NASA Ames Research Center.

Quantz, J. O. 1897. "Problems in the psychology of reading." *The Psychological Review: Monograph Supplements* 2 (1).

Spache, George D. 1962. "Is this a breakthrough in reading?" *The Reading Teacher* (Wiley) 15 (4): 258-263.

Yen, Tran Thi Ngoc. 2012. "The effects of a speed reading course and speed transfer to other types of texts." *RELC Journal* 43 (1): 23-37.

USM

BOOKS

Buzan, Tony. 2012. *Mind Maps at Work: How to be the best at work and still have time to play.* HarperCollins UK.

—. 1991. *Use Both Sides of Your Brain: New Mind-mapping Techniques to Help You Raise All Levels of Your Intelligence and Creativity, Based on the Latest Discoveries about the Human Brain.* Dutton.

Buzan, Tony, and Barry Buzan. 2006. *The Mind Map Book.* BBC Active. ★

Kesselman-Turkel, Judi, and Franklynn Peterson. 2003. *Note-Taking Made Easy.* Univ of Wisconsin Press.

McPherson, Fiona. 2012. *Effective Notetaking.* Wayz Press.

SCIENTIFIC JOURNALS

Agarwal, Pooja K., Patrice M. Bain, and Roger W. Chamberlain. 2012. "The value of applied research: Retrieval practice improves classroom learning and recommendations from a teacher, a principal, and a scientist." *Educational Psychology Review* (Springer US) 24 (3): 437-448.

Dunlosky, John, Katherine A. Rawson, Elizabeth J. Marsh, Mitchell J. Nathan, and Daniel T. Willingham. 2013. "Improving students' learning with effective learning techniques promising directions from cognitive and educational psychology." *Psychological Science in the Public Interest* (SAGE Publications) 14 (1): 4-58.

Karpicke, Jeffrey D., and Henry L. Roediger. 2008. "The critical importance of retrieval for learning." *Science* (American Association for the Advancement of Science) 319 (5865): 966-968.

Paul, Annie M. 2015. "A new vision for testing." *Scientific American* 313 (2): 54-61.

RAPID MATH

BOOKS

Flansburg, Scott, and Victoria Hay. 2004. *Math Magic: How to Master Everyday Math Problems, Revised Edition.* HarperCollins.

Handley, Bill. 2003. *Speed Mathematics: Secret Skills for Quick Calculation.* Wiley.

Julius, Edward H. 1996. *More Rapid Math: Tricks and Tips: 30 Days to Number Mastery.* Wiley.

Trachtenberg, Jakob. 2011. *The Trachtenberg Speed System of Basic Mathematics.* Edited by Rudolph McShane. Translated by Ann Cutler. Souvenir Press. ★

SCIENTIFIC JOURNALS

Delazer, M., A. Ischebeck, F. Domahs, L. Zamarian, F. Koppelstaetter, C.M. Siedentopf, L. Kaufmann, T. Benke, and S. Felber. 2005. "Learning by strategies and learning by drill—evidence from an fMRI study." *NeuroImage* (Elsevier) 25 (3): 838-849.

Delazer, Margaret, Frank Domahs, Lisa Bartha, Christian Brenneis, Aliette Lochy, Thomas Trieb, and Thomas Benke. 2003. "Learning complex arithmetic—an fMRI study." *Cognitive Brain Research* (Elsevier) 18 (1): 76-88.

Grabner, Roland H, Daniel Ansari, Gernot Reishofer, Elsbeth Stern, Franz Ebner, and Christa Neuper. 2007. "Individual differences in mathematical competence predict parietal brain activation during mental calculation." *Neuroimage* (Academic Press) 38 (2): 346-356.

Gruber, Oliver, Peter Indefrey, Helmuth Steinmetz, and Andreas Kleinschmidt. 2001. "Dissociating neural correlates of cognitive components in mental calculation." *Cerebral cortex* (Oxford University Press) 11 (4): 350-359.

Liu, Allison S., Arava Y. Kallai, Christian D. Schunn, and Julie A. Fiez. 2015. "Using mental computation training to improve complex mathematical performance." *Instructional Science* 43 (4): 463-485.

Wu, Tung-Hsin, Chia-Lin Chen, Yung-Hui Huang, Ren-Shyan Liu, Jen-Chuen Hsieh, and Jason J. S. Lee. 2009. "Effects of long-term practice and task complexity on brain activities when performing abacus-based mental calculations: a PET study." *European Journal of Nuclear Medicine and Molecular Imaging* 36 (3): 436-445.

Zamarian, L., A. Ischebeck, and M. Delazer. 2009. "Neuroscience of learning arithmetic—Evidence from brain imaging studies." *Neuroscience & Biobehavioral Reviews* 33 (6): 909-925.

INDEX

3

3D objects, 48

4

4D+, 50

A

Abdominal breathing, 42
Addition, 358
Alpha, 34
Alphabet list, 127, 166, 229
Amygdala, 74
Angular gyrus, 356
Annotate, 304, 305, 323, 325, 339, 340
Atkinson-Shiffrin model, 74
Attention, v, 28, 29, 30, 31, 33, 35, 36, 41, 45, 49, 50, 52, 53, 56, 70, 78, 80, 92, 111, 197, 244, 249, 255, 256, 258, 259, 276, 283, 295, 307

B

Background Sound, 56
Baseball bench, 156
Being systematic, 115
Beta, 34
Binary code, 176
Body list, 129, 229
Breathing, 42
Buddhist breathing, 42, 276, 304, 307, 338
Building block, 96, 318
Building your system, 227
Bundling, 156, 187, 193, 194, 207, 226, 236

C

Calendar, 203
Cards, 172
Cartoons, 86
Chemical notation, 189
Chess openings, 221
Circular grid, 151
Cognitive, 32, 74, 244

Comprehension, 30, 240, 242, 255, 265, 273, 278, 279, 282, 283, 284, 285, 295

Computer code, 178

Concentration, 21, 24, 27, 28, 29, 30, 31, 37, 42, 54, 60, 61, 62, 65, 69, 78, 84, 87, 105, 220, 250, 252, 253, 254, 276, 277, 278, 280, 295, 304, 306, 307, 338, 346, 353, 431, 437

Concentration Chapter, 27–66

Concentration rules, 61

Conscious awareness, 32, 71, 111

Consistent unique identifier, 96, 318

Corporate hierarchy, 222

Cortisol, 74

Countdown, 46

Creative linking, 80

Cube root, 406

D

Dan Tian, 45

Decay theory, 75

Decimals, 423

Deep learning., 328

Delta, 34

Dimensions, 48, 50, 85, 101, 104, 105, 110, 171, 175, 176, 177, 187, 206

Distinctive feature, 197, 198, 224, 225

Division, 397

Drills, 241, 243, 249, 265, 266, 281, 282, 294

E

Ebbinghaus, Hermann, 75

Effigy list, 126

Eidetic memory, 70

Emotions, 81, 83, 88, 90, 104, 235

Empty spaces, 155

Equity Volsurface, 224

Exaggerate, 87, 125, 160, 162, 164, 168

F

Facial memory, 195

Fastest speaker, 262

Fixations, 244, 251, 264, 265, 266, 267, 268, 269, 280, 286, 287, 289, 295

Flow, 253, 264, 271, 322, 323, 394

Foreign Vocabulary, 159, 164

Forgetting, 74, 75, 76, 110

Forgetting curves, 76

G

Gamma, 34
Gluing, 118, 235
Gluing toolbox, 89
Grid system, 145
Guide, 241, 254, 255, 256, 258, 260, 295

H

Higher roots, 411
Hippocampus, 74
Houses and Rooms, 132

I

Imaginary places, 140
Imagination is infinite, 85
Interference theory, 75

K

Kabbalists, 41
Key word, 310, 311, 314, 340, 341, 342

L

Layered reading, 251, 270, 271, 272, 274, 278, 280, 293, 295
Letting go, 37, 38, 40, 41, 44, 45, 46, 47, 49, 52, 53, 55, 56, 57, 58, 59, 65, 277, 282

Linear notes, 305, 309, 312, 313, 316, 325, 326, 327, 331, 332, 339, 344, 346, 348
Link system, 79, 118, 119, 122, 123, 159, 178, 179, 182, 189, 193, 223, 224, 225, 226, 235, 330, 342, 360
Loci, 130, 131, 133, 134, 135, 136, 137, 138, 140, 145, 173, 176, 178, 193, 194, 215, 221, 224, 226, 229, 231, 232, 235, 330, 342, 343, 377, 378, 393, 397, 398, 401, 403, 404
Loci system, 130
Logic, 80
Long term memory, 73, 74, 75, 77, 111, 112, 113, 114, 115, 144, 232, 236, 301, 302, 308, 309, 326

M

Mantra, 39, 40
Manual's instructions, 24
Maps, 223
Markers, 129
Mathematical formulae, 127, 182, 184, 191, 193, 321
Measuring of progress, 60, 62, 65, 167, 281, 429, 430

Meditation, 28, 32, 33, 35, 37, 40, 50, 51, 59, 65, 84

Memorise, 96, 112, 173, 190, 230, 231, 301, 305, 326, 330, 332, 342, 344, 346, 360, 406, 411

Memory, 21, 22, 33, 42, 48, 51, 68, 69, 70, 72, 73, 74, 75, 77, 78, 79, 80, 83, 88, 92, 101, 109, 110, 111, 112, 113, 115, 119, 131, 133, 134, 138, 140, 141, 174, 188, 229, 232, 235, 301, 307, 320, 327, 352, 353, 408, 413, 431

Memory Chapter, 67–238

Memory rules, 87

Mental arithmetic, 48, 114, 353, 357, 358, 431

Morse code, 223

Multiplication, 363

Multiplication arches, 376, 377, 380, 381, 383

Multiplication tricks, 364

Multitasking, 29, 30

N

Names and faces, 195

Neuroscience, 32

Non-Foreign Vocabulary, 164

Numbers list, 124

Numerical grid, 150, 155

O

Oenophiles, 212

of survival significance, 81

P

Paintings, 224

Palaces, cities and countries, 134

Parietal brain circuits, 356

Peg, 118, 122, 123, 124, 125, 127, 130, 134, 141, 142, 143, 145, 148, 154, 156, 157, 174, 175, 176, 177, 196, 199, 200, 201, 202, 204, 205, 217, 235, 377, 380, 381, 383, 397, 398, 403, 404

Peg system, 121

Pegging, 118, 122, 123, 124, 125, 139, 142, 143, 149, 155, 174, 197, 205

Perfumes, 224

Philatelists, 225

Phonetic alphabet, 94, 123, 127, 146, 206

Photographic memory, 70

Poems, 225

Presidents and Rulers, 199

Previewing, 272, 304, 324, 339, 346

Primal emotions, 78

Principal multiplication Technique, 376

Q

Qigong, 42

R

RANDBETWEEN(,), 425
Rapid Math Chapter, 351–432
Recipes, 226
Regressions, 241, 251, 253, 255, 280, 295
Reinforce, 301, 305, 334
Relaxation, 28, 32, 36, 62, 65
Relaxing scene, 54
Repetition, 39, 40, 73, 74, 75, 76, 111, 113, 114, 189
Retrieval practice, 328
Review, 110, 112, 133, 137, 139, 159, 163, 165, 184, 196, 230, 231, 236, 273, 301, 305, 308, 309, 311, 316, 325, 326, 331, 333, 339, 343, 344, 345, 346, 348
Revision-Map, 65, 66, 235, 237, 295, 297, 304, 305, 307, 308, 309, 311, 312, 325, 326, 327, 330, 331, 332, 339, 341, 343, 344, 346, 348, 349, 431, 432
Rhyme list, 129, 203, 204, 229

Rote, 21, 68, 76, 99, 113, 220

S

Sensory memory, 73
Short term memory, 73
Skimming, 254, 255, 256, 258, 264, 267, 272, 273, 284, 286, 287, 295, 304, 324, 339, 346
Sleep, 74, 114
Smell, 39, 51, 52, 55, 83, 104, 205
Sound barrier, 261
Spaced repetition, 76
Speed reading, 239, 272, 304, 322, 324, 338, 339, 346, 441
Speed Reading Chapter, 239–98
Spelling, 166
Square root, 416
Squaring, 386
Squaring trick, 386
S-shaped motion, 256
Standard grid, 146, 148, 150, 151
Stellated Dodecahedron, 49
Subconscious, 241, 275, 277, 278, 279
Subconscious reading, 241, 251, 275, 295, 304, 324, 339, 346

Substitution, 89
Subtraction, 391
Sub-vocalisation, 241, 251, 261, 262, 280, 286, 287, 295
Survival importance, 70
Symbols, 102
System, 96, 319

T

Table of cubes, 408
Tables for higher order powers, 413
Telephone numbers, 168
Theta, 34
Touch, 52
Trace Decay, 75
Transfer, 328
Tube/Underground map, 226

U

Ultimate Study Method Chapter, 299–349
Unique identifiers, 93, 95, 116, 161, 176, 177, 178, 179, 184, 190, 221, 318, 319

USM, 299, 301, 309, 324, 348

V

Varying reading speeds, 279
Vertical line, 198, 257, 258, 264, 268, 295
Visualise, 39, 42, 46, 48, 49, 50, 52, 53, 69, 81, 87, 91, 92, 93, 94, 95, 102, 122, 125, 132, 141, 148, 154, 156, 159, 160, 161, 162, 168, 169, 170, 174, 186, 187, 192, 200, 201, 202, 204, 206, 217, 290, 353
Visualising Letters, 40
Visualising numbers and symbols, 93
Visualising words, 91
Vowels, 97

Y

Yoga, 42

Z

Zero hour, 203, 205

CPSIA information can be obtained
at www.ICGtesting.com
Printed in the USA
BVOW06*1649061017
496713BV00007B/236/P